T0339485

The Future of Work, Technology, and Basic Income

Technological advances in computerization and robotics threaten to eliminate countless jobs from the labor market in the near future. These advances have reignited the debate about universal basic income. The essays in this collection offer unique and compelling perspectives on the ever-changing nature of work and the plausibility of a universal basic income to address the elimination of jobs from the workforce. The essays address a number of topics related to these issues, including the prospects of libertarian and anarchist justifications for a universal basic income, the positive impact of a basic income on intimate laborers such as sex workers and surrogates, the nature of "bad work" and who will do it if everyone receives a basic income, whether a universal basic income is objectionably paternalistic, and viable alternatives to a universal basic income. This book raises complex questions and avenues for future research about universal basic income and the future of work in our increasingly technological society. It will be of keen interest to graduate students and scholars in political philosophy, economics, political science, and public policy who are interested in these debates.

Michael Cholbi is Professor of Philosophy and Director of the California Center for Ethics and Policy at California State Polytechnic University, Pomona. He is the author of *Suicide: The Philosophical Dimensions* (Broadview Press, 2011), *Understanding Kant's Ethics* (Cambridge University Press, 2016), and *Procreation, Parenthood, and Educational Rights* (Routledge, 2017).

Michael Weber is Professor of Philosophy and Chair of the Department of Philosophy at Bowling Green State University. He has published widely in ethics and political philosophy on topics including rational choice theory, ethics and the emotions, and egalitarianism. He has also co-edited six volumes on applied ethics and political philosophy, including *Paternalism: Theory and Practice* (Cambridge University Press, 2013), *Manipulation: Theory and Practice* (Oxford University Press, 2014), *The Ethics of Self-Defense* (Oxford University Press, 2016), *Political Utopias: Contemporary Debates* (Oxford University Press, 2017), and *Religious Exemptions* (Oxford University Press, 2017).

Routledge Research in Applied Ethics

For more information about this series, please visit: www.routledge.com/
Routledge-Research-in-Applied-Ethics/book-series/RRAES

The Future of Work, Technology, and Basic Income

Edited by Michael Cholbi
and Michael Weber

Routledge
Taylor & Francis Group
NEW YORK AND LONDON

First published 2020
by Routledge
52 Vanderbilt Avenue, New York, NY 10017

and by Routledge
2 Park Square, Milton Park, Abingdon, Oxon OX14 4RN

Routledge is an imprint of the Taylor & Francis Group, an informa business

First issued in paperback 2021

Library of Congress Cataloging-in-Publication Data
A catalog record for this book has been requested

ISBN: 978-1-138-31606-5 (hbk)
ISBN: 978-1-03-209109-9 (pbk)
ISBN: 978-0-429-45590-2 (ebk)

Typeset in Sabon
by Apex CoVantage, LLC

Contents

Introduction

Michael Cholbi and Michael Weber

Many contemporary societies are "work centered," in the sense that work plays a variety of central economic, social, and psychological functions for the majority of the population.[1] In such societies, working is not merely the principal source of the income individuals need to support themselves.[2] It also serves as a source of identity, recognition, and sociability; is the chief avenue for the development and exercise of skills; and is perceived as a mark of adulthood and full inclusion in the community (Frayne 2015). Work-centered societies have largely succeeded in enticing individuals toward "the identification with and systematic devotion to waged work, the elevation of work to the center of life, and the affirmation of work as an end in itself" (Weeks 2011: 46).

Unsurprisingly then, involuntary unemployment is often a devastating financial, emotional, and physical setback for those in work-centered societies (Brenner 2005; Herbig, Dragano, and Angerer 2013; Calvo, Mair, and Sarkisian 2015; Margerison-Zilko et al. 2016). Yet many social forecasters anticipate that the work-centered society will erode in coming decades, as economic growth slows, climate change alters patterns of production and habitation, global populations age, loyalty between employers and employees declines, and temporary and "gig" employment increases (Frey and Osborne 2014; Brynjolfsson and McAfee 2014; Thompson 2015; Srnicek and Williams 2015; Stern 2016).

But of all the developments likely to chip away at the centrality of work, automation likely poses the greatest risk. Technological advance threatens to eliminate countless jobs. Recent well-publicized studies suggest that nearly half of existing jobs could be eliminated due to computerization and roboticization (Frey and Osborne 2013). As the Industrial Revolution proved, machines can be highly efficient in providing the "muscle" behind *manual* labor, and indeed, manufacturing employment continues to decline in part because of the continued introduction of labor-eliminating technology. But technologies currently under development will likely threaten different categories of labor. Digital "smart" technologies make it possible for machines to perform routine and repeatable *cognitive* tasks. As a result, computers are likely to substitute for workers in professions previously perceived as immune to automation, such as accounting, truck driving, medical diagnosis, and hospitality, just to name a few. The development of artificial intelligence could expand even further the range of jobs that can be done more efficiently and inexpensively by computers than by people.

Should this automation revolution materialize, societies, workplaces, and individuals will have to adapt to an economy in which there are likely to be a narrower range of job categories, reduced working hours, fewer available jobs overall, and unprecedented levels of non-cyclical unemployment. Such a revolution presents significant challenges, but opportunities as well. For instance, a decreased necessity for human labor could increase the opportunity for individuals to find fulfillment in their non-work or "leisure" time, the importance of which philosophers as distinct as Karl Marx, John Stuart Mill, and Bertrand Russell have emphasized (Mill 2001; Russell 1935; Sayers 2005). It could also open the door to improved work conditions, including the reduction of the authoritarian private government of employers emphasized recently by Elizabeth Anderson (2017). Nonetheless, given the centrality of work in such societies, and the widespread allegiance to work, an automotive revolution that profoundly impacts the economy and the nature of and need for human labor could be profoundly traumatic for many workers (Cholbi 2018). It would also surely require that we rethink social policies related to work and economic productivity. Most acutely, the prospective decline of work would likely force such societies to identify new ways for individuals to support themselves economically.

It is in this context that interest has increased recently in the idea of an universal basic income (UBI). UBI policies provide a minimal level of income to all individuals without condition and, arguably most importantly, without requiring them to work. UBI thus differs from public welfare approaches, common in the United States, the United Kingdom, and elsewhere, where recipients are required to work (or at least to seek work or perform workforce training). UBI is not a new idea, and has enjoyed support from theorists and leaders across the ideological spectrum, including classical liberal economists (Friedrich Hayek), anti-racism and anti-poverty activists (Martin Luther King, Jr. and Desmond Tutu), libertarian thinkers (Milton Friedman), feminists (Carole Pateman), Marxists (Antonio Negri), and a wide array of government official and entrepreneurs, including, most notably, Elon Musk. Nor is UBI without practical precedent: As of this writing, UBI experiments of various scales and forms have recently been undertaken in Canada, Finland, Kenya, the Netherlands, and the United States, with the Alaska Permanent Fund, which uses the state's energy revenues to provide every resident of the state an annual dividend, which has been in continuous operation since 1982.

The predicted emergence of a "crisis" in work, spurred by the aforementioned predictions about workplace automation, has put UBI in the intellectual spotlight. The articles in this volume offer a wide variety of discussions about UBI and changes in the nature of work. Taken together, they illuminate both the potential and the limits of UBI to address present and future challenges related to work and automation.

Several of the articles in this volume seek a deep philosophical foundation or justification for UBI, well aware that many would consider it a radical idea. Matt Zwolinski ("A Hayekian Case for Free Markets and a Basic Income"), for instance, defends basic income, perhaps surprisingly, by reference to the work of Friedrich Hayek, often regarded as a hard-line free-market libertarian. Zwolinski argues that Hayek's lifelong support for basic income, rather than being a fluke or an exception to his free market commitments, rested on Hayek's neo-republican understanding of freedom as the absence of coercion. For Hayek, freedom consists in the ability to live one's life according to one's own decisions and plans rather than being dominated by the will of others. Such a conception of freedom, Zwolinski argues, will require redistribution of resources in the form of a minimum income in order to ensure that individuals are not dominated by others.

In "An Anarchist Defense of the Basic Income," Jessica Flanigan argues that individuals have natural rights (e.g., rights against bodily interference) that public officials ought to protect. But public officials typically establish rules and conventions surrounding property that exceed these natural rights and do not rest on individuals consenting to these rules and conventions. Flanigan proposes basic income as a way to compensate individuals for the state's violating of their rights.

Justin Tosi ("Relational Sufficientarianism and Basic Income") argues that egalitarian theories of justice, including the relational forms of egalitarianism advanced by Elizabeth Anderson and Samuel Scheffler, struggle to justify basic income. Tosi turns instead to sufficientarian accounts of justice, according to which justice requires not equality in the distribution of some good but the assurance that each individual has enough of whatever good(s) serve as the currency of justice. A relational form of sufficientarianism, wherein each individual has a social status sufficient for decent, respect-based relations with others, provides a more credible rationale for UBI than any egalitarian view, Tosi concludes.

Some support UBI on the basis that, by comparison with traditional social welfare programs that provide "baskets" of essential goods (food, housing, etc.) rather than cash, UBI programs are less paternalistic because they offer recipients greater flexibility in the pursuit of their goals. Michael Cholbi ("The Anti-Paternalist Case for Unconditional Basic Income Provision") argues that an anti-paternalist case for UBI is more difficult to make than it appears. Those who support UBI on anti-paternalist grounds wrongly understand paternalism in terms of how having options affects liberty rather than, as Cholbi favors, in terms of how others intercede in their rational agency in ways that reflect judgments of the recipients' inferiority. Moreover, a basket of essential goods appears better equipped than UBI to prevent unequal social relations that paternalism can exploit or exacerbate.

A second group of contributors explore UBI in connection with work and the workplace, considering in particular how UBI intersects with the challenges that automation presents to work in work-centered societies. Evelyn Forget ("Work and Worth: Basic Income and the Social Meaning of Work") notes that basic income could play a number of desirable roles vis-à-vis work, providing incomes as steady jobs decline and contingent work increases, as well as enhancing opportunities for work-life balance, including opportunities to leave the workforce temporarily, to pursue volunteer or creative work, or to engage in leisure. That said, Forget asserts that work has value beyond a paycheck. Work is also inherently valuable, as it serves as a source of identity for citizens and shapes how we perceive ourselves and one another. Thus, Forget concludes, basic income cannot and should not alleviate some of the detriments of the current and future work environment, and as a result, reasonable disagreement should be expected about whether to require work as a condition of a basic income, especially for young workers near the beginnings of their careers.

Like Forget, Kory P. Schaff ("Work, Technology, and Inequality") emphasizes that work provides various non-pecuniary benefits, including self-realization, self-respect, and community. Technological advances that portend making labor obsolete thus have significant costs for workers in terms of their welfare. Basic income may ameliorate some of the economic downsides of declines in work, but in failing to address underlying property relations, it will not (Schaff argues) reduce inequality or compensate for the non-pecuniary losses workers are likely to suffer in the future.

John Danaher ("In Defence of the Post-Work Future: Withdrawal and the Ludic Life") splits with Forget and Schaff in viewing basic income as a measure to catalyze a desirable post-work future. Basic income is unlikely, according to Danaher, to be able to compensate individuals who lose meaning and fulfillment due to being perpetually unemployed. But given that work is genuinely bad, we should instead pursue a more ludic, game-like existence that affords us greater opportunities for human flourishing than lives centered on work.

In "Universal Basic Income and the Good of Work," Andrea Veltman engages with basic income critics who view it as antithetical to the traditional work ethic. Veltman sees many advantages in basic income, including the potential to enhance our positive freedom—our ability to effectively pursue our desires—by reducing our material dependence on work and increasing workers' power to bargain with employers for more advantageous working conditions. Moreover, basic income will change our motivations for working but not undermine them, according to Veltman. Nor, she concludes, will it threaten social norms of reciprocity that undergird belief in a social duty to work.

Veltman, like many basic income advocates, contends that it will not replace work but improve it. Frauke Schmode ("Basic Income and the Future of Bad Work") notes that little attention been paid to the likely impacts of basic income on "bad work." Bad work, on Schmode's analysis, is work that is both bad subjectively (from the standpoint of the worker's needs, preferences, values, or abilities) and objectively (with respect to the working conditions, remuneration, safety, autonomy, free time, etc.). While we might expect basic income will give workers greater leverage either to refuse bad work or to bargain to make it better, Schmode concludes that so long as bad work continues to exist, a neglected question of social justice—how to distribute the burdens of bad work in a society—would remain largely unaddressed.

The increased interest in basic income has coincided with greater attention to forms of labor that societies have sometimes marginalized or sought to prohibit. In "Basic Income and Intimate Labor," Vida Panitch considers how liberal and communitarian thinkers have approached "intimate labor," "work that is done primarily by women with intimate parts of their bodies or their intimate physical capacities in exchange for money, favors, or goods," including sex work and reproductive labor such as commercial surrogacy. Liberals and communitarians have largely debated whether the criminalization of such labor is an appropriate response to how such labor exploits women or commodifies their bodies. In contrast, Panitch argues that basic income is a more defensible response, allowing women to reject intimate labor if they wish, but protecting their right to work in fields of their own choosing. Liberal and communitarian thought, she concludes, lead away from criminalization and toward basic income as a policy solution to the potential harms of intimate labor.

As the research collected here attests, changing economic realities related to work and automation have given basic income new life as an object of both theoretical and practical investigation. These investigations, in turn, have profound implications for how we might relate to work—and to one another—in a future with dramatically different economic realities than those with which economically prosperous societies are accustomed.

Notes

1. According to the Organisation for Economic Co-operation and Development (OECD), the employment-to-population ratio in 2017 was over 50% in over 40 countries, and over 67% in 25 (https://stats.oecd.org/Index. aspx?DatasetCode=LFS_SEXAGE_I_R). In the United States, the ratio in 2017 was 70.1%, placing it above the OECD average of 67.8%, but well below leaders such as Iceland (85.8%), Switzerland (79.8%), and Sweden (76.9%). According to the United States Department of Labor (www.dol.gov/wb/stats/ stats_data.htm), the percentage of females in the labor force (57%) is lower

than it is for men. This is true in Iceland as well, where the female labor participation rate has hovered around 73% between 2015 and 2017 (www.theglobaleconomy.com/Iceland/Female_labor_force_participation/). The different rates of female and male participation in the labor force is important because it is relevant to the importance of unpaid labor even in "work-centered" societies, for example, child care and care for the elderly, which is typically done by women. According to the OECD (www.oecd.org/dev/development-gender/Unpaid_care_work.pdf), around the world women spend two to ten times more time on unpaid labor than men, resulting in discriminatory social institutions and stereotypes on gender roles, and gender gaps in labor outcomes such as labor force participation, wages, and job quality.

2. In the United States at least, income is not the only economic function of work, as it is often the source of health insurance (and a cluster of other benefits) for workers.

References

Anderson, E. 2017. *Private Government: How Employers Rule Our Lives (And Why We Don't Talk About It)*. Princeton: Princeton University Press.

Brenner, M.H. 2005. "Commentary: Economic Growth Is the Basis of Mortality Rate Decline in the 20th Century—Experience of the United States 1901–2000." *International Journal of Epidemiology* 34: 1214–1221.

Brynjolfsson, E. and McAfee, A. 2014. *The Second Machine Age: Work, Progress, and Prosperity in a Time of Brilliant Technologies*. New York: Norton.

Calvo, E., Mair, C.A., and Sarkisian, N. 2015. "Individual Troubles, Shared Troubles: The Multiplicative Effect of Individual and Country-level Unemployment on Life Satisfaction in 95 Nations (1981–2009)." *Social Forces*: 1625–1653.

Cholbi, M. 2018. "The Desire to Work as an Adaptive Preference." *Autonomy* 4.

Frayne, D. 2015. *The Refusal of Work: The Theory and Practice of Resistance to Work*. London: Zed.

Frey, C.B. and Osborne, M.A. 2017. The Future of Employment: How Susceptible Are Jobs to Computerization? *Technological Forecasting and Social Change* 114: 254–280.

Herbig, B., Dragano, N., and Angerer, P. 2013. "Health in the Long-term Unemployed." *Deutsches Ärzteblatt International* 110: 413–419.

Margerison-Zilko, C., et al. 2016. "Health Impacts of the Great Recession: A Critical Review." *Current Epidemiological Report* 3: 81–91.

Mill, J.S. 2001. *Utilitarianism*. Indianapolis: Hackett Publishing Co.

Russell, B. 1935. *In Praise of Idleness*. London: George Allen and Unwin Ltd.

Sayers, S. 2005. "Why Work? Marx and Human Nature." *Science and Society* 69: 607–616.

Srnicek, N. and Williams, A. 2015. *Inventing the Future: Postcapitalism and a World Without Work*. London: Verso.

Stern, A. 2016. *Raising the Floor*. New York: Public Affairs.

Thompson, D. 2015. A World Without Work. *The Atlantic*, July/August. https://www.theatlantic.com/magazine/archive/2015/07/world-without-work/395294/

Van Parijs, P. and Vanderborght, Y. 2017. *Basic Income: A Radical Proposal for a Free Society and a Sane Economy*. Cambridge, MA: Harvard University Press.

Weeks, K. 2011. *The Problem With Work*. Durham: Duke University Press.

1 A Hayekian Case for Free Markets and a Basic Income

Matt Zwolinski

Introduction

For better or for worse, there are now a substantial number of Americans who know the name of Friedrich Hayek only because his most popular book, *The Road to Serfdom*, was recommended by FOX News personality Glenn Beck as a prescient warning about the dangerous trajectory of the Obama Administration. Most of those people, I suspect, would be quite chagrined to discover that, consistently and throughout his entire career, Hayek defended the rather socialist-sounding idea of an "equal minimum income for all."[1]

There is certainly something of a paradox here. Hayek, one of the best-known free-market libertarians of the twentieth century, was also a defender of what many regard as the apotheosis of the welfare state—a basic income guarantee. And Hayek himself was little help in resolving this paradox. Although his support for a basic income guarantee was consistent throughout his career, Hayek never really provided much detail about *why* he supported it. Many readers were thus left with the forgivable impression that Hayek's support was a kind of fluke—an idiosyncrasy that reflects either (if you're sympathetic to libertarianism) a failure to think through the full logical commitments of his individualistic premises, or (if you're not) a trace of compassion and humanity that his libertarian ideology failed to fully extinguish.

The thesis of this chapter is that Hayek's support of a basic income guarantee was *not* a fluke. Or rather, since I wish to put the emphasis on positive political philosophy rather than Hayekian exegesis, that it need not be a fluke for those of us who draw inspiration from Hayek's ideas. What I shall argue is that a commitment to both the libertarian ideals of free markets and limited government, *and* to the idea of a basic income guarantee, *both* flow naturally from Hayek's fundamental commitment to individual liberty, understood as the absence of coercion.[2]

This thesis, I hope, will be of interest to more than just Hayekians. The Hayekian case for free markets and a basic income, as I understand it, is rooted in Hayek's distinctive understanding of the nature of freedom, and how that freedom operates in a market economy. That understanding of freedom, I will argue, has much in common with the neo-republican conception advanced by theorists such as Philip Pettit.[3] And it is superior to the standard, rights-based account of freedom adopted by libertarians such as Robert Nozick and Murray Rothbard.[4] Thus, one goal of this chapter is to convince non-Hayekian libertarians to adjust their understanding of freedom. This, I believe, will go a long way toward undermining a major source of resistance among libertarians to the idea of a basic income guarantee.

But I also think that non-libertarian republicans have something to learn from Hayek. Republicans in general, and Pettit in particular, have been adept at identifying sources of domination within the private sphere, and in suggesting various ways in which government can act so as to reduce the potential for domination. Where they have fallen short, I think, is in recognizing the ways in which market competition can itself serve as a powerful check against domination, and the ways in which even well-intentioned government policies can both reinforce existing and give rise to new forms of domination.[5] A second goal of this chapter is thus to convince those already attracted to the republican idea of liberty to adopt a more Hayekian understanding of the role markets and governments play in advancing or retarding freedom, and thus, I think, move in a more libertarian direction on questions of public policy.

This chapter is divided into four sections. In the first, I examine more closely Hayek's account of freedom and coercion, especially as developed in *The Constitution of Liberty*. In the second, I show how that account supports the libertarian position of free markets and limited government. In the third, I show how it supports a basic income guarantee. I conclude with the question of whether a guaranteed minimum income ought, as Hayek seems to have believed, to be contingent upon a willingness to work.

Hayek's Account of Freedom and Coercion

Early in *The Constitution of Liberty*, Hayek defines freedom as the absence of coercion.[6] In doing so, Hayek appears, at least to the casual reader, to be following the standard libertarian line. If freedom can be infringed only by coercion, then lack of power or lack of wealth would not appear to render an individual unfree.[7] Taxes and regulations imposed by the government, in contrast, *do* seem coercive and thus do seem to constitute an infringement of freedom on this view.

A close reading reveals, however, that Hayek's understanding of freedom diverges from that of the standard libertarian in terms of both its underling theory and its practical implications. In terms of theory, standard libertarians such as Rothbard and Nozick understand coercion as a moralized term that makes essential reference to the idea of individual rights. Libertarians believe, roughly, that *A* coerces *B* if and only if *A* proposes to violate *B*'s *rights* unless *B* complies with *A*'s demands.[8] Since governments do not have the right to seize an individual's justly held wealth without her consent, its threat to fine or imprison individuals who do not pay their taxes is viewed by libertarians as coercive. Taxation is theft.

As many critics of libertarianism (and some friends!) have argued, the logical implication of this theory of freedom (combined with the libertarian's underlying theory of rights rooted in self-ownership) would seem to be anarchism. Even a minimal state devoted solely to the protection of individuals' negative rights would still require coercive taxation to finance its activities. But if all taxation is a violation of individual rights, then freedom and even the smallest of governments are necessarily incompatible.[9]

Hayek rejects the idea that freedom and coercion should be understood in terms of abstract natural rights. Instead, Hayek holds that freedom consists of being able to live one's life "according to [one's] own decisions and plans, in contrast to . . . one who was irrevocably subject to the will of another."[10] Coercion, in contrast, consists of a state in which "one man's actions are made to serve another man's will, not for his own but for the other's purpose."[11]

According to Hayek, "coercion implies both the threat of inflicting harm and the intention to bring about certain conduct" by means of that threat.[12] The harm that is threatened will often take the form of physical violence, but Hayek notes that threats of brute force are not the only means by which coercion can be exercised.[13] One can also coerce by effectively withholding a resource or service that is crucial to the existence of another individual or the preservation of that he or she most values.[14] The owner of the only source of water in the middle of a desert, for instance, can wield coercive power through his ability to withhold that resource from others.[15] Even a "morose husband, a nagging wife, or a hysterical mother" might be said to exercise "coercion of a particularly oppressive kind," though in these cases any attempt to correct the coercion by means of government action would lead to "even greater coercion" and would thus be unacceptable in a liberal society.[16]

On this understanding of freedom, the activities of government *can* be coercive but need not be so. An absolute monarchy in which subjects' lives property were subject to the whim of the king would clearly be a situation rife with coercion, on Hayek's view. But, crucially, Hayek believed that a government consisting of general rules applied equally and impartially to all would *not* be coercive.[17] Such rules would, of course, restrict what individuals could do. But insofar as they are general and applied equally to all, they do not render any individual subject to the will of any other individual. They are, in Hayek's words, like "laws of nature"—stable facts of social existence around which individuals can learn to navigate and plan their lives. They do not place some citizens in a position of subordination, and they do not elevate others to a position of dominance.[18]

This view of freedom is not without its problems—some of which were pointed out by early libertarian critics of Hayek such as Ronald Hamowy.[19] But one advantage it seems to have over traditional libertarian theories is its focus on the actual character of social relationships. For libertarians, freedom is understood in terms of abstract rights, which are themselves understood in a historical sense.[20] And thus, for the libertarian, we can never tell simply by looking at the character of a social relationship whether it is a state of freedom or unfreedom. A man is being dragged, fighting, into a car by stronger men armed with guns. Is his freedom being infringed? That depends. Is he a criminal who is being justly arrested by the police (or, if you prefer, by the Dominant Protection Agency)? Then, despite all appearances to the contrary, the answer is no—his freedom, that is, his rights, are not being infringed. A soldier is told when to eat, when to sleep, what to wear, and who to kill by his superiors, on threat of severe punishment for disobedience. Is he free? The libertarian's answer is, not if he signed up for it. For the libertarian, it seems that there is no set of social arrangements so oppressive, no amount of being bossed around by others that is incompatible with freedom, so long as that situation *arose* in the right way. Whatever arises from a just situation by just steps, is itself just. And whatever arises from a free situation by freedom-respecting steps, is itself free.

Theodore Burczak has argued that the same is true of Hayek's account since, according to Burczak, Hayek makes the presence or absence of coercion in a proposal depend on how the conditions in which that proposal was made came about.[21] But this, I think, is a mistaken interpretation of Hayek's position. For Hayek, it doesn't matter *how* the wanderers in the desert became dependent on the monopolist. What matters is what the monopolist *does* with that power. If he threatens to withhold resources unless the others do as he wishes, he acts coercively. If he shares the water with them freely, he does not.

How is the monopolist's position different from other forms of conditional transactions in the marketplace? Note that for Hayek it is not the mere presence of monopoly in the background that makes the proposal coercive. Someone who wishes to be painted by a particular artist but must pay a very high fee to do so is not coerced. Hayek's explanation for this is that the painter's service, unlike the water in the desert, is something one can easily do without.[22] But as his later response to Hamowy makes clear, this is only part of the explanation. The deeper explanation is that, for Hayek, you do not have a *right* to the painter's services, whereas you do have a right to life-saving water in the case of an emergency.[23] Hayek admits that he lacks a full account of *why* we have such a right in the desert case, but presumably the fact that the water is vital to our survival is one part of the story, and the fact that the situation is such where the normal mechanisms of supply and demand are insufficient to produce desirable outcomes is another.

With this clarification, Hayek's account of coercion, and his analysis of the several cases he provides, appear to form a plausible and coherent whole. The key issue, for Hayek, is whether a proposal increases or decreases one's options, *relative to a baseline in which one's moral and legal rights are respected*. An offer of an unpleasant job from an employer is (generally) not coercive because it simply adds one option to whatever options one already has, and one does not generally have a *right* to work, or a paycheck, from any particular person. A gunman's threat of "your money or your life" is coercive because it *removes* options—specifically the option to keep both your money and your life—to which you are entitled and which you had before the gunman showed up. Finally, the desert monopolist's proposal to withhold water unless you do as he says is coercive because you have a *right* to a share of the water, and his threat to withhold it is essentially akin to the gunman's threat to take your life unless you hand over your wallet.

Freedom and the Market

Hayek's theory of freedom is in many respects similar to the neo-republican theory advanced most famously by Philip Pettit.[24] Like Pettit, Hayek takes something like the idea of *dominance* to be central to the understanding of freedom, where dominance is understood as being subject to the arbitrary will of another person, and freedom being understood as the absence (or the minimization) of dominance. The question I wish to take up in this section is—how well does a republican view of freedom such as this square with Hayek's embrace of the free market?

Contemporary critics of republicanism, such as Geoffrey Brennan and Loren Lomasky, argue that the view is "profoundly antimarket." I think this view is mistaken, but it is buttressed by the way in which advocates of republicanism such as Philip Pettit and Richard Dagger talk about markets.[25] At best, contemporary republicans take a stance of "complacency" toward markets, tolerating but hardly celebrating them. At worst, republicans are deeply skeptical of markets and view them as a troubling source of domination and unfreedom.

Both Pettit and his critics have a point. But in neither case is that point as strong as it is taken to be. The republican theory of freedom is not *inherently* hostile to markets, and markets are not *inherently* inhospitable to republican freedom.

Indeed, a Hayekian perspective on markets suggests that we can say quite a bit more than this. Markets are not only not inherently inhospitable to republican freedom; they are, in fact, often one of the most effective guarantors of that freedom.

The essence of market competition is the existence of alternatives, and the right to say "no" to proposals that fail to serve one's interests at least as well as one of those alternatives. In a competitive labor market, an employer who tries to force her employee to do something she doesn't want to do is constrained by that employee's ability to quit and find a job elsewhere.[26] Taking that exit option is not always easy, but in many cases it is sufficient to protect the freedom of all that the option *exists* and that *some* people take it. I almost never compare prices on toothpaste among the various stores at which I shop. But *some* people apparently do, and that is enough to keep the price competitively low for everyone.

The more competitive a market is, the more prices and other terms of agreements are regulated by the impersonal forces of supply and demand, and the less any particular market agent is able to impose his particular will on his partner in exchange. Of course, everything in the market has a price, and that price combined with budgetary restraints implies that no one will be "free" to do everything they might wish. But market competition does help to ensure that one's choices will not be determined by the particular will of other market agents. It limits the ability of market agents to *manipulate* your circumstances so that the thing they want you to do becomes your least painful option. Such non-manipulability is an important element of freedom on Pettit's view, and on Hayek's as well.

It is largely because Hayek views competition as such an effective check on coercion that he views government power with suspicion. For government is, after all, the only institution within society to claim and generally possess an effective monopoly on the use of force. And this monopoly on force is often used to establish and maintain *other* monopolies, such as on roads, on the delivery of regular mail, on the creation and enforcement of criminal law, and so on. Because individuals who value these services have nowhere else to go, they are often left with no practical alternative to complying with the government's demands. Indeed, this might very well be the essential difference between government and other organizations within society—most organizations can do nothing more than make proposals to which you are free to say "no"; government, in contrast, does not make proposals—it makes demands.

Insofar as those demands take the form of general rules equally applicable to all, Hayek suggests, the coercive nature of government might be kept to an acceptable level. But as legal rules become more numerous and complex, as ordinary individuals become unable to know in advance what actions are permitted and which are prohibited, as law enforcement becomes practically unable to enforce all the rules that they could, in theory, enforce; the extent of individual discretion increases and so too does the possibility of coercion. When that with which individuals have to comply is no longer "the law" but some bureaucrat behind a desk, or some officer behind a badge, with the practically unchecked power to apply the law in whatever way he or she sees fit, then individuals are no longer fully free.[27]

If, then, we follow Hayek in understanding freedom as the absence of coercion, and coercion as the state of being subject to the arbitrary will of another, his libertarian attitude toward both the market and the state make sense. Competition in the market means that individuals can say "no" to proposals that do not advance their interests, and thereby encourages firms to make offers that *do*. Because individuals are not dependent on any particular buyer or seller, no one is in a position to force them to accept terms that they do not like. In contrast, the lack of competition in government means that individuals will often have no choice but to accept proposals that are not in their interest. Competition protects choice and limits coercion; monopoly inhibits choice and makes coercion more likely. And government is the ultimate monopolist.

Of course, the Hayekian argument in favor of markets that I have just presented applies only to *competitive* markets. And this is a standard that we cannot simply *assume* all markets to meet. No real-world market lives up to the economist's standard of perfect competition with its full information, infinite buyers and sellers, and zero transaction costs. And some real-word markets fall short of even a more forgiving standard of competitiveness. Some markets have significant natural barriers to entry; others have barriers that have been artificially created by government policy. Some markets deal in highly differentiated products for which there are few substitutes; some are plagued by limited and asymmetric information.

In cases where competition is substantially lacking, significant opportunity for coercion may exist. In times or sectors of high unemployment, for example, a manager can use his discretionary power to compel workers to "voluntarily" work overtime, or to keep quiet about their political opinions, or to put up with harassing behavior and so on, on threat of being fired and plunged into unemployment. Hayek recognizes the possibility of such coercion, but views it as a relatively rare phenomenon in a market economy:

> There are, undeniably, occasions when the condition of employment creates opportunity for true coercion. In periods of acute unemployment the threat of dismissal may be used to enforce actions other than those originally contracted for. And in conditions such as those in a mining town the manager may well exercise an entirely arbitrary and capricious tyranny over a man to whom he has taken a dislike. But such conditions, though not impossible, would, at the worst, be rare exceptions in a prosperous competitive society.
>
> (Hayek 2013: 204)

Not every threat of termination will count as coercive on Hayek's view, or indeed on any defensible view of the matter. Whether the threat of termination is coercive will depend, at least in part, on how bad the consequences of termination would be for the employee. For instance, the threat of termination will not qualify as coercive if the employee has other acceptably good opportunities for employment. Nor, I believe, would it qualify as coercion for Hayek if the consequences of *unemployment* are not that bad—perhaps because the employee has a significant amount of savings to fall back on. Recall Hayek's example of the person who would very much like his portrait painted by a famous artist.[28] The artist's monopoly on his own services and his demand for a high price in exchange for them does not suffice to render his offer coercive, for Hayek. And the reason he does not act coercively is that the services he offers are ones that potential customers can easily do without. Similarly, an employer—even an employer who enjoys a degree of monopsony power—will not act coercively if her offer of employment is one which her potential employee can easily do without. I will return to this point in the next section.

Before turning to that section, I wish to raise one more issue regarding the relationship between market competition and coercion. At its best, market competition works to ensure that people's wages and other terms of employment are regulated by the impersonal forces of supply and demand, and not by the whim of any particular employer (or employee). But even in this best case, market competition ensures only that people are paid the fair market value of their labor. It does not ensure that people are paid *adequately* for their labor, at least if we understand "adequate" in some independent sense, such as what would be sufficient to maintain an acceptable standard of living. People whose productivity is very low, for instance, might still receive an inadequate wage under conditions of perfect competition. What, then, should we say about this category of persons, which might include those with a severe disability, or the very elderly? Does the market subject such persons to coercion?

That some persons in a competitive market are able only to earn a wage that is less than adequate for meeting their basic needs does not appear to be *itself* coercive. In cases such as these, wages are low because the productivity of labor is low, and because employers would lose money if they were to pay a wage that was higher. It cannot be said that employers are paying low wages in order to manipulate their employees' options, to bend them to their will, or to take special advantage of them. They are not threatening harm; they are, rather, offering a benefit that will improve the situation of workers, though perhaps not as much as those workers would like.

Even still, although less-than-adequate wages might not *themselves* be coercive, those who are dependent on them are certainly *vulnerable* to coercion from other sources. To be poor is to lack options, and when all of a person's small number of options are extremely bad, it is easy to imagine how an unscrupulous person or firm might exploit that vulnerability for her own advantage. A starving man can be made to act in accordance with your bidding by the "offer" of a loaf of bread, at least if yours is the only offer on the table. To be dependent on your survival on the will of another, and to be compelled to act in accordance with *his* will rather than your own, is, for Hayek, the essence of unfreedom.

The question remains, however, of how we should *respond* to that unfreedom. Legally prohibiting coercive proposals is one option, and in some cases it will be the most appropriate. When we ban threats of physical violence, we eliminate coercion and thereby expand (or at least preserve) the range of options of the potential victims of such threats. But what about the kinds of proposals involved in offering bad jobs to desperately poor people? Should we prohibit sweatshop labor? Notice that if we did so, the result would not necessarily be that the poor would be in a better position with respect to the range of options available to them. People work at sweatshops because they are the least bad option on the table. Taking that option away, without doing anything else to replace it, make those individuals worse off, not better.[29]

What individuals in circumstances like these need is an *expansion* of options, not a reduction. In this case, the minimization of coercion requires not prohibitions, but the provision of opportunities.

It is to the provision of those opportunities that we now turn.

Freedom and the Basic Income

The first step of a Hayekian argument for a basic income is to note that some redistribution is necessary in order to protect people from coercion. Lack of wealth, as we have noted, renders people vulnerable to coercion by others. An employee in a tight labor market must do what his boss tells him or else risk destitution. A wife who is dependent on her husband's paycheck may have to put up with abusive behavior simply in order to keep a roof over her head. In these cases and in many more, a person is unable to escape serious and pervasive interference by others because they lack the financial resources to stand on their own. Providing that person with money gives them options; it gives them the effective ability to say "no"; it gives them freedom.[30]

True, this freedom is achieved by state redistribution. And an opposition to state redistribution is thought to be central to the libertarian ideology. But we should note that the basic idea here is not so obviously different from other forms of policy that libertarians already accept. Leaving the anarchists to the side, most libertarians accept that the provision of police protection is a legitimate function of the state, necessary for the protection of individual rights. But police protection is not provided on a fee-for-service basis. It is funded out of general tax revenues, and then distributed to all persons on the basis of need. If, then, the libertarian can comfortably endorse the redistributive financing of *services* in order to protect individuals against coercion, why can she not also endorse the redistribution of *cash* for the same end? In both cases, the goal is to use coercion to limit coercion—to *minimize* the degree of coercion in society as a whole.

Of course, it is important to note the *limits* of the redistribution that can be justified on Hayekian grounds. The point of redistribution, on this view, is to protect individuals from coercion. And that is a fairly limited goal. It is much more limited, for instance, than the goal of securing *equality* among citizens, or of eliminating the effects of brute luck. A system of redistribution aimed at eliminating coercion will not have the aim of reducing suffering as such, but only a certain sort of suffering caused by the subjection of one individual to the will of another. Freedom from coercion is not the only thing that matters to individuals, of course. But the Hayekian view is that it is the only thing that can legitimately be *demanded* of others, as a matter of justice to be coercively enforced by the state.

Once we have established the necessity of some redistribution on Hayekian grounds, the second step is to determine what *form* that redistribution should take. My claim in this essay is that a Hayekian approach justifies a basic income—a cash transfer that is made equally available to all citizens. So why *this* form of redistribution rather than something else?

Once again, Hayek himself has relatively little to say on this matter. In laying out his position, Hayek writes:

> The assurance of a certain minimum income for everyone, or a sort of floor below which nobody need fall even when he is unable to provide for himself, appears not only to be a wholly legitimate protection against a risk common to all, but a necessary part of the Great Society in which the individual no longer has specific claims on the members of the particular small group into which he was born. A system which aims at tempting large numbers to leave the relative security which the membership in the small group has given would probably soon produce great discontent and violent reaction when those who have first enjoyed its benefits find themselves without help when, through no fault of their own, their capacity to earn a living ceases.
>
> (Hayek 1979: 55)

Hayek goes on to distinguish the assurance of a minimum income from the kind of "social justice" he famously criticized. There is a difference, Hayek argued, between a society that "accepts the duty of preventing destitution and of providing a minimum level of welfare" and one which seeks to "determine the 'just' position of everybody and allocates to each what it thinks he deserves."[31] Insofar as the latter task involves ensuring that "particular people get particular things, it requires a kind of discrimination between, and an unequal treatment of, different people which is irreconcilable with a free society."[32]

One of the themes of *The Constitution of Liberty* is the importance of laws consisting of general rules, equally applicable to all. And this might be thought to justify a *universal* basic income as opposed to some more targeted or means-tested form of transfer.[33] But Hayek himself was insistent that means-testing was essential to any justifiable system of state redistribution.[34] And anyway, I am skeptical that the ideas of "generality" and "equality" can really do much work here. A rule that says that *everyone* who makes less than $12,000 a year gets some help but anyone who makes more doesn't is general in the same way as a rule that says that *all* women over the age of 40 are entitled to annual mammogram, but women under that age (and men!) are not. In both cases, distinctions are made on the basis of relevant differences between persons. People are treated unequally in a sense, but this inequality of treatment seems quite compatible with whatever kind of equality we think ultimately matters in political life.

For this reason, I don't think the sort of basic income justified on Hayekian grounds is incompatible with means-testing—either on the front-end or the back-end. That is, either we redistribute only to those who truly need the help or we give money to everyone but take it back in the form of taxes from those who don't really need it.[35]

The point at which means-testing becomes problematic from a Hayekian perspective—though this is a point that Hayek himself seems never really to have considered—is the point at which the system of redistribution *itself* becomes a means by which some individuals are subject to the arbitrary will of others. To the extent that individuals must satisfy multiple bureaucrats with largely discretionary power that they really *deserve* the money, that they're trying hard to get a job and that they're not just lazy or on drugs or trying to game the system, to this extent individuals are put in a servile position where their ability to satisfy their needs depends on the permission of others who hold a monopoly power over the resources they require. A simple, relatively universal and automatic system of redistribution minimizes discretionary control, and thus frees individuals from this limiting and demeaning process.

Moreover, a system of *cash* transfers gives individuals the freedom to decide for *themselves* what they need, whether that is paying the rent, buying groceries, or saving for future consumption. A system of in-kind transfers, in contrast, puts those decisions in the hands of government, where they are at least as likely to be determined by the pleadings of powerful special interests as they are by genuine considerations of recipients' basic needs. One of the most powerful and consistent themes in all of Hayek's work is his insistence that government planners often lack "knowledge of the particular circumstances of time and place" that would be necessary to carry out their plans effectively.[36] For Hayek, that limitation was an important part of the case for decentralized (i.e., free market) economic planning. But insofar as cash grants decentralize decision-making regarding the most effective use of resources to those who are most familiar with the particularities of their own circumstances, the limitation of knowledge would seem to furnish a powerful argument for cash versus in-kind transfers as well.

Two elements in Hayek's thought—his belief in freedom as a condition of not being subject to the arbitrary will of another, and his well-known skepticism regarding the degree of particular knowledge available to government planners—push in favor of something very close to a universal basic income. But before we conclude our discussion, there is one more element to consider—Hayek's persistent insistence that social welfare payments be limited to those who are genuinely unable to support themselves through work.

Should There Be a Work Requirement?

It is often claimed that one of the defining elements that distinguishes a basic income guarantee from other forms of public assistance is *unconditionality*.[37] That description involves something of an overstatement. Almost all basic income schemes involve *some* conditions on who receives money—in some cases, it is restricted to citizens, in other cases, it is restricted to those above a certain age. But the truth behind the overstatement is that basic income schemes involve far *fewer* conditions than most other forms of public assistance. In particular, basic income schemes are almost always not conditional on recipients *working*, or willingness to work.

I have argued in this chapter that the Hayek's commitment to freedom as non-domination supports his call for provision of a minimum income for all. But that argument leaves open the question of whether that provision should come with strings attached. Should individuals be required to work, or at least be willing to work, in order to be eligible for a basic income?

Hayek apparently thought so. In *Law, Legislation, and Liberty*, Hayek wrote that

> The problem here is chiefly the fate of those who for various reasons cannot make their living in the market, such as the sick, the old, the physically or mentally defective, the widows and orphans—that is all people suffering from adverse conditions which may affect anyone and against which most individuals cannot alone make adequate provision but in which a society that has reached a certain level of wealth can afford to provide for all.[38]

In other words, the point of government transfer payments is to provide for those who are *unable* to provide for themselves. What about those who are able, but unwilling? On this question, Hayek is clear:

> I do not question any individual's right voluntarily to withdraw from civilisation. But what "entitlements" do such persons have? Are we

to subsidise their hermitages? There cannot be any entitlement to be exempted from the rules on which civilisation rests. We may be able to assist the weak and disabled, the very young and old, but only if the sane and adult submit to the impersonal discipline which gives us means to do so.[39]

As an example of the sort of "impersonal discipline" he had in mind, Hayek elsewhere suggested that "some voluntary service on military lines might well be the best form to provide the certainty of an opportunity for work and a minimum income for all."[40]

In these passages, Hayek appears to be at least tacitly endorsing a principle of reciprocity, a principle that has been employed by many critics of a basic income such Stuart White.[41] According to this principle, those who seek to benefit from the productive activities of society have a moral obligation to make some reciprocal contribution to society. There is no right to "free ride" on the productive activities of others, at least when one is capable of making a productive contribution oneself. It is, therefore, the argument continues, proper for governments to condition benefits on work, or willingness to work, as a means of discouraging free riding and ensuring that the reciprocity condition is met.

The reciprocity principle is a powerful one, and enjoys a great deal of both popular and philosophical support. It is possible, however, to defend a basic income without challenging that principle. For instance, even if it is true that individuals who benefit from the productive activities of society have an obligation to make *some* contribution in return, it is far from clear that that reciprocal contribution must necessarily take the form of paid labor. Artists, parents, and caregivers, for instance, all make (or are capable of making) an important contribution to society, but none of them is engaged in the sort of "work" that would qualify them for benefits under something like the Earned Income Tax Credit.[42]

Furthermore, even if the reciprocity principle is true, presumably some accommodation will have to be made for those who genuinely *cannot* make a reciprocal contribution. Those who are physically or mentally unable to work, for instance, presumably should not be excluded from receiving benefits in the way that someone is able but unwilling to work would. So even if the principle of reciprocity excludes *some* non-workers from receiving benefits, it should not be interpreted so as to exclude them all.

So far, the responses I have presented to the reciprocity principle are perfectly general. They are the kinds of responses that many defenders of a basic income have made before. But, interestingly, these responses actually become more powerful when combined with insights from Hayek's own thought. That is to say, the most powerful response to Hayek's objection to an unconditional basic income comes from Hayek himself.

In his discussions of the virtues of a market economy, and in particular his discussion of the role of a freely functioning price system within a market economy, Hayek repeatedly emphasizes the significance of the dispersed nature of knowledge. It is because knowledge of the particular circumstances of time and place is radically dispersed among all the individual members of an economy that central planning by a socialist state is bound to fail.[43] Such a state simply cannot know everything it would need to know in order to utilize resources efficiently. A market economy coordinates knowledge through means of price signals that indicate to buyers and sellers the relative supply of and demand for the various resources they use. But the price system works precisely because it economizes on knowledge. Buyers in the market will almost certainly not know all the reasons *why* a particular good they want has become more expensive; they only know *that* it has become so, and that they must, therefore, give up more of what they want in order to obtain it or do without.

In essence, Hayek's point is that government agents (or anybody else charged with making decisions about large, complex systems) are inevitably going to face a serious problem in obtaining knowledge of all the particular circumstances that would be relevant to determining how to effectively allocate resources. But this point has important implications for the two responses to the reciprocity argument just discussed. With respect to the first, suppose we grant that (i) reciprocity requires those who benefit from society's productive activities make some reciprocal contribution to society, and (ii) some kinds of activity other than paid labor can satisfy this reciprocity condition. We now face the challenge: *Which* kinds of activities are to count as satisfying the requirement, and which aren't? If Suzanne isn't working because she's trying to write the next great American novel, does that count? Does it count only if the novel has a reasonable prospect of success? If James isn't working because he's staying at home raising a child, does that count? What if he doesn't put much effort into being a father, neglecting his kids and watching television all day while they languish in the house unattended?

The point is not that these questions are unanswerable. Clever moral philosophers might very well be able to come up with a theory regarding precisely what counts as a reciprocal contribution, and what does not. The point is that *even if we had such a theory*, putting it into practice would require far more knowledge than governments can ever safely be assumed to possess. How could they know whether James is being a good father or a poor one? What sort of intrusive powers would we have to grant it in order for it to even *begin* to make that determination?

The same form of argument can be applied to strengthen the second response as well. If *some* people are exempt from the reciprocity condition because they are genuinely unable to make a reciprocal contribution, then government must have some means of determining who is unable to work, and who is simply unwilling. This determination will be made considerably more difficult by the fact that those who are merely unwilling will have a strong incentive to deceive government agents into believing they are unable, so as not to lose whatever benefits they might otherwise be entitled to. Here, again, making the correct decision will require considerable knowledge of the particular details of individuals' lives—knowledge that it will not be easy for government to come by, even if we were willing to grant them the considerable intrusive powers they would need in order to make the attempt.

Therefore, even if reciprocity is a valid moral principle, it does immediately not follow that governments should seek to apply it by conditioning benefits on some form of reciprocal contribution. The problem isn't the principle. The problem is that governments simply don't know enough to apply the principle correctly.

But, one might ask, why not try? Even if governments sometimes get it wrong, it might still be better to *approximate* reciprocity than to give up on the principle altogether. This response has some intuitive plausibility. But we cannot necessarily assume that *trying* to implement reciprocity will be better than not trying at all. Trying to implement reciprocity will result in a greater number of type 1 errors—a denial of benefits to those who are genuinely entitled to them. Not trying will result in a greater number of type 2 errors—conferral of benefits on those who are not entitled to them. Whether trying or not trying is better depends, in part, on the relative seriousness of these two distinct types of error.

The question of their relative seriousness is, of course, hard to resolve definitively, depending as it does on the relative weighting one assigns to a range of different moral considerations. Still, there are again resources within Hayek's own thought for concluding that we should be more concerned to avoid errors of type 1 than those of type 2. Errors of type 1 involve denying benefits to those who are entitled to them. And that, in turn, means that those individuals will be subjected to potentially severe and unjustifiable coercion in the marketplace. They will be forced to take demeaning jobs, or perhaps be (coercively) denied access to the basic necessities of life altogether. Errors of type 2, in contrast, mean that some people will get benefits who are not entitled to them, and that, eventually, taxes will, therefore, need to be somewhat higher than they would otherwise be in order to pay for those additional benefits. Hayek rightfully views taxation as coercive, so this consequence is not without moral import. Even still, there is a significant difference between the *degree* of coercion involved in increased taxes, and that involved in being destitute in a market economy. For this reason, someone like Hayek, who sets it as his goal to *minimize* the incidence of coercion, should be inclined to take type 1 errors much more seriously than those of type 2.

Conclusion

If we define a universal basic income as one that involves transfers that are both *unconditional* and in the form of *cash*, then Hayek did not endorse a universal basic income.[44] On the issue of whether transfers should be cash or in-kind, Hayek seems never to have addressed the issue one way or the other at all. But on the issue of unconditionality, Hayek clearly insisted that an individual's entitlement to an "equal minimum income" should be contingent upon a demonstrated inability to support herself through productive labor.

However, the question of what policies Hayek actually *endorsed* is different from that of what policies his principles *commit* him to. This chapter has argued that Hayek's broadly republican account of freedom, combined with his commitment to using the powers of the state to minimize coercion, and his deep skepticism of government's ability to acquire the knowledge necessary to make fine-grained decisions in a complex system, all strongly push in favor of a universal basic income. This case for the basic income is not Hayek's, but it is distinctively Hayekian.

I have not had much to say in this chapter about the *form* that a Hayekian basic income would take. My task here has been to articulate the Hayekian principles that justify a basic income, not to work out the precise details of what the value of that basic income ought to be, whether it ought to be distributed to individuals or families, whether it ought to be administered through the tax system or by some other means, and so on. These are all tremendously important questions.[45] And the Hayekian principles I have suggested here do suggest the general shape that some of the answers to them will take.

For instance, a Hayekian basic income will be aimed at providing a *minimum* income sufficient to provide people with some recourse against coercion. This will almost certainly be less sizable than the sort of basic income defended by Van Parijs, which has as its goal the ideal of *maximizing* the sustainable real freedom of the least well-off.[46] And in order to provide an effective check against domestic coercion, the income should probably be paid to individuals, rather than to heads-of-household as it might be if administered in the form of a negative income tax. Beyond these and other similar broad specifications though, Hayekian principles no doubt leave a wide range of optionality in the design of a basic income. *Some* form of minimum income is necessary to protect individuals against coercion, but the precise details of the system can, on good Hayekian grounds, vary with the particular circumstances of time and place in which it is considered for implementation.

Notes

1. (Hayek 2013: 427)
2. A similar coercion-based argument for a basic income has recently been advanced by Åsbjørn Melkevik. See (Melkevik 2017).
3. (Pettit 2006b)
4. (Nozick 1974; Rothbard 1982, 1973)
5. A notable recent exception is Robert Taylor. See (Taylor 2013, 2017).

6. (Hayek 2013: 57–58)
7. Though see (Cohen 2011) for a critique.
8. For critical discussion of the use of moralized concepts of freedom and coercion by libertarians, see (Cohen 1995; Weinberg 1997; Zimmerman 2002)
9. This was Rothbard's view (Rothbard 1973: Chapter 3), which Nozick famously went to great (though not entirely persuasive) lengths to reject in part 1 of (Nozick 1974).
10. (Hayek 2013: 59)
11. (Hayek 2013: 199)
12. (Hayek 2013: 200)
13. (Hayek 2013: 202)
14. (Hayek 2013: 203)
15. (Hayek 2013: 203)
16. (Hayek 2013: 205)
17. Hayek is actually somewhat unclear on whether such general rules are not coercive at all, or whether they are simply not the *kind* of coercion that we ought to worry about. In support of the former interpretation, Hayek writes that "in so far as the rules providing for coercion are not aimed at me personally but are so framed as to apply equally to all people in similar circumstances, they are not different from any of the natural obstacles that affect my plans" (Hayek 2013: 210). In support of the latter, however, Hayek repeatedly emphasizes that "to prevent people from coercing each other is to coerce them. This means that coercion can only be reduced or made less harmful but not entirely eliminated" (Hayek 1967).
18. (Hayek 2013: 221)
19. (Hamowy 1961)
20. Robert Nozick famously defends a historical account of distributive justice, but insofar as his view of freedom is moralized, such that a situation will count as unfree only if it involves a violation of individual rights, his account of freedom thereby takes on a historical character as well. See (Nozick 1974: Chapter 7).
21. (Burczak 2013: 51)
22. (Hayek 2013: 203)
23. (Hayek 1967)
24. (Pettit 1997)
25. See, for example, (Pettit 2006a).
26. "The individual provider of employment cannot normally exercise coercion, any more than can the supplier of a particular commodity or service. So long as he can remove only one opportunity among many to earn a living, so long as he can do no more than cease to pay certain people who cannot hope to earn as much elsewhere as they had done under him, he cannot coerce, though he may cause pain" (Hayek 2013: 203–204).
27. Considerations such as these partially explain Hayek's deep concern for the rule of law. See (Hayek 2013: part 2).
28. (Hayek 2013: 203)
29. I have discussed this issue in detail elsewhere. See (Zwolinski 2007; Powell and Zwolinski 2011).
30. This form of argument is fairly common among republicans. See, for instance, (Pettit 2007; Casassas 2007; Lovett 2009).
31. (Hayek 2013: 410)
32. (Hayek 2013: 376)
33. James Buchanan, however, appears to have endorsed this sort of argument. See (Buchanan 1997).
34. "The assurance of an equal minimum for all in distress presupposes that this minimum is provided only on proof of need and that nothing which is not

paid for by personal contribution is given without such proof. The wholly irrational objection to a "means test" for services which are supposed to be based on need has again and again led to the absurd demand that all should be assisted irrespective of need, in order that those who really need help should not feel inferior. It has produced a situation in which generally an attempt is made to assist the needy and at the same time allow them to feel that what they get is the product of their own effort or merit" (Hayek 2013: 427).

35. The fiscal equivalence of these two approaches, and thus the fiscal equivalence between a truly unconditional basic income and a Friedman-style negative income tax, can be demonstrated mathematically. See, for a recent example, (Fleischer and Hemel forthcoming).
36. This skepticism received its most famous expression in (Hayek 1945).
37. See (Van Parijs and Vanderborght 2017).
38. (Hayek 1979: 54–55)
39. (Hayek and Bartley III 1988: 153)
40. (Hayek 2007: 152)
41. (White 1997, 2006)
42. Building on this idea, one might argue that it is societies *without* a basic income that violate reciprocity, insofar as socially useful labor outside the sphere of paid employment do not receive just remuneration. For a development of this argument, along with an extended discussion of the relationship between reciprocity and the basic income, see (Widerquist 1999).
43. See (Hayek 1937, 1945, 1978; Hayek and Bartley III 1988).
44. I take these defining elements from (Van Parijs and Vanderborght 2017: chapter 1), which also specifies that any basic income must be an *individual* entitlement.
45. For a discussion of how and why these questions matter, see (Fleischer and Hemel forthcoming).
46. (Van Parijs 1995)

References

Buchanan, J.M. 1997. "Can Democracy Promote the General Welfare?" *Social Philosophy and Policy* 14(2): 165–179.

Burczak, T. 2013. "A Hayekian Case for a Basic Income." In *Basic Income and the Free Market: Austrian Economics and the Potential for Efficient Redistribution*, edited by G.L. Nell, 49–64. New York: Palgrave MacMillan.

Casassas, D. 2007. "Basic Income and the Republican Ideal: Rethinking Material Independence in Contemporary Societies." *Basic Income Studies* 2(2): 1–7.

Cohen, G.A. 1995. *Self-Ownership, Freedom, And Equality*. New York: Cambridge University Press.

Cohen, G.A. 2011. "Freedom and Money." In *On the Currency of Egalitarian Justice and Other Essays in Political Philosophy*, edited by G.A. Cohen and M. Otsuka. Princeton: Princeton University Press.

doi:10.1007/s10551-011-1058-8.

doi:10.1177/1470594x06064218.

Fleischer, M. and Daniel, H. forthcoming. "The Architecture of a Basic Income." *University of Chicago Law Review*.

Hamowy, R. 1961. "Hayek's Concept of Freedom: A Critique." *New Individualist Review* 1: 28–31.

Hayek, F.A. 1937. "Economics and Knowledge." *Economica* 4: 33–54.

Hayek, F.A. 1945. "The Use of Knowledge in Society." *American Economic Review* 35(4): 519–530.

Hayek, F.A. 1967. "Freedom and Coercion: Some Comments on a Critique by Mr. Ronald Hamowy." In *Studies in Philosophy, Politics, and Economics*, 348–350. Chicago: University of Chicago.

Hayek, F.A. 1978. "The Pretense of Knowledge." In *New Studies in Politics, Economics and the History of Ideas*, 25–34. London: Routledge.

Hayek, F.A. 1979. *Law, Legislation and Liberty, Vol. III: The Political Order of a Free People*. London and Henley: Routledge & Kegan Paul.

Hayek, F.A. 2007. *The Road to Serfdom*, edited by B. Caldwell. Vol. II, *The Collected Works of F.A. Hayek*. Chicago: University of Chicago Press.

Hayek, F.A. 2013. *The Constitution of Liberty: The Definitive Edition*, Vol. 17. London and New York: Routledge.

Hayek, F.A. and Bartley, W.W., III. 1988. *The Fatal Conceit: The Errors of Socialism*. Chicago: University of Chicago Press.

Lovett, F. 2009. "Domination and Distributive Justice." *The Journal of Politics* 71(3): 817–830. doi:10.1017/s0022381609090732.

Melkevik, Å. 2017. "No Malibu Surfer Left Behind: Three Tales About Market Coercion." *Business Ethics Quarterly* 27(3): 335–351.

Nozick, R. 1974. *Anarchy, State, and Utopia*. New York: Basic Books.

Pettit, P. 1997. *Republicanism: A Theory of Freedom and Government*. Oxford: Oxford University Press.

Pettit, P. 2006a. "Freedom in the Market." *Politics, Philosophy & Economics* 5(2): 131–149.

Pettit, P. 2006b. "The Republican Ideal of Freedom." In *The Liberty Reader*, edited by D. Miller, 223–243. Boulder: Paradigm Publishers.

Pettit, P. 2007. "A Republican Right to Basic Income?" *Basic Income Studies* 2(2): 1–8.

Powell, B. and Matt, Z. 2011. "The Ethical and Economic Case Against Sweatshop Labor: A Critical Assessment." *Journal of Business Ethics* 107(4): 449–472.

Rothbard, M.N. 1973. *For a New Liberty*. New York: Collier.

Rothbard, M.N. 1982. *The Ethics of Liberty*. Atlantic Highlands, NJ: Humanities Press.

Taylor, R.S. 2013. "Market Freedom as Antipower." *American Political Science Review* 107(3): 593–602. doi:10.1017/s0003055413000300.

Taylor, R.S. 2017. *Exit Left: Markets and Mobility in Republican Thought*. Oxford: Oxford University Press.

Van Parijs, P. 1995. *Real Freedom for All: What (if Anything) Can Justify Capitalism?*, edited by D. Miller and A. Ryan, *Oxford Political Theory*. Oxford: Oxford University Press.

Van Parijs, P. and Yannick V. 2017. *Basic Income: A Radical Proposal for a Free Society and a Sane Economy*. Boston: Harvard University Press.

Weinberg, J. 1997. "Freedom, Self-Ownership, and Libertarian Philosophical Diaspora." *Critical Review* 11(3): 323–344.

White, S. 1997. "Liberal Equality, Exploitation, and the Case for an Unconditional Basic Income." *Political Studies* XLV: 312–326.

White, S. 2006. "Reconsidering the Exploitation Objection to Basic Income." *Basic Income Studies* 1(2). doi:10.2202/1932-0183.1036.

Widerquist, K. 1999. "Reciprocity and the Guaranteed Income." *Politics and Society* 27(3): 386–401.

Zimmerman, D. 2002. "Taking Liberties: The Perils of "Moralizing" Freedom and Coercion in Social Theory and Practice." *Social Theory and Practice* 28(4): 577–609.

Zwolinski, M. 2007. "Sweatshops, Choice, and Exploitation." *Business Ethics Quarterly* 17(4): 689–727.

2 An Anarchist Defense of the Basic Income

Jessica Flanigan

Anarchists should support a basic income. If anarchism is the true theory of justice, then public officials may enforce laws that protect people's natural rights, such as rights against assault, because people who violate or threaten to violate the natural rights of others forfeit their rights against interference. In other words, natural rights, such as rights to one's body, are enforceable. This means that it is permissible for anyone, including public officials, to use of defensive force against a liable aggressor on behalf of oneself or others.

But if anarchism is the true theory of justice, then public officials may not permissibly use force or threats of force against people who are not liable to be coerced. Unless a person consents to a system of law enforcement, additional acts of law enforcement are unjust when officials use force. Certain property rules, which I call property conventions, are enforced even though they do not consist in the protection of people's natural rights and people did not consent to their enforcement. So if anarchism is true, then the enforcement of property conventions is unjust. When public officials commit an injustice, they ought to compensate to the victims of the injustice. Therefore, public officials ought to enforce property conventions that redistribute income in ways that compensate all citizens for the unjust enforcement of property conventions. A universal basic income is one kind of policy that could effectively compensate people.

My argument is similar to Thomas Paine's argument in *Agrarian Justice* for a ground-rent as compensation for the system of property that enables some people to cultivate the earth (Paine 2000). Paine acknowledges that people may have property rights in their labor and the value they add to the land by contributing to it, and that people may be better off on balance if governments enforce property conventions that incentivize the cultivation of the earth.[1] But even a system which promotes overall well-being violates natural rights because, on Paine's view, the earth is the "common property of the human race," meaning that all have natural rights to use it, which property conventions violate when they enforce claims to land which involve excluding people from using it.

Paine, therefore, concludes that everyone who benefits from the enforcement of conventional property rules, which violate people's natural rights to use the land, owe other members of the community compensation. Paine, therefore, supports ground-rent, to be paid into a common fund that would then distribute a grant to each person at the age of 21 "as compensation in part for the loss of his or her natural inheritance."[2] Paine's idea that public officials should enforce redistributive property conventions as compensation for their enforcement of property conventions that violate people's basic rights is the core of the anarchist case for the basic income.

In the first section, "Anarchism," I describe and briefly defend anarchism. If justice requires anarchism, then law enforcement is only just if people consented to the system of enforcement or if enforcement is used to protect people's natural rights. Law enforcement that does not meet these two conditions is unjust because enforcement requires the use of force or threats of force, which violates people's natural rights if they are not liable to be coerced. In the second section, "Property," I argue that property rights are at least partly conventional, and that anarchists should be concerned about the non-consensual enforcement of property conventions that exceed the protection of people's natural property rights. I build on this point in the third section, "Consent," where I argue that people do not consent to the enforcement of property conventions either. Therefore, the enforcement of property conventions violates citizens' natural rights and is, therefore, unjust. Yet it does not follow from the fact that the property system unjustly violates each person's enforceable negative rights that people ought to exercise their defensive rights against the government and disobey property rules or violently oppose officials who enforce them. Even if coercive property systems are not morally permissible because they entail unjustified violations of people's natural enforceable rights, a property system may nevertheless be the morally best available way of protecting people's natural enforceable rights.

In the fourth section, "Compensation," I make the case that officials should compensate citizens for the unjust enforcement of property conventions even if some kind of property system would be the morally best available way of protecting people's natural enforceable rights and all people are better off because of the enforcement of property conventions. I develop two arguments in favor of compensation. First, existing property systems are not the morally best available way of protecting people's natural enforceable rights because they force all people to participate in them to a greater extent than is necessary to ensure that people's natural rights are protected. Whatever property system is enforced, it should minimize the extent to which people subject to it are vulnerable to be the victims of the violence that enforcing it entails. Second, even the morally best system of property conventions would still fall short of the anarchist ideal. Non-consensual public enforcement of some property conventions is at best a second-best system that violates people's rights. I argue in the fifth section, "Basic Income," that a basic income is one way to compensate people for the enforcement of property conventions. A basic income could provide people with the assurance that their natural rights will be protected to a greater extent than existing property conventions do, and it would make space for people to live in society while avoiding the persistent threats from public officials that people in poverty currently face. A basic income would also serve the expressive function of acknowledging the harm that the coercive enforcement of a property system entails.

Anarchism

Anarchists are united in the conviction that people's moral permissions and obligations not change when some people act on behalf of a government or occupy a public role. Michael Huemer develops one of the best defenses of anarchism (Huemer 2013). To illustrate the appeal of the view, Huemer proposes that people answer questions about whether public officials are entitled to enforce laws by asking whether they would judge that their neighbor was entitled to act in the same way. This heuristic is useful for understanding the practical implications of anarchism. A public official can prohibit people from assaulting innocents because all people are entitled to use defensive force against liable aggressors for the sake of protecting others. But public officials may not prohibit people from using harmful substances or trading sex for money, just as it would be wrong if ordinary citizens used force and threats of force to prevent their neighbors from doing these things.

Following Huemer, the version of anarchism that I am defending assumes a particular conception of people's rights and obligations. First, I assume that people have natural rights, including (but not necessarily limited to) rights to their bodies, such as rights against acts of violence that prevent people from making decisions about their bodies. I use the term "rights" to refer to a pro-tanto, enforceable, entitlement to exclusively control something. Natural rights refer to the rights people have just because they are people. These natural rights include rights against murder, assault, and fraud, for example. They also include rights against threats of assault or murder. I use the term "coercion" to refer to announcements that threaten to violate a person's natural rights against violence, or whatever other natural rights she has (Pallikkathayil 2011; Wertheimer 1987). Even in a stateless society, people would retain rights against being assaulted or threatened.

Second, I am focusing on people's *enforceable* natural rights. People use the language of rights in different ways. Some use it to describe claim-rights against interference. This conception of rights broadly aligns with the will theory of rights or a list of negative rights against interference. This is the conception of rights that I am appealing to here. Others use the language of rights to refer to a broader set of interests, which includes a person's interests in acting freely, protection from interference, and interests in resources. I am not opposed to using the language of rights in this way. But for the purposes of the subsequent argument, I am focusing on negative rights against interference. These negative rights are enforceable in the sense that people are entitled to use defensive force or threats of defensive force against aggressors who violate or threaten to violate their natural rights. And bystanders would also be entitled to defensively intervene to enforce others' natural rights.

For the sake of this argument, I am assuming that people's negative natural rights against murder, assault, fraud, and threats of force are enforceable, but I am not assuming that people have natural positive rights or that, if they do, that they have enforceable positive rights. This means that if a person violates or threatens to violate a person's natural bodily rights, for example, that he forfeits his own rights against interference and is, therefore, liable to be threatened with defensive force. And I am also assuming that people are not liable to be threatened if they allow other people to suffer as a result of deprivation, even if people do have unenforceable positive rights to assistance. In other words, people forfeit their natural rights against interference only if they threaten to violate other people's natural rights against interference.

Third, I am assuming that people can waive their natural rights by consenting, which transforms an act that would have been an impermissible rights violation into a permissible encounter. John Simmons makes this point when he argues that it would be permissible for public officials to use force and coercion to enforce laws if people previously consented to a system of law enforcement that was backed by force and coercion (Simmons 1999). It is only in virtue of the fact that people do not consent to public officials' enforcement of laws that renders most law enforcement illegitimate. Together, these assumptions specify two sufficient conditions for the permissible use of force or threats of force against a person. First, if a person forfeits his or her rights against interference by threatening to violate another person's enforceable natural rights against interference, then the use of defensive force or threats of force is permissible. Second, a person can waive her natural rights against interference if she consents to be subjected to force or threats of force.

I have now sketched the broad outlines of anarchism. The main idea is that public officials do not have the authority to do things that would be impermissible if done by anyone else (Huemer 2013; Simmons 1999). Since use of force and coercion against people who are not liable to be interfered with is ordinarily impermissible, it is impermissible for public officials to interfere with non-liable citizens in these ways as well. The particular theory of rights I am assuming may be controversial, but it is flexible enough to accommodate various anarchist frameworks including individualist and left/egalitarian versions of anarchism.

It is worth emphasizing that anarchists do not think that that states should be without order or laws. Some people are liable to be coerced. Specifically, public officials have the authority to coerce people who violate or threaten to violate other people's natural rights because natural rights are enforceable. People who commit acts of violence or threaten others forfeit their rights against interference. For this reason, public officials are entitled to threaten wrongdoers or to use defensive force on behalf of others, just as any other person would have the authority to use defensive force or coercion against an unjust aggressor. Officials can also use force and coercion in cases where people authorize it by consenting beforehand. In these cases, officials do not violate people's rights because citizens can waive their rights. On the other hand, in all other cases, law enforcement is unjust because people are not liable to be coerced or subjected to force by public officials unless they waived or forfeited their rights against interference.

I have not argued for anarchism in this section, I have only described it. I am taking this conception of anarchism as a premise of the argument, though much more would need to be said for it in order to show that anarchism is true. Here are the contours of the view:

1. The moral landscape of permission and obligation is not different for public officials.
2. It is permissible to violate a person's natural, enforceable rights against force or coercion only if he or she is liable to be interfered with or if he or she consensually waives her rights against interference.
3. Therefore, it is permissible for public officials to use force or coercion only against people who are liable or people who waive their rights by consenting.

In general, people do not consent to the enforcement of most laws, and many laws that are enforced are not in the service of protecting people's natural rights. In these cases, law enforcement itself is an impermissible violation of people's natural rights because it entails the use of force or threats of force.

For those who basically accept the anarchist conception of political authority and obligation, the following argument shows that anarchist premises support surprising conclusions about the ethics of existing political institutions. For those who reject anarchism, they may nevertheless find that the practical implications of anarchism are more plausible than they thought.

Property

So far, I have focused on bodily rights when discussing people's enforceable natural rights against interference. But people could have other enforceable natural rights against interference that extend beyond the body as well. If people have natural enforceable property rights, meaning rights to exclude people from using things outside of their bodies, then people would also have rights against theft, in addition to the rights against force, fraud, and coercion that they have in virtue of their bodily rights.[3] If rights against interference extend beyond people's bodily rights, then it is permissible for public officials to enforce laws that protect people's property as well. And if there are natural enforceable property rights then public officials may not violate people's property rights unless they waived or forfeited their property rights.

People disagree about the existence of natural enforceable property rights. As a theory of political authority and obligation, anarchism doesn't take a stand on the scope of natural rights over external objects; it only holds that the entitlements people have to use and control external objects and the obligations people have to respect each other's claims to external objects do not depend on anything a government does. Whether public officials have the authority to use coercion to force citizens to respect each other's claims over external objects depends on whether people have such claims.

Some philosophers argue that all property rights are conventions, constructed by public officials, and that property rights would not exist in the absence of the state (Murphy and Nagel 2004). If all property rights are conventions and anarchism is true, then officials' use of force and coercion for the enforcement of individual's property rights would be impermissible. It is for this reason that some anarchist philosophers, such as Pierre-Joseph Proudhon, have argued that any enforcement of private property is unjust because it violates people's natural rights against interference (liberty) or rights to equal treatment (Proudhon 1876).

Yet some philosophers, including anarchists, do think that people have at least some natural enforceable property rights outside of their bodies, though they disagree about the scope of those rights.[4] One plausible natural enforceable property right is the right to the product of one's labor. For example, Huemer argues that people can have natural rights over external objects in limited cases, such as in the following case:

> Suppose you are exploring a remote wilderness region outside the jurisdiction of any government, when you come upon a clearing containing a rude hut. The hut appears to have been built by a hermit, who is its only inhabitant . . . over his vociferous protestations, you decide to spend the night in the hut, eat some of the food that the hermit has grown and gathered, and then paint the hut lime green. You don't need to do any of these things; you just do them for fun.
>
> (Huemer 2017)

In this case, Huemer argues that you act wrongly even if there isn't a government that establishes people's property rights over their homes. And in cases like these, people can have enforceable natural property rights over external objects in addition to the rights they have to their own bodies, meaning that the hermit would be entitled to use proportionate threats of force to exclude you from his hut and to prevent you from painting it lime green.

Huemer's example appeals to the intuition that the hermit has a greater claim to his hut because he built or maintained it. Dan Moller builds on this intuition. He argues that people have natural enforceable property rights in the product of their labor (Moller 2017). Moller then argues that since most of the wealth generated in developed economies is from the service sector, where people primarily use their labor to generate wealth, then most wealth is derived from things which people have natural enforceable rights over.

But even if we assume that some property rights are natural and enforceable in the way that bodily rights are, all existing property systems also involve the enforcement of conventional property rules. Consider three examples. First, following Paine's argument, the enforcement of property rights in natural resources is at least partly conventional even if natural resource rights are also partly natural, as Huemer suggests. That is, though a person may have a natural right to the fish he catches from the river, his right to the fish that he has not yet caught may be limited by conventions that determine each fishermen's entitlement to the uncaught fish. These conventions may emerge voluntarily and without state interference and develop to the point that they are coercively enforced, even against fishermen who did not consent to the conventions. In this case, enforcement of the fishing conventions might come to require the use of force to exclude fishermen who violate the conventions from the communal pool of resources.

Expanding on this insight, Michael Otsuka (2003: 20) argues that in virtue of the fact that ownership rights over land are conventional, public officials that enforce the conventions in land rights may also permissibly force farmers to provide some of their income to feed their hungry compatriots. We could say the same thing about people who benefit from the enforcement of fishing conventions. Otsuka contrasts these cases with cases where people's wealth issues solely from their bodies, which they do have natural rights to, such as if a person makes a sweater out of her own hair. The idea is that even if people own their bodies, they are not entitled to the unlimited use of natural resources outside their bodies, especially when using those resources requires enforcing rules that would violate the bodily rights of others or substantially disadvantage them in some other way.

Second, money is another non-natural property convention. Most currencies are printed by governments, usually by a central bank that controls the amount of money that is produced, and in so doing, determines the value the amount of money each person possesses. It is useful for public officials to create money because money lowers transaction costs and makes it easier to communicate information about the value of a good or a service. But when public officials create money, they also create a system of property conventions that are enforced with force and coercion against people.

Return to Huemer's example of the hermit and his hut. In the case of real property, it is intuitive that the hermit has an entitlement to his hut and it would be wrong to change his hut in ways he did not consent to, especially if doing so made the hut less valuable to him or others. But imagine that the hermit possessed $10,000 as well. It would not be the same kind of violation, if it were a violation at all, if you traded with his trading partners and thereby enabled them to raise the price of their goods, which effectively diminished the value of the hermit's financial holdings. He would not have the same complaint, for example, if instead making his house 2% less valuable as a house by painting it lime green you instead made his wealth 2% less valuable by trading with the local gasoline supplier, causing higher gas prices in response to increased demand. Nor would it be a comparable violation if the central banker that printed the money merely printed more of it, causing inflation and reducing the value of the hermit's wealth by 2%.

In this way, money is a very different kind of property than one's body or labor or Huemer's house in the woods. Though the scope of a person's authority over his body or time or over an external object that he has a natural right to is fixed, the rights conferred by money can vary. Central bankers can determine the value of each person's holdings, irrespective of his decisions about labor or his body, simply by changing interest rates or by pegging one currency to another. That it is not seen as a violation of a person's right to her money when this happens suggests that the nature of one's property right over money is largely conventional—not justified by an appeal to an independent standard of freedom, bodily rights, or more general natural rights against interference. Yet although money is a convention, it is a convention that each person is forced to participate in. The enforcement of a money system violates people's natural rights because people who do not comply with the money system may be subject to force and coercion even though they do not violate the enforceable rights of others.

Intellectual property rules are a third example of property conventions that are not derived from people's natural rights. Bryan Cwik suggests, for reasons that parallel Michael Huemer's argument for natural property rights over some external objects, that people may plausibly have limited natural enforceable property rights over certain kinds of ideas that are the product of their labor (Cwik 2014). I am skeptical that such rights are enforceable because if one person has an idea and acts on it, the landscape of permission and obligation does not change between people such that other people have a duty not to act on the same idea. People are not liable to be interfered with if they act on an idea that someone else happened to have first. But even though Cwik argues that people have limited rights to control the value of their ideas, it is unlikely that existing intellectual property conventions, which include the enforcement of patents for years, do not violate non-liable people's natural rights at some point.

Unlike the duty to respect people's natural enforceable rights, citizens do not have a duty to comply with conventional property laws. For this reason, people do not forfeit their natural rights when they violate property conventions. So the use of force and coercion for enforcement of property conventions is pro-tanto impermissible unless people consent to the conventions. The anarchist argument against the enforcement of conventional property rights can be stated like this:

1. It is permissible for public officials to use force or coercion only against people who are liable or people who waive their rights by consenting.
2. People who fail to comply with conventional property rules are not liable to be forced or threatened with force.
3. People do not consent to the enforcement of conventional property rules.
4. Therefore, public officials do not have the authority to use force and threats of force against people who fail to comply with conventional property rules. The public enforcement of conventional property rules is wrong.

The first is a statement of anarchism, which I am assuming for this analysis. The second and third statements are the crux of this argument. In this section, I argued that people who fail to comply with conventional property rules do not forfeit their natural rights against force and threats of force in virtue of this fact, as in the last statement. In contrast, people do forfeit their natural rights against force and threats of force to an extent when they violate more fundamental moral rules, such as the rule that people refrain from murder and assault.

Consent

If people consented to the enforcement of a set of property conventions, then it would be permissible for public officials to enforce those property conventions. We can imagine a voluntary system of property. For example, people could choose to use Bitcoin and consent to the enforcement provisions that protect people's claims to their digital currency. Or some people may voluntary join an Israeli kibbutz and thereby consent to a system of property conventions that distributed resources equally to all people, but which also allowed all participants to exit the system of property conventions at any time. And in the absence of the global property order that currently exists, we could imagine even more consensual property conventions that people voluntarily adopt.

But people do not consent to the enforcement of property conventions in general. For this reason, public officials' enforcement of property conventions is unjust. As it stands now, there is a global system of property that no one consents to but which all people are forced to comply with. This force and associated threats of force emerges within conventional property systems in two ways. First, as I have argued, all property claims are backed by law enforcement of one kind or another, and law enforcement is a kind of violence to the extent that it is not for the protection of people's natural bodily rights.

Second, people who lack property are subjected to violence in other ways, because the property system deprives them of the means of living outside of it. Consider black markets as an example of this. Existing property rules deprive some people of the benefits of law enforcement but provide those benefits to others (De Soto 2000). Those who live outside the property system are vulnerable not only to violence from public officials for making trades or enforcing contracts that are prohibited by the property rules of their society, but also to the violence associated with black market property systems that having a publicly enforced property system was designed to solve.

In other words, any property system, to the extent that it enforces property claims for some but not others, to the extent that it upholds rules concerning money and intellectual property, picks winners and losers. And when it does, it cannot say to the losers that they deserve what they get, since the particulars of the system are conventions which are not themselves grounded in more fundamental natural rights. It is in this sense that all existing property systems are unjust (Goff 2017).

These arguments may seem to imply that people are morally permitted to ignore or even forcibly resist the enforcement of property conventions, in virtue of their natural defensive rights. This is true, but people also have moral reasons to not forcibly resist the enforcement of property conventions because, in practice, resistance is likely to involve violating the non-liable bystanders' natural rights and the harms of resistance to property conventions is potentially disproportionate to their injustice. Even though the enforcement of property conventions is unjust because it violates people's enforceable natural rights, enforced property conventions may nevertheless be the best available institutions to protect people's natural rights on balance. So it would be a mistake for a revolutionary anarco-communist to conclude from the foregoing case against property conventions that violently overthrowing the government is permissible. Government-enforced property systems and violent revolutions are wrong for the same reasons—they both involve coercing people who are not liable to be coerced.

It would also be a mistake to conclude from the fact that public officials impermissibly violate non-liable citizens' natural rights by enforcing property rules that they have sufficient reasons, all things considered, to stop enforcing property rules. Officials can vastly improve almost everyone's well-being by upholding a property system. Current economic systems that are broadly capitalist are so much better for people than communist societies or the feudal systems of the past. Agrarian societies were, in the long term, much better for humanity than the hunter-gatherer systems that preceded it. Since property systems can substantially promote overall and long-term well-being, this consideration potentially weighs against the fact that enforcing property conventions violates the natural rights of everyone subject to them.

Therefore, public officials have moral reasons to continue to enforce beneficial property conventions even though they also have moral reason not to. The very same reasons to judge that coercive property systems are unjust are also reasons to support certain property systems as non-ideal mechanisms for protecting people's natural rights, given concerns about the infeasibility of a fully voluntary society and problems with people's non-compliance with their duties to respect each person's natural rights (Valentini 2012). There is also a sense in which public officials who enforce property rules may commit acts of dirty hands, where they violate their duties to respect other people for the sake of the axiological benefits they can achieve through doing so.

The moral reasons for and against enforcing property systems issue from two different moral points of view. From the deontic point of view, which refers to enforcement, all state-run property systems are impermissible. From the axiological point of view, which refers to the goodness of various states of affairs, state-run property systems are good because they are more conducive to well-being and flourishing than alternative systems, and some systems are better than others for the same reason. On one hand, when a person violates another person's rights, she is liable to be defensively interfered with and punished or required to pay compensation to the victim whose rights she violated. On the other hand, if well-being is morally significant at all, then a person may have a most moral reason to nevertheless violate someone's rights for the sake of well-being in some circumstances.

Compensation

Since some property systems violate people's natural rights but are on balance beneficial and overthrowing them would be a greater rights violation and harm in terms of welfare, public officials have sufficient moral reasons to continue to enforce rights-violating property conventions, and citizens do not have sufficient moral reasons to overthrow existing property conventions. Nevertheless, even if coercive property systems are the morally best available way of protecting people's rights, this claim does not imply that existing coercive property systems are morally permissible or that people are not wronged by being forced to participate in them.

For one thing, all existing enforced property conventions not only violate citizens' enforceable rights but also pick winners and losers in ways that are genuinely detrimental to some of the people whose enforceable rights are violated. For another, even an ideal property convention that made everyone as well off as any property system could would not be justified if it violated their rights. For these reasons, public officials should compensate all citizens for the injustice that enforcing property conventions entails.

Consider an analogy to sports. Say everyone in a park would benefit greatly if they spent their Saturday engaged in a cooperative endeavor like a sports game, because otherwise fights would break out from some people's idleness, it would be difficult to coordinate anything more fun, and the park would generally be in a state of chaos. So some people decide to get together and force everyone to play lacrosse. Say they choose on the basis of a vote, after hearing all sides. Still, some people don't want to play lacrosse; they want to play tennis, which advantages the quick and the clever, or football, because they are physically strong. Some people are not sports players and just want to ride the bench or watch from the stands. Forcing everyone to play is an injustice. It may be a beneficial injustice, but it is wrong all the same. Once that injustice has been done, the game-makers owe it to those who lose out to minimize the harmful effects of that injustice.

Even if all people in the park benefit from the game-makers' interference, they are still entitled to compensation for being forced to use the park in accordance with the game-makers' orders. Since the game-makers force everyone to comply with the rules that designate the park to be used for lacrosse, they owe accommodation to the people who opposed lacrosse that will enable those detractors to refrain from playing. The game-makers should permit all people to forego the potential fun they would have playing lacrosse and provide a bench for abstainers to use where they can decline to participate and watch the game without penalty.

Since all non-voluntary property systems violate people's natural rights, all citizens who are forced by public officials to abide by conventional property rules are like the people of the park who are forced to play a game they never consented to. Even if they benefit on balance, they are owed compensation for the injustice of a state-imposed property system and the compensation should enable them to refuse from playing the game, which they never consented to, as much as it feasibly can. Thomas Paine developed an argument like this when he argued that all governments owed people compensation for the enforcement of property conventions that gave some people an entitlement to profit from the land and to exclude others from doing the same. Paine's key insight was that public officials may not justify violating people's natural rights on the grounds that doing so ultimately provides people with morally significant benefits on balance.

The claim that the people who benefit from public officials' coercive violation of natural rights are owed compensation for the officials' beneficial violation may appear counterintuitive at first, but the principle is intuitive in other contexts. For example, Seana Shiffrin argues that it may be wrong to have children when doing so exposes a child to substantial suffering or illness, and that parents may thereby incur duties to compensate their children even if the children are not (and cannot be) worse off due to their conception (Shiffrin 1999). Shiffrin illustrates this point by describing an analogous case where a wealthy person in an airplane drops gold bricks that substantially benefit the recipients. If the wealthy person injures a person's arm in dropping the brick he would owe compensation to his victim even if the victim benefited on balance.

It is also wrong to violate a person's natural rights in order to benefit her paternalistically. For example, it would be wrong for a physician to forcibly perform surgery on an informed patient who competently refused a lifesaving intervention, even if doing so would benefit her on balance (Eyal 2012). Similarly, it would be wrong for a public official to prohibit people from making exploitative or imprudent contractual agreements on the grounds that it would benefit them on balance to be deprived of their economic rights (Flanigan 2017). Many liberal philosophers reject paternalism on the grounds that it violates people's natural rights and is disrespectful to people who are subject to it. In these cases, pubic officials cannot cite the on-balance benefits of violating important liberties as the sole justification for doing so.

Just as it is wrong to expose people to morally significant forms of suffering or to violate people's natural rights in order to benefit them on balance, it is also wrong to treat people unfairly on the grounds that it benefits them on balance. For example, imagine that a racist airline refused to allow a person to board their plane, and the flight then crashed, killing everyone on board (Woodward 1986). The fact that the victim of racial discrimination ultimately benefited from being excluded from the flight does not silence his claim against the airline for discriminating against him on the basis of race.

In all these cases, the fact that a rights-violating, unfair, or injurious form of interference was beneficial and beneficent does not silence claims for compensation. The coercive enforcement of property systems always violates the rights of those who did not consent to them and can be injurious or unfair to those who are immiserated by the enforcement of a particular set of property rules. For these reasons, public officials are obligated to compensate the citizens they have wronged even if the property systems they enforce are on balance beneficial, and even if they act beneficently.

Compensation serves three functions. First, compensation has an expressive function. Providing compensation for wrongdoing is one way of acknowledging the wrongful act and recognizing the moral status of the victim.[5] In general, the law expresses social norms, but it can also change social norms by changing one aspect of the public's expression of its values (Sunstein 1996). Punishment is one area of law where the expressive force of legal norms is especially salient. When public officials punish people, they should express disapproval or reprobation in proportion to the wrongfulness of the crime (Feinberg 1965). Similar norms may inform a theory of compensatory duties. When compensation for wrongdoing is warranted, it should also be proportionate to the magnitude of wrongdoing committed (Klepper 1990; Varuhas 2014). Just as public officials may express disapproval that is proportionate to the wrongfulness of criminals' actions by imposing punishment, they ought to express repentance that is proportionate to the wrongfulness of their own actions by providing citizens with compensation.

Second, compensation has a restorative function, and this second aspect of compensation can inform a theory of what kind of compensation is proportionate to the wrongdoing of imposing a property system on all citizens. Though compensation cannot make a wrongful act right, it can address some of a victim's legitimate grievances pertaining to the wrongdoing (Coleman, Hershovitz, and Mendlow 2015). In the case of the injustice of state-enforced property systems, compensation ought to address the legitimate grievances that the victims may cite against the property system, namely that it treats them unfairly, that they are injured by the threats or acts of force that are used to enforce a property system and, most important, that it violates their natural rights. A just form of compensation would, therefore, mitigate citizens' unfair disadvantages and exposure to injury while enabling them to exercise their natural rights as much as is feasible in light of the continuing enforcement of property rules.

Third, compensation has a relational function. If a person has been wronged, it is important to publicly acknowledge the wrongdoing in order to acknowledge her equal status within the moral community even if an injustice cannot be remedied (Radin 1993; Darwall 2009). This third aspect of compensation can also inform the kind of compensation public officials owe citizens for the unjust enforcement of property norms. Namely, whatever form compensation takes it should not undermine citizens' equal status further, meaning that it ought not be stigmatizing or paternalistic. Officials' initial act violating people's natural rights for the sake of enforcing property rules is itself an act of unjust subordination. Officials should not further subordinate citizens when compensating them for their initial wrongdoing.

Finally, the provision of compensation should be minimally burdensome on non-liable bystanders. This means that compensation for public officials' wrongdoing should not be financed in ways that amount to collective punishment of innocent members of a political community. On the other hand, to the extent that organizations can be collectively responsible for wrongdoing even when none or few of their members acted wrongly, individuals acting on behalf of those organizations may reasonably be expected to apologize or compensate the victims of collective wrongdoing (Shockley 2007). In these cases, the burdens of providing compensation ought to be fairly distributed among members of the organization (Crawford 2007; Smiley 2017).

Basic Income

Since the enforcement of property conventions is unjust, public officials ought to compensate people. In this section, I argue that the compensation should take the form of a universal basic income. A universal basic income is a cash payment given unconditionally to all adult citizens.[6] My argument for the basic income is theoretical; I am not advancing a particular schedule or level of income payments, as long as they effectively compensate people for the injustice of a coercively enforced property system in ways that are minimally burdensome to non-liable bystanders and proportionate to the injustice. In light of these conditions, whatever form or level of payments would most effectively enable people to "opt out" of participation in the property system while still maintaining the benefits that the property system provides, such as economic growth and innovation, is the form and level of income that I support (e.g., Van Parijs 1997).

There are four reasons to favor a basic income as the best form of compensation for the enforcement of a property system. First, a basic income would provide people with more protection for their natural rights than existing property conventions. For example, unlike existing property conventions that force people to work within the property system in order to meet their basic needs, a basic income would enable people to live in society without participating in the property system as a laborer. Second, the current property system is backed by threats of force, and these persistent threats are disproportionately burdensome to people who are disadvantaged by the property conventions themselves. A basic income would insulate people from the harmful effects of some of the threats that are used to enforce property conventions. Third, a basic income is expressively better than existing anti-poverty programs and better restores a relationship of equals between citizens. For example, a basic income is less paternalistic than in-kind benefit programs and the basic income also explicitly acknowledges the harm that the coercive enforcement of property norms entails, thereby silencing some people's concerns about whether beneficiaries are deserving of benefits. Fourth, a basic income also restores egalitarian relations between citizens because it is universal. This aspect of a basic income encourages solidarity among citizens in contrast to existing entitlement programs that induce a zero-sum mindset and class resentment, and which benefit the politically powerful at the expense of the disadvantaged.

The first reason that compensation for the enforcement of conventional property rules should take the form of a universal basic income is that it enables citizens to largely opt out of the property system by choosing not to work. Though a universal basic income cannot justify the injustice of property laws, the basic income is a form of reparation for those whose rights are violated when they are forced to comply. Unlike other justifications for a basic income, this argument does not rely on an empirical hypothesis that a basic income will improve well-being, nor does it assume that people have positive rights to assistance. This justification for a basic income is compatible with both libertarian and egalitarian theories of distributive justice. Any publicly enforced property system, whether capitalist or socialist, equally violates all people's natural rights by forcing them to comply.

Another reason to favor the basic income as a way of compensating people for the wrongful enforcement of conventional property rights is that it serves the aforementioned three functions of compensation while meeting the desiderata of proportionality and minimal harm to bystanders. A basic income for all would acknowledge the fact that all citizens are wrongfully forced by public officials to comply with illegitimate property conventions. It would also address the valid grievances that people may have about the enforcement of property conventions, such as the grievance that property conventions not only violate their bodily rights, but also limit people's freedom in other ways, for example, by forcing people to work and participate in a property system they did not consent to. And a basic income would also acknowledge all citizens' equal rights against interference, which publicly enforced property systems violate, and would reaffirm each person's equal moral status with respect to public officials.

A basic income is also expressively better than existing anti-poverty programs for two reasons. First, unlike the anti-poverty programs favored by public officials on the left and right, the basic income is not paternalistic. Compare a basic income to a program that provides poor families with food vouchers, but allows public officials to dictate which kinds of food they may buy. It is insulting that public officials claim to know which foods families should choose better than they do. Such policies stigmatize and subordinate poor citizens (Anderson 1999). The same can be said of anti-poverty programs favored by the left, such as public health insurance, that prevent poor families from spending the money as they see fit.

Second, because the basic income is justified as a form of compensation for the coercive enforcement of a property system, it silences concerns about whether recipients are deserving of public benefits. So unlike existing anti-poverty programs, which are beset with complaints about the "undeserving poor" receiving too many benefits, a basic income program would not encounter such complaints because all people who are subject to coercive property rules are deserving of compensation and entitled to spend it however they see fit. Such a system would be especially beneficial for women who work in the home and are currently disadvantaged by anti-poverty programs that require recipients to seek paid labor (Pateman 2004).

Egalitarian anarchists should also support the basic income on the grounds that it fosters solidarity between citizens and restores a sense of civic virtue. When anti-poverty programs are restricted to a subset of citizens, it causes citizens who are excluded from the programs to resent the benefits that people in the program receive. And when only a subset of citizens receives benefits, it also encourages rent-seeking, as that subset seeks to expand its own share of collective resources at the expense of other groups. Or, in other cases, citizens don't acknowledge that they receive public welfare benefits, which also diminishes their support for welfare programs that could benefit their compatriots (Mettler 2011).

In some cases, targeted welfare programs not only foster resentment and rent-seeking, but also can exacerbate existing inequalities between citizens and enable politically powerful subsets of a population to exploit and subordinate less powerful groups (Rothstein 2017). Social security is an example of this phenomenon. Social security is a limited basic income program for senior citizens. Senior citizens are an especially powerful political force in the United States, and groups that lobby on behalf of older Americans advocate for regressive tax policies that enrich the old at the expense of the politically powerful young Americans (Wilkinson 2005).

The basic income is a revisionary proposal, and one might worry that enforcing it will be more burdensome to non-liable bystanders than the status quo. But there should be no presumption in favor of property conventions that minimize officials' interference with the choices that people with lots of money make, relative to a property conventions that minimize officials' interference with people's choices on balance. This explains why concerns about burdening non-liable bystanders are misplaced against the basic income. A basic income would likely require that taxpayers pay even more taxes than they currently do.[7] And public officials do coercively require all taxpayers to finance the enforcement of a property system. But taxpayers cannot claim that they are entitled to the particular level of benefits they receive from the property system and that an alternative property system would, therefore, be a violation of their rights. When officials violate all citizens' entitlements by forcing them to comply with the rules of a state-run property system, they do not establish a presumptive claim in favor of maintaining whatever particular system they imposed. Though there are moral reasons to prefer the enforcement of a broadly market-based property system, those reasons do not derive from taxpayers' alleged entitlement to keep their income.

Conclusion

The foregoing arguments in favor of a basic income show that support for redistributive policies does not require accepting the claim that public officials have the authority to coerce people or that people have natural duties to obey public officials. Even anarchists have reason to support policies that protect people from deprivation and promote freedom on balance, not as an ideal but as a non-ideal solution to fact that public officials currently enforce property norms that violate people's fundamental rights.

Critics of redistribution might object that the enforcement of a basic income further empowers the state to coerce people and is, therefore, contrary to the anarchist ideal. This is a natural objection because anarchists are generally against state interference with people's private choices. But the choices that people make about conventional property are not choices that they are entitled to make in the first place. So while people who value money and have a lot of it may think it is wrong for public officials to redistribute their money to others, they would be mistaken. The fact that public officials enforce conventions that constitute and protect people's money in the first place is wrong because it violates the rights of everyone, including those who do and do not have a lot of money according to the conventions. So while redistribution would entail interference with the choices that people with lots of money make, so does a non-redistributive conventional property system. The moral considerations against redistributive property systems are also considerations against the enforcement of conventional property rules, and if officials enforce property rules, they ought to enforce redistributive ones.

A more serious objection, from an anarchist's perspective, is that a basic income policy is incompatible with open borders and the moral demands of global justice (Howard 2006). Anarchists ought to support open borders for the same reasons they ought to oppose the enforcement of conventional property rules. Borders are conventions that public officials establish and enforce, which violate people's natural rights such as their rights against violence and freedom of movement. But if public officials must distinguish citizens from non-citizens in order to provide citizens with a basic income as compensation for the enforcement of conventional property rules, then it may seem as if open borders and the basic income are incompatible. Or, more pragmatically, one may worry that as an empirical matter, states that engage in redistribution are less likely to welcome foreigners and democratic support for redistribution could decline.

Anarchist proponents of a basic income may reply in three ways. First, the principle that public officials owe compensation to the victims of the enforcement of conventional property rules, including currencies and intellectual property protections as well as borders, is an argument in favor of giving some kind of compensation to foreigners as well. Second, the argument for a basic income could be compatible with the ideal of open borders. Officials could refrain from violating people's natural rights by enforcing a border and then compensate them for the violations that the enforcement of other conventional property rules entails. Third, to the pragmatic worry that redistributive states are less welcoming to foreigners even if they need not be, this empirical phenomenon need not undermine the case for either open borders or a basic income, it merely illustrates that in some cases, officials fall short of satisfying their duties of justice. And in a world where all states enforce conventional property rules and borders, any policies that compensate people for these violations of their natural rights improve upon the status quo.

One might also object to this argument on the grounds that a fully voluntary society is impossible, so people's rights are not violated if counterfactually they would have been worse off in all feasible alternative political systems. But the anarchist case for a basic income as compensation for the enforcement of conventional property rules does not assume that people would be better off if conventional property rules were never enforced. It also does not assume that a world without property conventions is possible. Rather, the anarchist case for a basic income illustrates a role for ideal theorizing, even if a political ideal is infeasible and even if people ought not try to achieve it. To anarchists, the ideal political community is a voluntary, non-violent association where everyone respects each other's natural rights. This ideal is incompatible with the enforcement of conventional property rules because enforcing such rules violates people's rights. Yet the enforcement of conventional property rules seems either inevitable, or if it is not, then a society that does not enforce conventional property rules would likely risk falling short of the anarchist ideal of non-violence in other ways.

For these reasons, anarchists should not support policies that dismantle conventional property rules, which could risk making people vulnerable to further acts of violence. Rather, anarchists ought to support basic income policies that compensate people whose rights are violated by officials' enforcement of conventional property rules.

Notes

1. Paine writes, [T]he earth in its natural state . . . is capable of supporting but a small number of inhabitants compared with what it is capable of doing in a cultivated state. And as it is impossible to separate the improvement made by cultivation from the earth itself, upon which that improvement is made, the idea of landed property arose from that inseparable connection; but it is nevertheless true, that it is the value of the improvement only, and not the earth itself, that is individual property (Paine 2000). Karl Widerquist also defends the basic income on the grounds that it is a form of compensation that gives people the freedom to not work (Widerquist 2013).
2. Paine also proposed that the fund be used to finance a retirement program for people over the age of 50 and a program to care for people with disabilities (Paine 2000).
3. Proponents of self-ownership argue that people's bodily rights are property rights, which entitle them to prevent other people from using their bodies

without their consent Critics of self-ownership often reject the property meta-phor for bodily rights, but these disagreements will not undermine the subse-quent argument I develop in this section. Other critics of self-ownership worry that it is arbitrary or too extensive (Cohen 1995; Sobel 2012), but my argu-ment doesn't rely on marginal claims of self-ownership. Rather, it rests on less controversial "core cases" of bodily rights and rights against violence.

4. At times, this disagreement is taken as a sign that people's natural rights over external objects are indeterminate. Some Kantians seem to suggest that the fact that property rights over external objects are both natural and yet inde-terminate in the absence of a state is a reason to think that anarchism is false. This argument assumes that a state is needed to solve the indeterminacy prob-lem associated with the enforcement of people's natural property rights. But if property claims are vague and indeterminate in the state of nature, then states' norms of coercive enforcement for property claims will also be inde-terminate. Public officials don't have a privileged epistemic status that enables them to know how to settle vague property claims, nor would the presence of public officials settle property norms that are indeterminate due to metaphysi-cal vagueness. States are useful because the appropriation of any resource, if it is legitimate, imposes duties on other people not to forcibly interfere with that appropriation and establishes a right of the property holder to use force to defend the appropriation. But everyone else is not obviously liable to be interfered with on the grounds that someone appropriated an external object. And knowing that others may not recognize a property claim, the owner lacks assurance that his negative rights will not be violated as well. In this way, the institution of property makes people vulnerable to acts of violence. The state settles the assurance problem by monopolizing the violence it requires to enforce property claims, which minimizes instances of violence. But the use of state violence is justified in these cases only if it is for the protection of people's enforceable rights, a state cannot settle the scope of those rights in the first place.

5. This expressive function is usually associated with punishment, which goes beyond mere compensation for an injury or a violation to express further disapproval of a rights violation (Feinberg 1965). Yet compensation can also serve this expressive function, which is clear when we consider the expressive nature of denying a person or a group compensation for a rights violation in cases of historical and enduring injustice (Posner and Vermeule 2003; Valls 2003).

6. Conditional payments may be justified for children, just as compensatory benefits or inheritances for children may be required to meet conditions that ensure that the benefits or inheritances are used in ways that further the child's interests. On the other hand, if unconditional payments better promoted chil-dren's interests, then I would favor unconditional payments to children as well (Levy, Matsaganis, and Sutherland 2014).

7. Though some proponents of a basic income, for example, Charles Murray, argue that a basic income need not require higher taxes (Murray 2016).

References

Anderson, E.S. 1999. "What Is the Point of Equality?" *Ethics* 109(2): 287–337.

Cohen, G.A. 1995. *Self-Ownership, Freedom, and Equality*. Cambridge: Cambridge University Press. https://books.google.com/books?hl=en&lr=&id=oeUQjOLNY-wC&oi=fnd&pg=PR9&dq=self+ownership+cohen&ots=e-kkiHs-cm&sig=eGPHUOy2-JWrrbacjYVl8Uzb_LI.

Coleman, J., Hershovitz, S., and Mendlow, G. 2015. "Theories of the Common Law of Torts." In *The Stanford Encyclopedia of Philosophy*, Winter 2015 edition, edited by E.N. Zalta. http://plato.stanford.edu/archives/win2015/entriesort-theories/.

Crawford, N.C. 2007. "Individual and Collective Moral Responsibility for Systemic Military Atrocity." *Journal of Political Philosophy* 15(2): 187–212.

Cwik, B. 2014. "Labor as the Basis for Intellectual Property Rights." *Ethical Theory and Moral Practice* 17(4): 681–695.

Darwall, S. 2009. *The Second-Person Standpoint: Morality, Respect, and Accountability*. Cambridge, MA: Harvard University Press.

De Soto, H. 2000. *The Mystery of Capital: Why Capitalism Triumphs in the West and Fails Everywhere Else*. Basic Civitas Books. https://books.google.com/books?hl=en&lr=&id=vnK3A5uFpqQC&oi=fnd&pg=PA1&dq=hernando+de+soto+property+rights&ots=WxASGKJ9AI&sig=gMl89x3iF2O0A8WpSQuuGr76jwY.

Eyal, N. 2012. "Informed Consent." In *The Stanford Encyclopedia of Philosophy*, Fall 2012 edition, edited by E.N. Zalta. Metaphysics Research Lab, Stanford University. https://plato.stanford.edu/archives/fall2012/entries/informed-consent/.

Feinberg, J. 1965. "The Expressive Function of Punishment." *The Monist* 49(3): 397–423.

Flanigan, J. 2017. "Rethinking Freedom of Contract." *Philosophical Studies* 174(2): 443–463.

Goff, P. 2017. "If Your Pay Is Not Yours to Keep, Then Neither Is the Tax." *Aeon*, 21 September. https://aeon.co/essays/if-your-pay-is-not-yours-to-keep-then-neither-is-the-tax.

Howard, M.W. 2006. "Basic Income and Migration Policy: A Moral Dilemma?" *Basic Income Studies* 1(1). doi:10.2202/1932-0183.1001.

Huemer, M. 2013. *The Problem of Political Authority: An Examination of the Right to Coerce and the Duty to Obey*, 1st edition. Houndmills, Basingstoke, Hampshire; New York: Palgrave Macmillan.

Huemer, M. 2017. *Is Wealth Redistribution a Rights Violation?* https://philpapers.org/rec/HUEIWR [Accessed May 18].

Klepper, H. 1990. "Torts of Necessity: A Moral Theory of Compensation." *Law and Philosophy* 9(3): 223–239.

Levy, H., Matsaganis, M., and Sutherland, H. 2014. *Simulating the Costs and Benefits of a Europe-Wide Basic Income Scheme for Children*. UNICEF Policy and Strategy. www.unicef.org/socialpolicy/files/CPI_Manos_January_2014.pdf.

Mettler, S. 2011. *The Submerged State: How Invisible Government Policies Undermine American Democracy*. University of Chicago Press. https://books.google.com/books?hl=en&lr=&id=sL0rSuBu-v8C&oi=fnd&pg=PP8&dq=submerged+state&ots=NNwXdf3Ae4&sig=I3jjtOd4agD4EZF_JigXs9gJkGs.

Moller, D. 2017. "Property and the Creation of Value." *Economics & Philosophy* 33(1): 1–23. doi:10.1017/S0266267115000395.

Murphy, L. and Nagel, T. 2004. *The Myth of Ownership: Taxes and Justice*, New Ed edition. Oxford; New York: Oxford University Press.

Murray, C. 2016. *In Our Hands: A Plan to Replace the Welfare State*. Rowman & Littlefield. https://books.google.com/books?hl=en&lr=&id=Gx9ADAAAQBAJ&oi=fnd&pg=PR5&ots=GZD9wcV4Il&sig=9GHOCvp4ljzxJwgcECJrp9xBP5o.

Otsuka, M. 2003. *Libertarianism Without Inequality*. Oxford: Clarendon Press.

Paine, T. 2000. *Agrarian Justice*. Raleigh, NC: Alex Catalogue. http://schalken bach.org/library/henry-george/grundskyld/pdf/p_agrarian-justice.pdf.

Pallikkathayil, J. 2011. "The Possibility of Choice: Three Accounts of the Problem With Coercion." *Philosopher's Imprint* 11(16). www.philosophersimprint.org/011016/.

Pateman, C. 2004. "Democratizing Citizenship: Some Advantages of a Basic Income." *Politics & Society* 32(1): 89–105. doi:10.1177/0032329203261100.

Posner, E.A. and Vermeule, A. 2003. "Reparations for Slavery and Other Historical Injustices Essay." *Columbia Law Review* 103: 689–748.

Proudhon, P.-J. 1876. *What Is Property? An Inquiry Into the Principle of Right and of Government*. B.R. Tucker.

Radin, M.J. 1993. "Compensation and Commensurability." *Duke Law Journal* 43(1): 56–86. doi:10.2307/1372746.

Rothstein, R. 2017. *The Color of Law: A Forgotten History of How Our Government Segregated America*, 1 edition. New York; London: Liveright.

Shiffrin, S.V. 1999. "Wrongful Life, Procreative Responsibility, and the Significance of Harm." *Legal Theory* 5(2): 117–148.

Shockley, K. 2007. "Programming Collective Control." *Journal of Social Philosophy* 38(3): 442–455.

Simmons, A.J. 1999. "Justification and Legitimacy." *Ethics* 109(4): 739–771.

Smiley, M. 2017. "Collective Responsibility." In *The Stanford Encyclopedia of Philosophy*, edited by E.N. Zalta, Summer 2017 edition. Metaphysics Research Lab, Stanford University. https://plato.stanford.edu/archives/sum2017/entries/collective-responsibility/.

Sobel, D. 2012. "Backing Away From Libertarian Self-Ownership." *Ethics* 123(1): 32–60.

Sunstein, C.R. 1996. "On the Expressive Function of Law." *University of Pennsylvania Law Review* 144(5): 2021–2053. doi:10.2307/3312647.

Valentini, L. 2012. "Ideal vs. Non-ideal Theory: A Conceptual Map." *Philosophy Compass* 7(9): 654–664. doi:10.1111/j.1747–9991.2012.00500.x.

Valls, A. 2003. "Racial Justice as Transitional Justice." *Polity* 36(1): 53–71. doi:10.1086/POLv36n1ms3235423.

Van Parijs, P., et al. 1997. *Real Freedom for All: What (If Anything) Can Justify Capitalism?* OUP Catalogue. https://ideas.repec.org/b/oxp/obooks/9780198293576.html.

Varuhas, J.N. 2014. "The Concept of 'Vindication' in the Law of Torts: Rights, Interests and Damages." *Oxford Journal of Legal Studies* 34(2): 253–293.

Wertheimer, A. 1987. *Coercion*. Wiley Online Library. http://onlinelibrary.wiley.com/doi/10.1002/9781118785317.weom020106/full.

Widerquist, K. 2013. *Independence, Propertylessness, and Basic Income: A Theory of Freedom as the Power to Say No*. Springer. https://books.google.com/books?hl=en&lr=&id=o6yTqTHFnJkC&oi=fnd&pg=PP1&dq=karl+widerquist+basic+income+compensation&ots=X76Ml3WH58&sig=q8FOH88vjXUDRndBtepZ8VGvSYU.

Wilkinson, W. 2005. *Noble Lies, Liberal Purposes, and Personal Retirement Accounts*. Social Security Choice Paper No. 34. Cato Institute.

Woodward, J. 1986. "The Non-identity Problem." *Ethics* 96(4): 804–831. doi:10.1086/292801.

3 Relational Sufficientarianism and Basic Income

Justin Tosi

People are attracted to egalitarianism for many reasons. One popular reason for its appeal is that it expresses a strong concern for improving the material conditions of the least advantaged. For many egalitarians, that is also probably the most attractive feature of the view.

The topic of this volume, then, presents the class of egalitarian described with an interesting dilemma. Proposals for universal basic income policies have enjoyed a surprisingly broad base of support. Versions of an unconditional basic income have been endorsed by politicians in South Africa, Scotland, Finland, and Switzerland. And both private and public experiments with a basic income are underway. The idea has also drawn support from unexpected parts of the ideological spectrum. In this book, for instance, there are arguments supporting a basic income from the perspectives of both classical liberalism and anarchism.[1]

But what should egalitarians think of a universal basic income? On the one hand, a universal basic income policy would probably make the least advantaged members of society materially better off—perhaps even substantially so. But on the other hand, the adoption of such a policy would leave the distribution of goods (or welfare, or capabilities, or whatever one takes to be the correct currency of egalitarian justice) far short of the egalitarian ideal. The amounts of money typically proposed for a basic income are not so large that they would significantly reduce disparities in wealth. Perhaps some egalitarians would favor the adoption of a universal basic income, hoping that it would put us on the path to more ambitious redistributive policies. Others might be wary of such a policy, fearing that it would restrict the imaginations of policymakers so that they focus on minor issues around the basic income rather than on the possibility of more radical egalitarian measures. But let us set such strategic concerns aside and focus only on what sort of philosophical evaluation egalitarians should make of basic income policies.

Brian Barry considered precisely this question, and he concluded that egalitarians should oppose the basic income if they took any of three common foundations for their egalitarian commitments. Utilitarians could not accept an unconditional basic income, he argues, because whether a person should work depends on whether that person's doing so would contribute to the maximization of utility. Luck egalitarians should oppose a basic income because such a policy would treat those who simply choose not to work similarly to those who, through no choice of their own, are unable to work. It would, therefore, fail to distinguish between cases of brute luck and option luck, as the former would enjoy greater life satisfaction than the latter. Finally, and most interesting for my purposes, Barry argues that those who are egalitarians for reasons of solidarity or fellowship should reject a basic income because it would create a two-class society of the employed and the unemployed:

> [I]f we take economic equality to be an equal material standard of living . . . a system of basic income would create a society that was markedly unequal because of the gap that would have to be created between those on the basic income and those in employment.[2]

I suppose many egalitarians would agree with Barry's assessment. But perhaps an egalitarian who remembers being drawn to her beliefs about distributive justice out of a concern for the least advantaged will recognize in his remarks the thinking of what Adam Smith terms the "man of system." Such a man "seems to imagine that he can arrange the different members of a great society with as much ease as the hand arranges the different pieces upon a chessboard," and "is often so enamored with the supposed beauty of his own ideal plan of government, that he cannot suffer the smallest deviation from any part of it."[3] If commitment to a theory of egalitarian justice would lead one to reject a universal basic income as unjust, then perhaps that is a strike against such a theory. For those who became egalitarians because they wanted to help the least advantaged, then this might be a good time to search for another theory. Alternatively, those who think basic income policies are an attractive idea might be on the lookout for a broader theory of justice that would endorse them.

This chapter develops a tentative sketch of such a theory. Basically, I will take it as a set point that a universal basic income is a just policy and search for an explanation of why that might be. If a basic income strikes us as a fair and just idea compatible with our vision of a good society, why is that so? The answer I defend below is that most recent theorizing about distributive justice and egalitarianism is wrong. A just society is not one in which people must enjoy equal holdings, equal welfare, equal capabilities, or even equal social status. It is, rather, one in which everyone enjoys sufficient social status. I call this view relational sufficientarianism.

Distributive Egalitarianism and Its Discontents

Much of the debate among egalitarians in the post-Theory of Justice era has been about the currency of distributive justice—or the "equality of what" debate.[4] The idea unifying participants in this debate has been that there is some thing X that must be equalized across persons, and our task as moral and political philosophers is to figure out whether it is resources, welfare, capabilities, or something else. And once we have settled that crucial question, the correct public policy is the one that best approximates an equal distribution of that thing.

I would like to discuss two popular views that arose, at least in their contemporary form, as reactions to this debate. The first view is called relational egalitarianism and has been defended most prominently by Elizabeth Anderson and Samuel Scheffler.[5] Relational egalitarians argue that egalitarianism is fundamentally about the elimination of social hierarchy, and the equality worth caring about is relational equality. Anderson in particular chides distributive egalitarians for missing this point by fixating on the distribution of goods at the exclusion of all else. Historically, she points out, egalitarian movements have been concerned with bringing about equality of social conditions, in which people interact with one another in a democratic society of persons with equal status. It is not clear what the distributive implications of this view are, and to my knowledge, no one has attempted to work them out.[6] But critically, equal social relations are not reached simply by distributing things—and certainly not by distribution of a single good.

Is relational egalitarianism any more friendly to basic income policies than are the forms of distributive egalitarianism considered earlier? The differences between employed and unemployed members of society in terms of material holdings, welfare, and so on are not as likely to offend relational egalitarians. It is not necessarily a problem for social relations among free and equal citizens if a basic income makes little headway in lessening the gap between most and least advantaged along whatever metric favored by distributive egalitarians.

But I think relational egalitarians' focus on equal status creates new problems. First is what we can call the jobs problem. Consider the differences in status that might emerge as a result of some having careers—some of which might even be enjoyable—and others being underemployed or even entirely dependent on the basic income. For better or worse, many peoples' self-esteem is bound up with their work. It is important to them that they be able to see themselves as productive members of society who support themselves and their families, and who make a positive contribution to their community through remunerative work.[7] Thus, if the basic income is supposed to address the issue of rising unemployment due to automation, it does not satisfy the primary concern of relational egalitarians. Simply giving people money does not make them feel like the social equal of their fellow citizens when what they really need is a job.[8]

For lack of a better term, we can call a second problem the problem of rubbing it in. A basic income would open up lucrative new frontiers in conspicuous consumption. Most proposals for a basic income are universal, in the sense that everyone would get a basic income payment. Some with far greater sources of income would no doubt seek out opportunities to signal how unimportant their basic income is to them, and businesses would undoubtedly meet their demand with creative offers, all of which would cost exactly as much as the full basic income payout for individuals. Resorts would offer lavish "basic income weekend getaways." Michelin-starred restaurants would design a special "basic income menu." Even charities might get in on the act, offering convenient ways to brag to your friends that you had donated your entire basic income payout, since you certainly don't need it![9] The idea behind all offers would be to blow your entire basic income as frivolously and demonstrably as possible. Perhaps some people would choose an even simpler route, and share a video of themselves simply burning the money. In any case, enterprising minds would find ways to turn the amount of money representing a basic income into a symbol of the lower class and use it to create social distance between that class and themselves. A basic income could thus be used as a weapon against the possibility of a society of equals.

The other view that stands in opposition to distributive egalitarianism is sufficientarianism.[10] Sufficientarianism is also a doctrine about distributive justice, but it holds that equality is not the correct distributive ideal. Instead, what matters from the standpoint of justice is that people have enough. Harry Frankfurt summarizes the case for sufficientarianism as a reaction to distributive egalitarianism this way:

> What I believe [egalitarians] find intuitively to be morally objectionable, in the types of situations characteristically cited as instances of economic inequality, is not the fact that some of the individuals in those situations have *less* money than others but the fact that those with less have *too little*.[11]

As Frankfurt presents it, sufficientarianism is an error theory of egalitarianism. That is, it offers support for an alternative theory by identifying an understandable mistake that many egalitarians have made in their account of their intuitions.

This same type of move will make an appearance later in the chapter, so it is worth lingering for a moment to explain what I mean by this characterization of Frankfurt's argument. Here is an example of an error theory in a different context. When people look at a straw submerged in liquid, they sometimes think that the straw is bent. Their understandable mistake is a failure to consider that, by the principle of refraction, light waves change direction when they change speed. The different medium of the liquid causes the light waves to change speed, and thus direction, causing an optical illusion. When children hear this explanation, they often protest that it cannot be true. They are looking right at the straw, and they would not make such a stupid mistake. This is not a good objection to the principle of refraction, for the obvious reason that the principle undercuts the evidence on which the objection is based.

Paula Casal offers the following objection to Frankfurt's argument: "The claim that all egalitarians, including some of the most sophisticated philosophers, believe that equality matters only because they confuse 'being poorer than others' and 'being poor' is rather implausible."[12] There are two obvious instances of equivocation in this objection. Frankfurt is not accusing *all* egalitarians of making this mistake, nor does he suggest that this is the *only* reason anyone is an egalitarian. Rather, he is picking the most plausible reason for a non-instrumental concern for distributive equality and showing that even it is not a good reason.[13] There are, undoubtedly, distributive egalitarians who base their beliefs on still worse mistakes. (For instance, John Rawls associates some forms of egalitarianism with envy.)

Frankfurt's argument is attractive in part because of the prevalence in ordinary political discourse of the mistake he identifies. Defenders of equality often cite a concern for poor people as the first and strongest reason in favor of redistribution. Rightly so. Surely it is not implausible that many of those who are convinced by these popular appeals come to believe that a concern for the poor is the most compelling basis for egalitarianism. Nor is it implausible that a philosopher's intuition could be, in some sense, rooted in this belief. So there is reason to be suspicious of an intuition that equality is intrinsically valuable, even if that intuition belongs to a sophisticated philosopher.[14] Thus, it is a mistake to dismiss sufficientarianism in much the same way that children dismiss the principle of refraction.

According to sufficientarians like Frankfurt, a society's distribution of goods is just when everyone meets a threshold of sufficiency. If that condition is met, then it does not matter if some have more than others. Thus, unless the currency of distributive justice is jobs, sufficientarians will not have the same objection to basic income policies as relational egalitarians. And as long as the basic income is high enough to meet the threshold of sufficiency, it would seem that sufficientarians would endorse such a policy.

I suppose our search could end here, as we have identified a view of distributive justice that endorses the basic income.[15] But I think there is an important grain of truth in relational egalitarianism. What is the point of isolating the question of what justice demands in the distribution of goods from the question of what justice demands of social relations more generally? We might not like what relational egalitarianism has to say about basic income policies institutionalizing unacceptable social relations, but that does not mean we should expel all relational considerations from our theorizing. Instead, I suggest we explore a theory that combines what is good about sufficientarianism with what is good about relational egalitarianism. The resulting view is relational sufficientarianism.

Relational Sufficientarianism: The Basic Idea

Relational sufficientarianism applies the requirement of sufficiency to social relations rather than distributions. Unlike distributive sufficientarianism, this view does not demand that people *have* enough—or at least that is not its fundamental demand. Like its egalitarian counterpart, relational sufficientarianism does not concern itself directly with the distribution of goods. Instead, it says that society should aim at bringing about sufficiently decent relations and any intervention in the distribution of goods should serve that fundamental aim. The basic demand of the view, then, is that everyone should have social status that is sufficient for decent relations, or those in which everyone is treated with sufficient respect. What are sufficiently decent relations? I do not have a full theory addressing that question to present here, but I take it that at minimum they would include everyone's rights being respected, social mobility (i.e., absence of rigid hierarchical structures), and access to important goods.[16] Notably, they do not include equal social status. They might, however, require equal status in some domains, as sufficient status might sometimes just be equal status. One obvious candidate is equality before the law.

Like its distributive counterpart, relational sufficientarianism can fruitfully be understood as an error theory, but this time of relational egalitarianism. Relational sufficientarianism says that proponents of relational egalitarianism confuse a concern that relations be decent for a concern that they be equal. Again, the error theory interpretation of relational egalitarianism is supported by the cases people appeal to in support of the view—that is, ones in which people are treated horribly. Here is how one relational egalitarian, Carina Fourie, begins a paper on equal social status:

> In the US, black people were often expected to step off the pavement to get out of the way of approaching whites. In apartheid South Africa, black people were expected to call white men "Baas", which means "Boss" in Afrikaans, and white women, "Madam". Although typically this is what black people would call their white employers, they were often expected to call any white people, including strangers, "Baas" or "Madam". White people, on the other hand, would often refer to adult blacks as "boy" or "girl". These are examples of what can be called social inequality.[17]

We hardly need any assistance from relational egalitarianism to see that the treatment described in these cases is morally repugnant. The people in these cases do not need equal social status across the board to have their situations remedied. They do not need a workplace without hierarchical management, for instance, or the elimination of other voluntary associations that admit of distinctions of status. They need to have their rights respected and not to be treated as absolute subordinates in all things. In other words, there is an awful lot of space between apartheid and a society in which all have equal social status. Relational sufficientarians reject arrangements like the former while denying that a just society requires anything as extreme as the latter.

So relational sufficientarianism differs from relational egalitarianism in its view of the demands of justice concerning social status. It too focuses on promoting a certain kind of relations, but it denies that we should aim for equal status and the elimination of social hierarchy. Instead, we should aim for relations in which everyone has sufficient status and so is treated well enough in interpersonal relations. To paraphrase one of Harry Frankfurt's slogans for distributive sufficientarianism, if everyone were treated well enough, it would be of no moral consequence whether some were treated better than others.

There could be more or less fine-grained approaches to relational sufficiency. The coarsest possible view would hold that in some overall summary sense, there should be no social class (or set of persons) whose status is so low that they are not treated sufficiently well. At the other end of the spectrum, one could hold that no one should be subject to insufficiently decent treatment in any of the various spheres of life, however one divvies those up. I find the latter option more plausible and illuminating, but I will not attempt to work the view out here.

Status Relations in a Just Society

Let us now turn to a more detailed comparison of the case these two relational views offer for their accounts of status relations in a just society. Again, relational egalitarians argue that social hierarchy should be eliminated, whereas relational sufficientarians hold that hierarchy is unproblematic so long as everyone is treated with sufficient respect. Samuel Scheffler offers the clearest rejection of hierarchy. Scheffler writes that social equality matters to us "because we believe that there is something valuable about human relationships that are, in certain crucial respects at least, unstructured by differences of rank, power, or status." But, he admits, "differences of rank, power, and status are endemic to human social life."[18] So how can we explain our toleration of hierarchy? Scheffler says that tolerable hierarchies are either instrumentally valuable, "or else it is not necessary, in order for a relationship to qualify as having an egalitarian character, that it should be altogether unmarked by distinctions of rank or status."[19]

I think that this is simply not true of all tolerable hierarchies, unless we interpret "egalitarian character" so broadly that it has nothing to do with social equality. Here is a story in which hierarchy is not instrumentally valuable and still unproblematic. A philosopher was seated at a conference dinner next to John Rawls sometime after the publication of *A Theory of Justice*. Apparently during his military service, Rawls contracted trench foot, and it bothered him for the rest of his life, making it uncomfortable to wear dress shoes. Rawls explained this situation to his dining companion and asked permission to take off his shoes. The man replied, "You're John Rawls. You can do whatever you want!" Now, unless this person went around screaming at graduate students who made similar requests, it would be ridiculous to classify anything about this story as a social injustice. And if he did respond that way to requests from lesser philosophers, it would be unjust only because of his failure to treat another person with respect, not because of his special deference to Rawls. That is because what matters is that we treat such requests with sufficient understanding, even if we're more understanding for people of a certain social status than others. It seems to me that nothing valuable is promoted by this deference to philosophical royalty that would excuse the presence of social hierarchy.

But perhaps Scheffler's other condition is active in this case, and this is a relationship of egalitarian character that happens to include a limited distinction of rank. Those of us who have worked in political philosophy for a while have all met people who knew Rawls and speak of him with such reverence that no impartial observer could describe their relationship as "having an egalitarian character" with a straight face. To outsiders, these encomia to Rawls are sometimes a bit weird, but there is nothing wrong with the relationships described therein.

We can find a less personal example in which hierarchy is clearly appropriate by considering the workplace. There some people have more power in their firm in virtue of their position. It could be objected that hierarchies within firms are acceptable only because they are instrumentally valuable. I do not doubt that company hierarchies are effective means of, for example, increasing productivity, but the fact that they are so effective does not entail that they are justified only because of their instrumental value. Hierarchy within a firm need not be in competition with justice, as it might be a result of justice. Suppose a principle of desert is true and people should be rewarded with increased status in the spheres of life in which they invest their efforts effectively. That people get deserved promotions is unproblematic (and even laudable) so long as other people are not denied access to important goods as a result.

But, it might be objected, what about workplace tyranny? Some employers use company hierarchy to dominate their employees. They make them take drug tests without any occupational justification for doing so. They place unreasonable restrictions on dress, what can be done during breaks, and so on. It is not hard to find accounts of people making justified complaints of lousy, arbitrary treatment from a boss who has been corrupted by power. But none of this provides a case for workplace democracy, or the elimination of hierarchy within firms. It just suggests that some employers don't treat their workers sufficiently well. But once again, there is a lot of space between sufficiently decent treatment and equal status within the firm.

Finally, someone might object that I have been unfair to relational egalitarians. A society of equals is not as demanding as I am making it out to be. Perhaps there is a place for earned and forfeited status in such a society. Here is Scheffler again, on the limits of hierarchy under conditions of social equality:

> [T]he participants in putatively egalitarian relationships must work out the terms of those relationships for themselves. . . . They must establish for themselves the divisions of authority and labor and the patterns of mutual dependence that will characterize their dealings with each other, and they must determine what kinds of role differentiation their relationship can sustain while remaining a relationship of equals.[20]

It is fair to withhold judgment about the specifics of what character relationships can take on while remaining egalitarian, as reasoning in the abstract cannot possibly account for all the potential complications. But it also seems fair to insist that relational egalitarianism can allow only so much hierarchy before it is no longer requiring that we treat one another as social equals, but merely as moral equals. And if all the view says is that we should treat one another as moral equals (i.e., with sufficient respect), and in some special cases that requires social equality, then I have a more accurate name for it: relational sufficientarianism.

The Threshold of Sufficiency

There is one final reason worth considering here to favor relational sufficientarianism to distributive sufficientarianism. The latter view has always faced what I will call the threshold problem: What counts as enough? Distributive sufficientarians have tried to solve this problem by specifying two kinds of thresholds, both of which face enduring objections. Some have offered absolute thresholds. Frankfurt says that we will have reached the point of sufficiency when we have no significant additional desires that would be satisfied with further resources.[21] Roger Crisp says that sufficiency requires enough to support 80 years of high-quality life—an account he proposes as adequate for all possible beings.[22] Basic questions of plausibility aside, absolute thresholds generally seem either too low for developed societies, or too high for developing ones.

The second strategy is to propose a relative threshold, according to which what counts as enough depends on how much some relevant class of others have. This would solve the problem just noted for absolute thresholds, as the demands of sufficiency would vary by a society's stage of economic development. As critics have pointed out, however, this method of specifying a threshold conflicts with Frankfurt's claims about well-being that motivate sufficientarianism in the first place.[23] Frankfurt rejects egalitarianism in part because he says what others have should make no difference to your well-being. But of course if this is true, what counts as enough resources for a person should not depend on what others have, either.

Relational sufficientarianism is better equipped to address the threshold problem. What it means to treat people with respect varies by circumstance. One variable determining what decent social relations require is plausibly the level of economic development and wealth of a society. The resource requirements of relational sufficiency can thus vary depending on facts about a society that impact how its members relate to one another. Rousseau expressed something like the view I have in mind when he wrote that "no citizen should be so rich as to be capable of buying another citizen, and none so poor that he is forced to sell himself."[24] The amount of wealth required to satisfy that criterion would vary according to social and economic conditions. Relational sufficientarianism thus does not restrict itself to absolute thresholds of distributive sufficiency. And it is consistent with Frankfurt's claim that well-being is non-comparative, as the reason for varying the threshold does not depend on the mere fact of others' high well-being. Instead, relational sufficientarianism holds that what counts as enough resources will depend on what is necessary to bring about sufficiently decent relations in a particular society.

It is worth emphasizing one more nice result that falls out of this view. In some political circles, it has lately been a depressingly popular talking point to disparage the less advantaged members of developed societies who complain that they are living in relative poverty. "How can anyone complain about poverty when they have access to a refrigerator, something their ancestors would never have even dreamed of?" is a common instance of the move I have in mind. For relational sufficientarians, this is an easy claim to put to rest. They can complain because what it means for a preindustrial society to show sufficient concern for the well-being of its members bears little relation to what it means for us to do so.

Conclusion

It is time now to deliver on the promise I made at the outset of a view that can embrace a basic income policy. I have worked out only the bare bones of relational sufficientarianism, but I hope it is clear enough that it is better suited than the other views to serve as a theoretical backing for a basic income. For one thing, relational sufficientarianism can endorse a basic income that ensures everyone has enough. And it can tolerate differences in the payment amount for societies at different stages of development. More critically, it can avoid the jobs problem faced by relational egalitarianism, as the view endorses only limited concern for differences in social status brought about by employment status. And it is unconcerned with the problem of rubbing it in that relational egalitarians might bristle at. So unless a lack of employment options causes social relations to become indecent despite a basic income, relational sufficientarians could endorse such a policy.

Notes

1. See essays by Zwolinski and Flanigan.
2. Brian Barry, "Equality Yes, Basic Income No," in *Arguing for Basic Income: Ethical Foundations for a Radical Reform*, ed. Philippe Van Parijs (London: Verso, 1992), 140.
3. Adam Smith, *The Theory of Moral Sentiments* (Indianapolis: Liberty Fund Inc., 1985), 233–234.
4. G.A. Cohen, "On the Currency of Egalitarian Justice," *Ethics* 99, no. 4 (1989): 906–944; Amartya Sen, "Equality of What?" in *The Tanner Lectures on Human Values*, ed. Sterling McMurrin (Cambridge: Cambridge University Press, 1980), 196–220.
5. See, for example, Elizabeth S. Anderson, "What Is the Point of Equality?" *Ethics* 109, no. 2 (1999): 287–337; Samuel Scheffler, *Equality and Tradition: Questions of Value in Moral and Political Theory* (New York: Oxford University Press, 2010).
6. Though at least one person has argued that someone should. See Christian Schemmel, "Why Relational Egalitarians Should Care About Distributions," *Social Theory and Practice* 37, no. 3 (2011): 365–390.
7. Robert Nozick famously poses the experience machine thought experiment, in which he asks whether you would plug into a machine for life that provides you with any subjective experience you want, though you are essentially dead for purposes of the external world. Anyone who teaches this thought experiment has likely seen in many students a powerful revulsion at the thought of plugging in and making no contribution to society. I suspect that similar thinking is behind the negative reaction some have to the admittedly far less extreme idea of a basic income as a replacement for the loss of opportunities to work. Robert Nozick, *Anarchy, State, and Utopia* (New York: Basic Books, 1974), 42–45.
8. Michael Cholbi has argued elsewhere, however, that the stated desire to work is an adaptive preference. See his "The Desire for Work as an Adaptive Preference," *Autonomy* 4 (2018): 1–17.
9. Cf. Justin Tosi and Brandon Warmke, "Moral Grandstanding," *Philosophy and Public Affairs* 44, no. 3 (2016): 197–217.
10. For a recent and thorough defense of distributive sufficientarianism, see Liam Shields, *Just Enough: Sufficiency as a Demand of Justice* (Edinburgh: Edinburgh University Press, 2018).
11. Harry Frankfurt, "Equality as a Moral Ideal," *Ethics* 98, no. 1 (1987): 32.
12. Paula Casal, "Why Sufficiency Is Not Enough," *Ethics* 117, no. 2 (2007): 305.
13. Given that philosophers have had such difficulty finding a basis for equality, this might well be the most plausible reason. For one such discouraging search, see Richard J. Arneson, "What, If Anything, Renders All Humans

Morally Equal?" *Peter Singer and His Critics*, ed. Dale Jamieson (Oxford: Blackwell, 1999), 103–128.

14. For another example, Ronald Dworkin writes: "It is, I think, apparent that the United States falls far short now [of the ideal of equality]. A substantial minority of Americans are chronically unemployed or earn wages below any realistic 'poverty line' or are handicapped in various ways or burdened with special needs; and most of these people would do the work necessary to earn a decent living if they had the opportunity and capacity." Ronald M. Dworkin, *A Matter of Principle* (Cambridge, MA: Harvard University Press, 1985), 208.

15. As we will see, though, sufficientarianism as described so far might have trouble specifying a society-specific basic income level.

16. Because I will not be giving a full account of what kind of relations are sufficiently decent, and this view is new and the general idea unfamiliar, it would be understandable if one felt uneasy about it. For instance, readers might worry that some nasty conceptions of sufficient relations are in this family of views. But that is true of relational egalitarianism, too, before one narrows down the set to what is reasonable. So to provide some reassurance, I take it that any satisfactory account of decent relations would rule out historical caste societies, slave societies, and societies in which women are second-class citizens.

17. Carina Fourie, "What Is Social Equality? An Analysis of Status Equality as a Strongly Egalitarian Ideal," *Res Publica* 18, no. 2 (2012): 107–108.

18. Scheffler, *Equality and Tradition*, 225.

19. Scheffler, *Equality and Tradition*, 226.

20. Scheffler, *Equality and Tradition*, 226.

21. Frankfurt, "Equality as a Moral Ideal," 37–38.

22. Roger Crisp, "Equality, Priority, and Compassion," *Ethics* 113, no. 4 (2003): 762.

23. Casal, "Why Sufficiency Is Not Enough," 301.

24. Jean-Jacques Rousseau, *The Basic Political Writings*, 1st ed. (Indianapolis: Hackett Publishing, 1987), 170. Rousseau's statement may have implications for a ceiling on permissible holdings, as might my own view. But I will leave that issue aside for purposes of this chapter.

Bibliography

Anderson, E.S. 1999. "What Is the Point of Equality?" *Ethics* 109(2): 287–337.

Arneson, R.J. 1999. "What, If Anything, Renders All Humans Morally Equal?" In *Peter Singer and His Critics*, edited by D. Jamieson, 103–128. Oxford: Blackwell.

Barry, B. 1992. "Equality Yes, Basic Income No." In *Arguing for Basic Income: Ethical Foundations for a Radical Reform*, edited by P. Van Parijs, 128–140. London: Verso.

Casal, P. 2007. "Why Sufficiency Is Not Enough." *Ethics* 117(2): 296–326.

Cholbi, M. 2018. "The Desire for Work as an Adaptive Preference." *Autonomy* 4: 1–17.

Cohen, G.A. 1989. "On the Currency of Egalitarian Justice." *Ethics* 99(4): 906–944.

Crisp, R. 2003. "Equality, Priority, and Compassion." *Ethics* 113(4): 745–763.

Dworkin, R.M. 1985. *A Matter of Principle*. Cambridge, MA: Harvard University Press.

Fourie, C. 2012. "What Is Social Equality? An Analysis of Status Equality as a Strongly Egalitarian Ideal." *Res Publica* 18(2): 107–126.

Frankfurt, H. 1987. "Equality as a Moral Ideal." *Ethics* 98(1): 21–43.

Nozick, R. 1974. *Anarchy, State, and Utopia*. New York: Basic Books.

Rousseau, J.-J. 1987. *The Basic Political Writings*, 1st edition. Indianapolis: Hackett Publishing.

Scheffler, S. 2010. *Equality and Tradition: Questions of Value in Moral and Political Theory*. New York: Oxford University Press.

Schemmel, C. 2011. "Why Relational Egalitarians Should Care About Distributions." *Social Theory and Practice* 37(3): 365–390.

Sen, A. 1980. "Equality of What?" In *The Tanner Lectures on Human Values*, edited by S. McMurrin, 196–220. Cambridge: Cambridge University Press.

Shields, L. 2018. *Just Enough: Sufficiency as a Demand of Justice*. Edinburgh: Edinburgh University Press.

Smith, A. 1985. *The Theory of Moral Sentiments*. Indianapolis: Liberty Fund Inc.

Tosi, J. and Warmke, B. 2016. "Moral Grandstanding." *Philosophy and Public Affairs* 44(3): 197–217.

4   The Anti-Paternalist Case for Unconditional Basic Income Provision

Michael Cholbi

Let us suppose that all individuals are unconditionally entitled to a social minimum, some amount of economic resources provided them independently of their labor or other productive activity. What form ought this social minimum take? Traditional social welfare programs typically offer some "basket" of essential goods such as food, housing, health care, and (in some cases) income assistance. Some libertarians or liberals argue that an unconditional social minimum should instead take the form of a government-administered basic income, a direct transfer of cash to recipients, on the grounds that providing the social minimum in the form of a basket of essential goods is objectionably paternalistic.

This anti-paternalist case for a basic income over other forms of a social minimum is often gestured at but rarely developed or theorized in a very detailed way. The aim of my discussion is, therefore, to consider whether there is a plausible anti-paternalist case to be made in favor of providing an unconditional social minimum in terms of a basic income rather than in terms of a basket of in-kind goods.

Notice that an unconditional social minimum of whatever form is almost certainly less paternalistic than a social minimum that comes with various strings attached. Indeed, many of the conditions governments sometimes attach to the receipt of a social minimum appear to be paternalistic: To require that recipients submit to drug testing or forego procreation is to make the provision of the social minimum contingent upon incursions into recipients' liberty, autonomy, or agency so as to ensure that recipients live in ways that the state (or other citizens) believe they ought to. Making the provision of a social minimum unconditional thus removes one avenue for state-provided benefits to be paternalistic. But this provides no anti-paternalistic basis for favoring an unconditional basic income over an unconditional basket. Hence, the further question of whether considerations of paternalism favor an unconditional income over an unconditional basket of in-kind goods remains.

The remainder of my discussion will thus consider the plausibility of several anti-paternalistic bases for arguing for a basic income rather than other forms of a social minimum. My conclusion will be that making an anti-paternalist case for basic income over a basket of essential goods is more difficult than it first appears. Making such a case first requires showing that a basic income is at least as effective in promoting well-being as a basket of in-kind goods. In the first section, "Paternalism and Welfare," I critique this proposition, as well as pointing out that an anti-paternalist case for a basic income cannot rest on this proposition alone. The second and third sections, "Liberty-Based Accounts of Paternalism" and "Rational Will Accounts of Paternalism," consider how an anti-paternalist case for a basic income fares in light of the two most fully developed accounts of the nature and wrongfulness of paternalism, the liberty- or autonomy-based account offered by Gerald Dworkin and the more recent "rational will" account. The third section defends the latter account and suggests how an in-kind social minimum might, in comparison with an unconditional basic income, represent a form of "weak" paternalism. However, in the fourth section, "Paternalism, Justice, and Entitlement," I propose that because states are entitled to prescribe the means by which individuals may pursue just outcomes, individuals would not be treated paternalistically if states opt to provide a social minimum in terms of a basket of goods rather than in terms of a basic income.

In arguing that there is not a strong anti-paternalist case for a basic income over a basket of in-kind goods, it is not my intention to argue against a basic income. Indeed, I am both dispositionally opposed to paternalism and highly sympathetic to the cause of an unconditional basic income. But the best case for the latter ought not appeal to its puta-tively anti-paternalistic credentials.

Paternalism and Welfare

That providing citizens cash rather than in-kind goods is a move away from paternalism is a claim often advanced on behalf of an unconditional basic income, but it is rarely argued for or analyzed in detail.

One of the few explicit attempts to defend this claim is made by lib-ertarian Matt Zwolinski.[1] He favors a guaranteed basic income in part because it is ostensibly less paternalistic than existing social welfare pro-grams. The state ought not make its provision of social welfare dependent on recipients living as the state sees fit, Zwolinksi argues. This extends to the nature of the goods the state provides:

> [B]enefits are often given in-kind rather than in cash precisely because the state doesn't trust welfare recipients to make what it regards as wise choices about how to spend their money. This, despite the fact that both economic theory and a growing body of empirical evidence

suggest that individuals are better off with the freedom of choice that a cash grant brings.

Here, Zwolinski appeals to several different normative considerations: (i) that in-kind benefits indicate that the state "doesn't trust" recipients of the social minimum, (ii) that a "cash grant" provides recipients with greater "freedom of choice," and (iii) that individuals are "better off" under a basic income than with an in-kind basket of goods. Let us address these considerations in reverse order.

A basic income might well prove a more efficient method of maximizing individuals' well-being. With a basic income, individuals could make spending decisions tailored to their own economic circumstances and goals. Rather than receiving a particular amount in housing vouchers, for example, individuals could opt to use their basic income in more flexible ways (buying more health care insurance and less expensive housing, say). The latitude thus provided by basic income may well result in greater individual well-being.

Whether an unconditional basic income improves well-being is an empirical question, and systematic efforts to explore this question are comparatively new. That said, pilot studies of basic income schemes have found positive impacts, in terms both of direct and indirect measures of well-being. Studies of the GiveDirectly program conducted in Kenya in 2011–2013 found that recipients of a monthly unconditional income reported reduced stress and greater self-esteem, especially among female recipients.[2] Evelyn Forget's research on a basic income program carried out in the 1970s in Manitoba found that recipients had fewer doctor visits and hospitalizations for mental health issues and high school students were less likely to drop out.[3] These results are not surprising in light of extant research on income and well-being. While additional income contributes to well-being, this effect "tops out" (in the US, the effect kicks in around $75,000 USD per annum[4]), and in general, the security and reliability of one's income matters nearly as much as its size. More theoretically, an unconditional basic income seems likely to improve well-being by enhancing individuals' control over their lives,[5] especially greater control over their work environments.[6] It may also reduce the load that scarcity places on our "cognitive bandwidth" and better enable effective long-term decision making.[7]

There are, however, two difficulties in inferring that a basic income does better than a basket of in-kind goods with respect to promoting well-being. The first is that the aforementioned research and the theoretical findings that predict it do not carefully distinguish between an unconditional basic income and other forms of an unconditional social minimum, such as a basket of in-kind goods. What this research appears to show is that greater overall economic security redounds positively to well-being. It does not show that enabling this security via a basic *income*, as opposed to in some other form, does better in promoting well-being. The primary explanatory factor behind the increases in well-being seems to be the *unconditionality* of basic income and how it enables individuals to counteract employment-related economic volatility. If so, then there are grounds for supposing that an equally unconditional basket of goods (including, say, medical care, food vouchers, and housing[8]) could have the same positive eudaimonic effects.

Moreover, there are reasons to think a basket of in-kind goods may be more efficacious on this front. If the phenomenon known as *ego depletion* is genuine, then a basic income could make recipients less well-off than a basket of in-kind goods. Ego depletion occurs when individuals' limited pool of mental resources for self-control and complex choices are taxed to the point that later decisions manifest reduced self-control and poor choice making.[9] In distributing an in-kind basket of goods, a state makes particular choices on behalf of recipients. In comparison, a basic income leaves individuals greater latitude over how to capitalize on their basic income. Because it requires recipients to make more choices regarding how to dispose of their social minimum, a basic income is likely to place greater demands on recipients' decision-making powers and thus invite disadvantageous ego depletion. Yet even if a basic income would not result in greater ego depletion, we may have other reasons related to well-being to prefer the narrow range of choices that an in-kind social minimum would provide. Choice takes time and energy that could instead be devoted to enjoying goods that increase well-being. In addition, the availability of choice can also induce self-doubt and anxiety, create unrealistic expectations regarding the outcomes of our choices, and lead to subsequent regret when choices fall short of those expectations. Choice has eudaimonic value, but its value is subject to diminishing marginal returns past which we enter the domain of "choice overload."[10]

I do not contend that these considerations demonstrate that a basic income does worse than a basket of in-kind goods in promoting well-being. It could be that a basic income lands us in the proverbial "sweet spot" regarding the availability of choices and options, that is, it provides us just enough control or range of choice to be better for us than either no social minimum or a social minimum provided as in-kind goods. Or it may be true that to whatever degree a basic income is detrimental to well-being because it requires us to make more choices, we can offset this with self-discipline or self-nudging. Or (as I suspect to be the case) basic income versus a basket of in-kind goods may be a wash as far as overall well-being goes. The crucial point, however, is that existing evidence far from decisively settles the matter in favor of a basic income. We simply need more research on that question.

Yet even if a basic income is superior to an in-kind social minimum with respect to promoting well-being, this fact does not ground a recognizably anti-paternalistic case for the former. For appealing to how basic income is purportedly more efficient in promoting individual well-being seems to miss the philosophical thrust of opposition to paternalism. As we shall see momentarily, paternalism, and its objectionability, can be understood in different ways. However, at the heart of all opposition to paternalism is the conviction that individuals are entitled to a high degree of deference with respect to their self-regarding choices. As Mill famously put it, a person is "amenable to society" for his conduct when it concerns others, but "in the part which merely concerns himself . . . over himself, over his own body and mind, the individual is sovereign."[11] This need not imply that our duty not to interfere with conduct that is solely self-concerning is "absolute," as Mill maintained. Perhaps (contrary to Mill) a person's good can sometimes be so profoundly at stake as to make her good a "sufficient warrant" for interfering with her self-concerning conduct. But in such cases, anti-paternalists will understand her good as a counter-vailing consideration, one that overcomes whatever moral presumption exists against interfering with her self-concerning conduct. A person's good is not itself an anti-paternalistic basis for not interfering with a person's self-concerning conduct, even if (as a matter of fact) refraining from paternalism often maximizes a person's good. And few anti-paternalists would subscribe to a presumption against interference so weak that it would be outweighed whenever interference would advance a person's good. In other words, in order for anti-paternalism to have any teeth, it must sometimes be the case that persons have a right not to be interfered with with respect to their self-concerning choices *despite* others having reason to believe that those choices will be less than optimal from the standpoint of that person's good. If paternalism is at all morally objec-tionable, then individuals sometimes have the right to make mistaken choices, and even to act on those mistaken choices, in the realm of their self-concerning affairs.

Hence, to rest an anti-paternalistic case for a basic income (as Zwolin-ski does in part) on whether it does better than a basket of essential goods in promoting individuals' good is to appeal to a rather diluted picture of the anti-paternalistic constraint on interference with self-regarding con-duct. Indeed, such an appeal seems to lack anti-paternalistic credentials altogether. We must, therefore, look elsewhere for an anti-paternalistic basis for favoring a basic income over a basket of in-kind goods.

Liberty-Based Accounts of Paternalism

Zwolinski's brief remarks contain the seed of a second anti-paternal-istic defense of a basic income: In comparison with an in-kind basket of goods, a basic income would offer recipients greater "freedom of choice." And according to Gerald Dworkin's near-canonical definition of paternalism, to restrict a person's freedom of choice so as to improve the person's welfare is paternalistic. Dworkin defines paternalism as follows:

X acts paternalistically towards Y by doing (omitting) Z if and only if:

1. Z (or its omission) interferes with the liberty or autonomy of Y.
2. X does so without the consent of Y.
3. X does so only because X believes Z will improve the welfare of Y (where this includes preventing his welfare from diminishing), or in some way promote the interests, values, or good of Y.[12]

If this conception of paternalism is correct conceptually and captures what is morally objectionable about paternalism, then an anti-paternalistic case for a basic income and against an in-kind social minimum begins to come into view. Suppose that a policymaker believes that a basket of in-kind goods better serves the interests of recipients of the social minimum. If she provides that social minimum as a basket of goods rather than as a cash transfer, the policymaker interferes with recipients' liberty or autonomy. For if the recipients are entitled to the social minimum, to provide that minimum in terms of a basket of goods rather than a basic income imposes significant limits on recipients' options. A cash payment can presumably be used to buy most any basket of goods the recipient saw fit. She could use all of her payment on rent or on medical care; one-third each on rent, medical care, and food; and so forth. A basket of goods, on the other hand, fixes how her social minimum will be allocated to these component goods. The policymaker who opts for the basket of goods thus impinges on the options available to recipients of the social minimum, thereby impeding them from exercising their liberty or autonomy in ways that a cash payment makes possible. This choice is therefore paternalistic, and on the assumption that concerns about paternalism carry any moral weight, we have reason to favor a basic income over a basket of in-kind goods.

Before considering how strong an anti-paternalist case for a basic income this argument generates, let us first address a worry about whether it even qualifies as an anti-paternalistic argument. On its face, opting for a basket of goods over an income transfer does not seem to involve "interference" with recipients' liberty, as Dworkin's definition of paternalism requires. As noted earlier, any unconditional social minimum is likely to be less paternalistic than any conditional social welfare scheme because determining whether recipients meet the conditions set by the latter scheme will almost certainly involve interferences with their liberty or autonomy. The state will interfere with recipients' liberty or autonomy by requiring them to conscientiously seek employment or to submit to drug testing, and so forth. Hence, *relative* to the baseline of a conditional social minimum, an unconditional social minimum will almost certainly be less paternalistic, irrespective of whether that unconditional minimum takes the form of a basic income or a basket of in-kind goods. Nevertheless, an unconditional basket of in-kind goods, even if it represents an expansion of recipients' liberty or autonomy in comparison with a conditional social minimum, clearly places greater constraints on their liberty and autonomy than does a basic income. The interference with liberty or autonomy here is comparative but real.

So should the fact that a basic income would offer recipients a greater range of options than a basket of goods count in its favor by virtue of its being less paternalistic? The guiding assumption behind this argument is that limiting a person's available options for her own benefit restricts her liberty or autonomy in ways that are worryingly paternalistic. This assumption, I suspect, is doubtful.

One reason for such doubt is that the converse of this assumption is false: Increasing the options available to a person is not incompatible with treating her paternalistically, nor does increasing her available options rebut the charge of paternalism. For one, the scope of a person's liberty or autonomy seems restricted to options that are meaningful or "live" to her. Suppose that a restaurateur concerned about her regular customers' health makes use of research regarding product placement, and so forth, to redesign her menu.[13] She places the healthier entrees (chicken and seafood) near the top left of the menu, the less healthy entrees (beef and pork) at the bottom center. At the same time, she adds ten new items to the menu. However, because the restaurant is a Memphis-style barbecue joint, she knows full well that these new items (plain boiled tofu, for instance) will virtually never be ordered. The restaurateur has plainly acted paternalistically despite the fact that she has given her diners more options overall. The options she has provided to the barbecue aficionados are options that they are very unlikely to choose. The scope of their liberty or autonomy has been expanded in ways that are merely formal, and so the restaurateur cannot rebut the claim that she has acted paternalistically by citing the fact that she expanded the diners' options overall.

Similarly, paternalistic manipulation can occur when one person attempts to *inundate* a person with options. George Tsai has observed that giving a person an enormous number of options and then forcing him to make a rapid decision leads to predictable patterns of choice (e.g., choosing the first or last option mentioned) that can be put to paternalistic purposes.[14]

Examples such as these speak against the thesis there is some positive relation between the number of options available to a person and the scope of her liberty or autonomy (or at least, their scope as it bears on whether an act or policy is paternalistic). Thus, they also speak obliquely against the thesis pertinent to the debate about a basic income versus a basket of in-kind goods, namely, that a basic income is preferable on anti-paternalist grounds to a basket of in-kind goods because the latter restricts liberty or autonomy more than the former. After all, if expanding the number of options available to a person does not by itself make an act or policy *less* paternalistic, why should restricting the number of options available to a person by itself make an act or policy *more* paternalistic?

Still, expanding and restricting options could be asymmetric in this respect, so that expanding a person's options bears no clear relation to whether an act or policy is paternalistic, but restricting a person's options has clear implications, to wit, that it renders an act or policy (more) objectionably paternalistic. But the relationship between an act or policy's limiting a person's options and its being paternalistic is no less haphazard than the parallel relationship between expanding a person's options and treating her paternalistically.

Consider an example mirroring our earlier restaurateur: Suppose she already has a number of menu items that are rarely ordered and wants to encourage her customers to make healthy dining choices. She removes the rarely ordered items and (as before) places the healthier items at eye level on the menu. Here, she acts paternalistically but her removing the rarely ordered items, thereby limiting her customers' options, is incidental to her act's being paternalistic.

There are also instances of paternalism in which a person's liberty or autonomy are essentially unaffected. Jonathan Quong argues that refusing to lend a friend money because you believe she will squander the money is paternalistic, despite the fact that the range of options available to her is precisely the same as it was before your refusal.[15] In this case, paternalism occurs even though the paternalistic act has no effect on the scope or significance of the options available to the friend.

The liberty-based account of paternalism thus errs in supposing that how a paternalistic act or policy affects the number or range of options available to those targeted for paternalism bears any intrinsic relationship to the act or policy's qualifying as paternalistic. But as we have seen, expanding a person's options can be paternalistic, limiting a person's options seems incidental to paternalism as such, and some instances of paternalism do not affect a person's options at all. The scope or range of a person's liberty or autonomy is often affected by being treated paternalistically, but this fact does not define the nature of paternalism.

If restricting a person's liberty or autonomy is not central to paternalism, what accounts for the near-canonical status of the liberty- or autonomy-based account? My own speculation is that the prominence of state paternalism (and the concordant neglect of interpersonal paternalism) in philosophical discussions of paternalism have led to a misunderstanding of the role of coercion (and other means by which options can be limited or curtailed) in paternalism. When the state engages in paternalism toward its citizens, it can use only the tools at its disposal, and its coercive powers (to imprison, levy taxes, and the like) are its principal tools. These tools, in turn, operate primarily by increasing the costs of certain options agents might pursue. State paternalism, in other words, exerts its paternalistic force by attempting to limit (or foreclose outright) options otherwise available to citizens. But to see the limiting of options as essential to paternalism is to confuse what paternalism is with the methods states use to engage in it.[16]

Rational Will Accounts of Paternalism

Making an anti-paternalist case for a basic income would, therefore, seem to require a different conception of the nature and objectionability of paternalism. In recent years, an alternative picture of paternalism has emerged, one that resonates with Zwolinski's remark that states typically do not "trust welfare recipients to make . . . wise choices about how to spend their money."

On what I call *rational will* accounts of paternalism, paternalism has two defining features.[17] First, when acting paternalistically, an individual or institution attempts to motivate the target of their paternalistic action to behave in ways that reflect the paternalizer's judgments regarding what is best for their targets. The paternalistic actor thus aims to decouple the target's judgment from the target's choices and actions, interposing her own judgment so as to influence the target's choices and actions in a way that the paternalistic actor sees as better for her. Paternalism thus involves the attempted substitution of the paternalistic actor's judgment regarding her target's good for that of her target. For adherents of the rational will view, this substitution of judgment is central to what makes paternalism morally objectionable in the first place. To attempt to guide others' self-regarding choices by one's own lights is to wrongfully intrude into a domain of agency concerning which they are owed deference and respect.

Second, the rational will account posits that paternalizers believe that their targets are, with respect to some self-regarding judgment, less rationally competent than they are. This second feature is closely coupled with the first: While it is not impossible to intercede in another's self-regarding choices believing that she is as competent, or more competent, with respect to making such choices, doing so would make paternalism nearly unintelligible. Why, if one is acting paternalistically, that is, for the putative benefit of one's target, would one think paternalism is justified unless one thought that the target's judgment was inferior to one's own with respect to the choices singled out for paternalistic intercession? A paternalistic actor who believes her judgment is not superior to her target seems to be instrumentally irrational, inasmuch as her presumed end (promoting her target's good) is not, by her lights, best realized through her paternalistic action.

Notice that, in contrast to the liberty-based account, the rational will account understands paternalism in terms of the reasons that motivate the paternalistic actor rather than any particular means used by that actor. A paternalist can use whatever means she finds most suitable in order to compel her target to guide her self-regarding choices in ways the paternalist judges best for her. These means can involve limiting (or expanding) the options available to her target, but are not restricted to efforts to shape the options available to her target. The rational will account is thus better situated than the liberty-based account to explain the secondary role that limiting liberty or autonomy has in rendering an act or policy paternalistic.

For proponents of the rational will view, the *mistrust* that paternalistic actors exhibit is key to its moral objectionability. Paternalists do not trust their targets to exercise prudence on their own behalf. The objectionability here stems from how paternalism amounts to a derogation of the status of its target. Rather than viewing the target as an equal participant in social life, thereby entitled to others' deference to his own judgments regarding his good, paternalists view the rational wills of others as impediments to be circumvented by their judgments regarding the target's good. It is often the case that we believe others are prone to misjudgment regarding their own good and how best to achieve it. Setting aside this mistrust of their self-regarding judgments, even when it is justifiable in light of our past evidence about those judgments, is critical to respecting others as our equals. A social world lacking such respect is one that places little stock in the notion that individuals and their rational wills are freestanding sources of authority regarding their own good.[18]

The rational will account is more independently credible than the liberty-based account of paternalism. More germane for our purposes, it puts the anti-paternalistic case for a basic income over a basket of goods on a firmer footing. The rational will account would seem to imply that providing a social minimum in terms of a basket of in-kind goods rather than a basic income reflects an implicit attitude of the state or its policymakers, to wit, they cannot "trust welfare recipients to make . . . wise choices about how to spend their money." To opt for a basket of in-kind goods over a basic income appears to rest on judgments to the effect that the recipients of the social minimum are less competent than the state or its policymakers in determining how their well-being is best realized. The rational will account thus seems to provide an anti-paternalistic reason to favor a basic income over a basket of in-kind goods.

All the same, it is not evident that the rational will account of paternalism better serves the cause of a basic income over an in-kind social minimum. Recall that central to the rational will account is the paternalizer's judgment that her target is comparatively deficient in making self-regarding judgments. This derogation of the target's status, according to the rational will account, indicates a lack of respect for the target and her will as an independent source of reasons. But notice that in the case of a universal and unconditional social minimum, no such comparative appraisal is issued. Because all members of the polity receive the social minimum without condition, there is no suggestion that any *particular* recipient is deficient in judgment, prudence, self-control, or the like. Those who as a matter of fact have poor self-regarding judgment are not singled out by a universal social minimum policy. Granted, one might see such policies as justified, at least in part, by the observation that human agents in general often lack the volitional or agential capacities to make wise judgments regarding their own well-being. Finitely rational agents, to use Kant's term, will frequently not plan well, gather evidence about their options, weigh these options carefully, and so on. This shared vulnerability to various species of practical irrationality seems to favor a guaranteed social minimum as a way of placing a floor underneath us, a floor we need in order to be equal participants in shared social life at all. Yet this rationale for a social minimum carries none of the inegalitarian connotations that, according to the rational will account at least, make paternalism disrespectful, arrogant, and morally troubling. The message of a universal and unconditional social minimum is not that the most unfortunate should bear the stigma of being supported by the public treasury.[19] Rather, the message is that all have a claim to society's economic productivity as a matter of right. The message is one of solidarity rather than of the kind of hierarchy of competence that the rational will accounts finds ratified by paternalism.

The universality and unconditionality of a social minimum thus speaks against its being put to paternalistic uses, or at least, being put to uses that the rational will account of paternalism understands as morally objectionable. Still, opting for an in-kind social minimum over a basic income may carry a whiff of paternalism, inasmuch as the state appears to dictate to its members how it may use the social minimum to which they are entitled. Again, the fact that a universal social minimum does not single out any recipient as especially incompetent in guiding her own affairs suffices, in my estimation, to show that, whatever form a social minimum may take, its provision is not paternalistic. But it nevertheless seems possible that an in-kind basket of goods is more objectionably paternalistic than a basic income even if neither is paternalistic as such.

In one respect, this objection has already been answered: If the allegation is that an in-basket of goods is more paternalistic than a basic income because the latter leaves agents with options for how to exploit their social minimum that the former does not, then the allegation rests on the claim that what renders an act or policy paternalistic is that it limits a person's options for her own good. And as we observed in the second section, that fact does not seem to define paternalism or explain what renders paternalism *pro tanto* objectionable. Better to look, as the rational will account does, to the motivations of paternalistic actors than their methods in order to grasp the nature of paternalism.

Furthermore, even if providing an in-kind basket of goods is more paternalistic than providing a basic income, this provides a weak basis for favoring a basic income, because the paternalistic intercessions in question engage with powers of choice that are fairly peripheral to our agency. As I argue elsewhere,[20] paternalistic acts or policies can intercede in different powers that define rational choice. They can attempt to prevent us from *recognizing* some end as worthy of rational consideration; they can lead us to *discriminate* in favor of some ends over others; or they can attempt to lead us to pursue ends to which we are antecedently committed in ways that the paternalizer believes will make the *satisfaction* of those ends more probable. Because these powers vary in how central they are to our practical identities and in how much mistrust a paternalizer shows by interceding in them, the strength of our reasons to object to paternalism directed at us depend on which of these three powers the paternalistic act or policy intercedes in. We have the greatest reason to object when a paternalistic act or policy intercedes in our power to recognize ends, since the paternalist thereby indicates that our entertaining certain ends as possible objects of choice is so antagonistic to our well-being that we ought not even be permitted to consider those ends. Our capacity to entertain ends as possible objects of choice resides near the heart of our ability to make rational judgments about our own good. In contrast, we have the least reason to object to paternalistic intercessions in our power to satisfy ends to which we are already committed. Our judgments regarding how to satisfy our ends reside near the margins of our conceptions of the good, inasmuch as they are not judgments about goodness as such but about causal or metaphysical relations—about how to realize various states of affairs we have already decided it is worthwhile to pursue. Such judgments are not, therefore, robust reflections of our practical identities, and to the extent that a paternalistic intercession in our power of deciding how best to satisfy our ends shows mistrust, it shows mistrust in judgments of fact rather than of value.

I cannot make a full case here for the philosophical merits of understanding paternalism in terms of our rational powers. Nevertheless, I anticipate that many will find it intuitively credible that paternalism that interferes with the means by which we pursue our ends ("weak paternalism") is less objectionable than paternalism that attempts to influence the ends we pursue ("strong paternalism"). If so, then it follows that whatever anti-paternalistic reasons there are to favor a basic income over an in-kind social minimum reside toward the lower end of the anti-paternalistic spectrum. In opting for an in-kind social minimum over a basic income, policymakers would not be dictating to us "how to live our lives" in any very normatively substantial sense. They would not be attempting to influence what religion we practice, whom we marry, what careers we pursue, what dietary practices we adopt, and so forth. That policy decision reflects judgments about what means are most conducive to citizens' realizing their chosen ends, and so long as the means are sufficiently generic in their instrumental utility (as housing, medical care, food vouchers, and other typical items in the in-kind basket are), then the objection that the state is imposing some conception of how to live seems exaggerated at best.

Paternalism, Justice, and Entitlement

I argued in the previous section that to the extent that an in-kind basket of goods is more paternalistic than a basic income, this is a relatively benign form of weak paternalism wherein the state determines the means by which individuals could pursue their chosen ends. In this section, I argue that it is not even clear that providing a social minimum in terms of an in-kind basket would be paternalistic at all.

An unconditional social minimum, in whatever form, is presumably justified as a means to some just outcome. Candidates for that just outcome include assuring a minimal level of individual welfare; empowering workers (individually and collectively) to improve their conditions of employment; enabling individuals to pursue a wider array of goods, including less work-centered lifestyles, and so forth. An apparently anti-paternalistic defense of basic income might assert that individuals are entitled to the means they desire or see fit in order to realize that just state of affairs. If the state aims (say) to improve individual welfare or empower workers, then perhaps individuals should be given the maximal liberty possible in order to realize such goals, in which case a basic income, inasmuch as it gives individuals greater liberty than an in-kind social minimum, is preferable on anti-paternalistic grounds.

The error in this reasoning is the assumption that, in the realm of state policy at least, individuals are entitled to whatever means they see fit in order to realize just outcomes. A state may permissibly mandate that individuals utilize the means it prescribes in order to realize just outcomes without thereby treating individuals paternalistically. A state that aims to create an educated citizenry does not treat its citizens paternalistically when it limits state support to accredited educational institutions; a state that aims to improve its citizens' health does not treat its citizens paternalistically when it refuses to reimburse citizens for care provided by untrained medical practitioners; a state that aims to encourage homeowners to maintain their dwellings in habitable condition does not treat its citizens paternalistically when it mandates standards for plumbing or electrical wiring; and so forth. Such policies are not instances of weak paternalism because, although they do impose limits on the means citizens may take in the pursuit of desirable social outcomes, citizens are not entitled to choose the means they think are best suited to realizing those outcomes. Democratic policymaking is public and collaborative, involving both shared deliberation and the encumbering of shared resources (e.g., tax revenue). As such, individuals are not entitled to determine on their own what means they will use to pursue just outcomes. In policymaking contexts then, choosing means to just outcomes does not fall within individuals' "legitimate domain of judgment or action."[21] Admittedly, when the state prescribes means in this way, it relies on collective judgments about which means are most instrumentally effective in realizing these just outcomes. In this regard, the state does not entrust individuals to decide such matters for themselves. It may, therefore, appear that the state thereby shows the mistrust that, according to the rational will view of paternalism outline in the previous section, characterizes paternalism and renders it morally objectionable. But prescribing means need not reflect mistrust of individuals, and more importantly, a policy that mandates particular means is paternalistic only when choosing means to just outcomes falls within individuals' legitimate domain of judgment or action. The determination of what means the state will endorse or facilitate in the pursuit of just outcomes does not fall within individuals' legitimate domain of judgment or action. In this respect, paternalism assumes a distinction between properly public choice and a realm of "private" individual authority.

Notice that this conclusion is compatible with a general presumption in favor of allowing individuals to choose whatever means are consistent with realizing just or socially desirable outcomes. At the same time, though, this conclusion underscores that when it comes to the provision of public benefits, communities may rightfully operate according to their own objective (or at least intersubjective) determination of how such benefits are best provided instead of deferring to individual judgments. And when individuals are not entitled to act on their judgment of appropriate means in the first place, we do not treat them paternalistically when our public policies dictate those means to them.

Hence, in opting to provide a social minimum in terms of a basket of in-kind goods instead of as a basic income, states do not treat their members paternalistically, for such choices lie within their domain of choice rather than in the members' domains of choice. Of course, this is not an argument in favor of the social minimum taking the form of a basket of in-kind goods. It does, however, show that there is not a compelling argument in this area for its being paternalistic to do so.

Conclusion

As indicated at the outset, any unconditional social minimum will almost certainly be less paternalistic than the systems of social welfare in place in many communities, systems that subject their beneficiaries to intrusive and insulting compliance conditions. Opponents of paternalism should thus welcome the prospect of communities transitioning from conditional to unconditional social minima. As it turns out, though, there is not a compelling anti-paternalistic basis for a social minimum to take the form of a basic income rather than a basket of goods. No matter if we think of paternalism in terms of limiting agents' options or in terms of mistrusting their judgment, providing a basket of goods rather than a basic income is not more paternalistic. But these same considerations illustrate that there is also not a compelling anti-paternalistic case for the social minimum to be provided as a basket of goods. Perhaps surprisingly, paternalism is largely immaterial to the moral question of how a social minimum should be provided. Deciding what form a social minimum takes should thus be decided on other grounds, most notably, what form will best realize the outcomes that provide an unconditional social minimum its rationale.

Notes

1. "The Pragmatic Libertarian Case for a Basic Income Guarantee," *Cato Unbound: A Journal of Debate*, August 4, 2014. https://www.cato-unbound.org/2014/08/04/matt-zwolinski/pragmatic-libertarian-case-basic-income-guarantee, accessed 17 July 2017.
2. Johannes Haushofer and Jeremy Shapiro, "The Short-Term Impact of Unconditional Cash Transfers to the Poor: Experimental Evidence From Kenya," *Quarterly Journal of Economics* 131 (2016): 1973–2042. doi:10.1093/qje/qjw025.
3. "The Town With No Poverty: The Health Effects of a Canadian Guaranteed Annual Income Field Experiment," *Canadian Public Policy* 37 (2011): 283–305.
4. Angus Deaton and Daniel Kahneman, "High Income Improves Evaluation of Life But Not Emotional Well-being," *Proceedings of the National Academy of Sciences* 107 (2010): 16489–16493. doi:10.1073/pnas.1011492107.
5. Richard M. Ryan and Edward L. Deci, "Self-determination Theory and the Facilitation of Intrinsic Motivation, Social Development, and Well-Being," *American Psychologist* 55 (2000): 68–78.
6. Chris Yuill, "Health and the Workplace: Thinking About Sickness, Hierarchy and Workplace Conditions," *International Journal of Management Concepts and Philosophy* 3 (2009): 239–256.
7. Anandi Mani, Sendhil Mullainathan, Eldar Shafir, and Jiaying Zhao, "Poverty Impedes Cognitive Function," *Science* 341 (2013): 976–980.

8. Housing insecurity appears particularly crucial for well-being, especially children's well-being. See Edward Scanlon and Kevin Devine, "Residential Mobility and Youth Well-being: Research, Policy, and Practice Issues," *Journal of Sociology and Social Welfare* 28 (2015): 119–138.

9. Some of the earliest studies supporting the existence of ego depletion are Roy E. Baumeister, Ellen Bratslavsky, Mark Muraven, and Dianne M. Tice, "Ego Depletion: Is the Active Self a Limited Resource?" *Journal of Personality and Social Psychology* 74 (1998): 1252–1265. doi:10.1037/0022-3514.74. 5.1252. For recent methodological concerns about studies supporting ego depletion, see Evan C. Carter and Michael E. McCullogh, "Publication Bias and the Limited Strength Model of Self-Control: Has the Evidence for Ego Depletion Been Overestimated?" *Frontiers in Psychology* 5 (2014): 823. For an exploration of some ethical and political implications of ego depletion, see Michael Cholbi, "The Implications of Ego Depletion for the Ethics and Politics of Manipulation," in *Manipulation*, ed. C. Coons and M.E. Weber (Oxford: Oxford University Press, 2014), 201–220.

10. Barry Schwartz, *The Paradox of Choice* (New York: Harper Collins, 2004) is a well-known exposition of the downside of an overabundance of choices.

11. *On Liberty* [1859], Chapter 1, ¶9.

12. Gerald Dworkin, "Paternalism," *Stanford Encyclopedia of Philosophy*, 2014. http://plato.stanford.edu/entries/paternalism/, accessed 3 August 2017.

13. Brian Wansink and Katie Love, "Slim By Design: Menu Strategies for Promoting High-Margin, Healthy Foods," *International Journal of Hospitality Management* 42 (2014): 137–143.

14. "Rational Persuasion as Paternalism," *Philosophy and Public Affairs* 42 (2014): 78–112.

15. *Liberalism Without Perfectionism* (Oxford: Oxford University Press, 2011), 77.

16. This, as I see it, is also the essential mistake of the "libertarian paternalist" advocacy of nudges: The mere fact that a strategy does not limit a person's options does not settle whether it is paternalistic or whether it is objectionable *qua* paternalistic.

17. I used the term "rational will" account in my "Paternalism and Our Rational Powers," *Mind* 126 (2017): 123–153. Others who advance kindred accounts include Seana Shiffrin, "Paternalism, Unconscionability Doctrine, and Accommodation," *Philosophy and Public Affairs* 29 (2000): 205–250; Quong, *Liberalism Without Perfection*; and Daniel Groll, "Paternalism, Respect, and the Will," *Ethics* 122 (2012): 692–720. These authors may take issue with the details of the rational will account as I present it here.

18. Some claim that the objectionability of paternalism is expressive, that is, that it *consists in* the fact that paternalism expresses disrespect of, or insults, its target. See John Kleinig, *Paternalism* (Totowa, NJ: Rowman and Allenheld, 1983), 38; Joel Feinberg, *Harm to Self* (Oxford: Oxford University Press, 1986), 23–24; Elizabeth Anderson, "What Is the Point of Equality?" *Ethics* 109 (1999): 287–337; Shiffrin, "Paternalism, Unconscionability Doctrine, and Accommodation"; and Nicolas Cornell, "A Third Theory of Paternalism," *Michigan Law Review* 113 (2015): 1316. As a supporter of the rational will account, I agree that paternalism has insulting expressive content but deny that this is fundamental to the phenomenon. Rather, paternalistic acts are insulting only because they reflect judgments that disrespect, mistrust, and so forth, its target, and it is these judgments (or more accurately, incorporating these judgments into one's treatment of

the target) that make paternalism objectionable. That the target may feel insulted by paternalistic acts or that the acts express insulting judgments is conceptually subordinate.

19. Phillipe van Parijs, "Basic Income: A Simple and Powerful Idea for the Twenty-First Century," *Politics and Society* 32 (2004): 14.
20. "Paternalism and Our Rational Powers," 133–144. For a brief account of this argument, see "Identity Threat," London School of Economics, *theForum*, May 2017. http://blogs.lse.ac.uk/theforum/identity-threat/
21. Shiffrin, "Paternalism, Unconscionability Doctrine, and Accommodation," 216.

5 Work and Worth

Basic Income and the Social Meaning of Work

Evelyn L. Forget

The role that work plays in organizing our lives and our society is changing rapidly. Workers displaced by technology need secure incomes as regular jobs with good wages and decent benefits disappear and are replaced by part-time and contingent work. Simultaneously, the polarization of the labor market has increased the material and social gaps between the successful and the less successful. A basic income can fill the gaps in our social programs and provide secure incomes for the low-waged, the unemployed, and the insecurely employed. It can also provide everyone, including those with portable skills in high demand, the opportunity to pursue work-life balance—to take temporary or permanent leave from the workforce to pursue volunteer work, creative work or caregiving opportunities, or simply to engage in leisure on its own terms.

This freedom to pursue leisure, however, raises an issue for many: Work is more than a paycheck. It is the primary way we exercise our rights and responsibilities as citizens. As children, we are educated (in part) for the labor market. As adults, we expect to earn enough to support ourselves and our families through the labor market. As seniors, we expect to live off what we have saved and invested. Moreover, pensions, income assistance, and disability support for those who cannot support themselves are funded primarily through taxes on earned income. Participation in the labor market affects how we perceive and value ourselves and one another.

This chapter argues that work is inherently valuable to human beings. We want to work because work provides tangible rewards that go far beyond the paycheck we receive. It documents the social dislocation that can occur when vulnerable segments of the labor market are deprived of the opportunity to work, and it recognizes that while a basic income can offset some of the personal and social consequences of being out of work, there is still a positive value attached to work in and of itself. The chapter ends by addressing the question of whether we should require those who receive a basic income to work for their own benefit and concludes that reasonable people might disagree in the case of young people at the beginning of their careers.

The Human Meaning of Work

Contrary to the visionaries of Silicon Valley, there is and there will continue to be plenty of work for human beings to do. Every time technological change disrupted labor markets in the past, more new jobs were created than were destroyed. Some reports breathlessly forecast a future in which self-driving cars and trucks displace from the US workforce 1.6 million truck drivers, 800,000 delivery truck drivers, 180,000 taxi drivers, 160,000 Uber drivers, 500,000 school bus drivers, 160,000 transit bus drivers, not to mention the 445,000 auto repair shop workers who will no longer required to repair the consequences of higher accident rates associated with human driving error, and the hospital workers no longer required to patch up human victims, and the many associated jobs for well over 4 million US jobs lost to just one foreseeable change (Lee 2015; Gao, Kaas, Mohr, and Wee 2016). Yet, if such a report were commissioned at the beginning of the twentieth century, would we read about the promising new industry based on the internal combustion engine that would soon create millions of jobs worldwide not only for truck drivers but also in supporting industries, or would we list the horses, drivers, buggy manufacturers, farmers, train makers and engineers, and others who would soon be displaced? In the nineteenth century, 80% of jobs were in agriculture; today, about 2% of jobs are in agriculture, largely because of technological change that substitutes machinery for human labor. In our own time, do we celebrate all the new jobs for "content creators" unleashed by the internet, or do we focus on the death of journalism? When Gutenberg introduced his press, there were people mourning the loss of jobs for scribes, and the invention of the wheel no doubt caused consternation among the bearers who would no longer be in such demand. We are not very good at imagining the real changes that the future will bring, and we always pay more attention to what we are losing than on what we are about to gain. There will be changes, but one change we need not fear is the elimination of work for humans to do. It is far more important to recognize and prepare for the fact that the new jobs being created are of much poorer quality than the jobs that are left behind. It matters that people earn less and have less security in their work.

Human labor is still the source of all the goods and services we consume. It is where many of us find the human interaction that gives our life structure and meaning. Work provides an opportunity to learn and practice new skills. Economists have always undervalued this aspect of work. We treat labor is a necessary evil. Adam Smith, for example, writes:

> What everything is really worth to the man who has acquired it . . .
> is the toil and trouble which it can save to himself, and which it can
> impose upon other people. . . . Labour was the first price, the original
> purchase-money that was paid for all things. It was not by gold or by
> silver, but by labour, that all the wealth of the world was originally

purchased; and its value, to those who possess it, and who want to exchange it for some new productions, is precisely equal to the quantity of labor which it can enable them to purchase or command.

(Smith 1776 BK I, Ch. 5)

Throughout the history of economics, the negative features of work are emphasized. Work is a "disutility" that is undertaken only if workers receive a wage high enough to outweigh the unpleasantness that labor imposes. This view is common to Judeo-Christian thought in which work is imposed as a curse on the first man, whereas Aristotle and Plato saw labor as the destiny of slaves but imagined other human beings to aspire to a life of leisure and freedom (Sayers 2005: 607–608). There are exceptions: Marxian economists saw work as negative only because of its organization under capitalism (Sayers 2005). Other socialist writers, such as William Morris and Henri de Saint-Simon, also emphasized the historical contingency of the negative value we associate with work. Early in the twentieth century, institutional and social economists emphasized the inherent value of work and attempted to improve its quality, but these efforts lost influence after the Second World War (Rutherford 2011).

More recently, a new area of economics that expands its traditional focus has emerged in the Economics of Happiness, which is based on the premise that human beings can report on aspects of their own well-being. These reports can then be subjected to statistical analyses. Proponents of the Economics of Happiness have documented the satisfaction that can stem from work itself. The 2017 World Happiness Report, for example, portrays employed individuals scoring higher on "life evaluation" and "positive affect" than unemployed individuals (see Fig. 5.1). Even after we control for factors such as marital status, family income, sex, family structure, and age, the unemployed still report significantly less well-being than those with full-time employment.

Not all jobs are equal, to be sure. Those that offer greater opportunities for self-actualization and control over one's time are associated with higher levels of life satisfaction than jobs with greater levels of control and supervision (Fig. 5.2).

The happiness of men is more affected by employment variables than the happiness of women. In high-income countries, self-employed people are happier than those with full-time employment. Women who work part-time voluntarily are happier than those working full-time. Involuntary part-time employment and being out of the labor force are associated with lower levels of happiness. Some characteristics of jobs that are associated with improved well-being are higher wages, job security, autonomy, the opportunity to learn new things, support from others on the job, and opportunities for advancement. Other characteristics reduce perceived well-being, such as job insecurity, dirty or dangerous work, lack of control, jobs that interfere with family time, and worry about work outside job hours (Helliwell, Layard, and Sachs 2017).

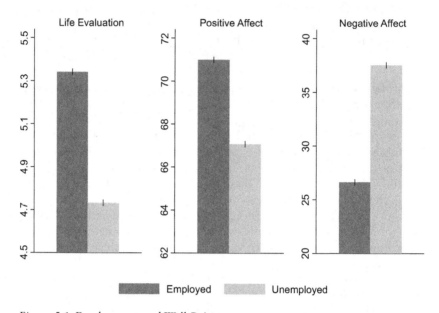

Figure 5.1 Employment and Well-Being

Source: Helliwell, J., Layard, R., & Sachs, J. 2017. World Happiness Report 2017, New York: Sustainable Development Solutions Network.

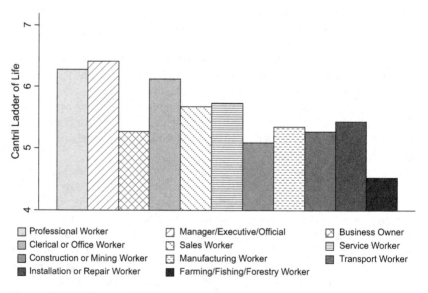

Figure 5.2 Job Type and Well-Being

Source: Helliwell, J., Layard, R., & Sachs, J. 2017. World Happiness Report 2017, New York: Sustainable Development Solutions Network.

On a less theoretical level, we know that people value work because of their desperation to acquire it when there is no material advantage to doing so. Most food banks rely on volunteer labor and the volunteers are, disproportionately, people with lived experience of poverty. Many are not in the labor force because of documented disabilities or mental health issues that make it difficult to keep a job even though they might not qualify for disability support. Working at the food bank does not increase their entitlement to a food basket; they get one whether they work or not. It does not earn them any other material rewards except, perhaps, a modest lunch and a bus ticket. The work can be hard and dusty; there are not many opportunities to perfect high-level skills. However, no food bank has difficulty attracting volunteers from among its clients. People value the job. Their reasons vary: Some like the social aspects of work, whereas others want to feel useful. Work helps to structure our lives.

Basic Income and Social Well-Being

Basic income has usually been justified on individual and materialistic grounds, but social factors may be just as important. Anne Case and Angus Deaton have spent a lot of time in the past decade investigating the US malaise and they make a stark case.

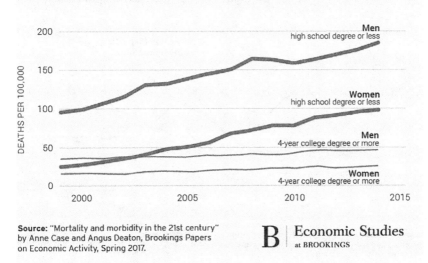

White non-Hispanic midlife mortality from "deaths of despair" in the U.S. by education

Ages 50–54, deaths by drugs, alcohol, and suicide

Source: "Mortality and morbidity in the 21st century" by Anne Case and Angus Deaton, Brookings Papers on Economic Activity, Spring 2017.

B | Economic Studies
at BROOKINGS

Figure 5.3 Midlife Mortality from "Deaths of Despair"

The obverse of social well-being may well be the "deaths of despair" that Case and Deaton document. (Case and Deaton 2017) Looking specifically and 50- to 54-year-olds, they document a rise in deaths by suicide, drugs, and alcohol specifically among those with a high school degree or less. Their explanation is that the upsurge in these deaths is the result of economic dislocation. Even though others in the US economy have fared worse in economic terms, specifically low-income minorities, Case and Deaton have argued that it is the "crushed aspirations" of these white workers that have led them to despair. Whereas others have found solace for job loss in family relationships and community, this group chose to replace stable marriages with serial monogamy, to drop out of the labor market entirely, and to replace their participation in traditional communal churches with attendance at "prosperity gospel churches" that emphasize individual identity. These are all aspects of an unhealthy society.

A basic income could offset the economic consequences of job loss and it might go further and help to protect the social institutions—stable families, traditional churches, and community involvement—that support healthy societies. Angus and Deaton did not find comparable deaths of despair in other countries that have faced similar economic challenges in recent years.

They attribute the different international experience to the fact that most other high-income countries investigated still have well-functioning

Midlife mortality from "deaths of despair" across countries
Men and women ages 50–54, deaths by drugs, alcohol, and suicide

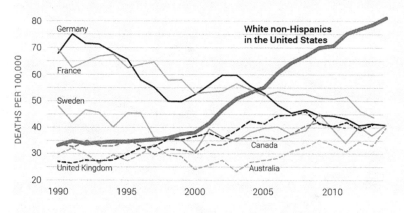

Source: "Mortality and morbidity in the 21st century" by Anne Case and Angus Deaton, Brookings Papers on Economic Activity, Spring 2017.

B | Economic Studies
at BROOKINGS

Figure 5.4 "Deaths of Despair" Across Countries

social safety nets, including at least basic welfare and social medicine, unlike the social welfare system in the United States.

These despairing 50- to 54-year-olds would have entered high school in the early 1970s. Think about the life chances experienced by someone who did not finish high school in the mid-1970s. Young white men who left high school could find good jobs, often in agriculture, agriculture-servicing industries, and manufacturing. Since the 1970s, the number of people employed in agriculture has collapsed and factories have closed in the face of increased international competition and, especially, automation. These young men who left school early found work, but their jobs were far less secure than they must have seemed in the 1970s. Since then, men without a high school diploma would have struggled to find and keep work. High school graduates are much less likely to experience periods of unemployment than those without a high school diploma, and when they are laid off, they are more likely to be re-employed at comparable wages to those they left behind. Their lifetime earnings will be higher and the opportunities they offer their children greater. These young men struggled relative to their lucky contemporaries who had different opportunities and finished high school. A basic income would provide not only income security to these families, but also resources that would allow children to continue their education and to engage and re-engage in job training.

Should We Impose a Work Requirement on Those Who Receive a Basic Income?

If work is so important to our lives, should we impose a work requirement when we offer people a basic income? The argument that we need such a requirement is left over from outdated thinking: We need a work requirement only if we believe work is such an unpleasant activity that people will take a job only if they are forced to do so.

Some work is so essential that society cannot function without it, yet it does not fit well into the paid labor market. Young children, old people, and some people with extreme disabilities require substantial caregiving, and all of us rely on assistance from others to a greater or lesser extent. Yet caregiving has never fit well into a formal labor market. When we try to commodify caregiving, we tend to devalue the work. This is most apparent in nursing homes; no matter how professional and caring the workers, these are rarely places where people want to spend their last days. Most people say they would prefer to die at home. A mother at home with preschoolers today faces social pressure to justify her decision not to use daycare. Women have traditionally provided the bulk of this care work. No one would argue that a society can survive and flourish without someone undertaking these activities. They might be commodified or they might be provided outside the market, but society does require that they be provided. Similarly, creative work is an important part of flourishing societies, yet the market does a limited job of encouraging it. Long ago, artists required the financial support of patrons and, more recently, the state has provided grants to a limited number of applicants. How would society be different if everyone who thought they had something worth saying had the economic freedom to engage in creative work?

Not everyone is a caregiver or an artist, and not everyone aspires to be either. If people receive a basic income without a work requirement, some people will nonetheless choose to work for pay because that is how they find human contact and satisfaction in their lives. Some will work for a wage or the inherent value of the work itself, whereas others will work because they enjoy the social interaction or structure that work provides. Some will decide that the job they have is not worth the wage it commands. They will either seek a different job, volunteer, or do something else with their time. The job will then be done by someone else who makes a different decision about the value of the wage and the nature of the job. If no one chooses to take the job at the wage offered, then the wage will have to increase, or a technology that can replace the human labor will need to be found, or the job will simply not be done. If the job is important enough to society that it needs to be done, and it must be done locally, its wage will increase. If the wage does not increase, then it reflects our social decision to do without the product of that labor. As economies grow and develop, many previously necessary jobs do disappear. Few people in North America or Europe have the households of servants that earlier generations "needed" and that are still considered essential to middle-class life in places like India or Indonesia. It is also possible that work will be exported to other countries in which workers are prepared to do that work for less than labor in high-income countries might demand. Some would argue that this provides new opportunities for these workers who will, assuming there is no compulsion, benefit as a consequence. Others might note that consumers in high-income countries will benefit at the expense of exploited labor broad. If so, the solution lies not in doing without a basic income but instead in advocacy for labor rights abroad and consumer education at home.

There will no doubt be some people who choose not to do important work that falls outside the market, volunteer labor, or work for pay. If a basic income is provided without a work requirement, some people will not work at all. Some will fish all day or daydream under an apple tree: As utilitarian Jeremy Bentham argued, "Prejudice apart, the game of push-pin is of equal value with the arts and sciences of music and poetry. If the game of push-pin furnished more pleasure, it is more valuable than either." (Bentham 1830: 94) According to Aristotle, we would expect the innate differences between individuals to lead to differential use of non-working time, and that for many people, leisure will be a social activity:

Everyone wishes to share with his friends, the occupation of their existence. This is why some drink together, others dice together, others go for athletics and hunting together or philosophy, each type spending their time together in the pursuit that gives them the most satisfaction of their lives.

(Aristotle, *The Nicomachean Ethics*, 1172a.)

We know that work is associated, on average, with increased well-being. Should we force basic income recipients to work for their own good? This is a moral argument and not an economic one. If the economy does not need the labor of these folks enough to pay them a wage sufficient to command it, why should we worry about how they spend their time? There is, of course, the fear that idle hands will cause social mischief. If that turns out to be the case, then we need to worry directly about the specific problem of criminality or mischief rather than abolishing leisure for the many law-abiding human beings who prefer idleness to work.

Leisure is essential to civilization. Whereas economists tend to label "leisure" as any period not devoted to work for pay in the market, philosophers have always had a more nuanced view. Aristotle writes:

Hence, when all such inventions were already established, the sciences, which do not aim at giving pleasure or at the necessities of life, were discovered, and first in the places where men first began to have leisure. This is why the mathematical arts were founded in Egypt; for there, the priestly caste was allowed to be at leisure.

(Aristotle, *Metaphysics*, 939a3)

Indeed, almost all of the great achievements of past centuries in the arts, sciences, music, philosophy, and scholarship were created by people who had, for all intents and purposes, the equivalent of a basic income that purchased for them the leisure required to engage in important work. They were daughters and younger sons of aristocratic families who did not need to work for money, or talented individuals who had attracted a patron who could finance their scientific undertakings, or they had a living provided by the Church which regarded support for some scientific and artistic activities as an important investment.

Leisure—not entertainment, but time to contemplate—is essential to the well-being of societies. Leisure becomes an activity in itself rather than simply the absence of work. Martha Nussbaum asks, in *Creating Capabilities*, if a young girl named Vasani who lives in rural India has leisure:

Does she have any time for leisure? Can she ever just sit and think, or enjoy something beautiful, or enjoy tea with friends?

(Nussbaum 2011: 10).

Basic income offers all individuals not only access to the resources to live a modest but dignified life, but also the opportunity to participate in leisure. The fundamental characteristic of basic income is that everyone becomes the judge of how to spend his or her own time and money without the help and assistance of people who believe themselves to know better. In our society, leisure may be a more difficult good to obtain than most commodities. We are raised from infancy to achieve, but we are not encouraged to dream.

Should We Impose a Work Requirement on Young People Who Receive a Basic Income?

The idea that individuals should be free to make their own decisions and pay the consequences is usually limited to adults with the capacity to make judgments. Young people at the beginning of their careers are adults under the legislation of most countries. They are free to sign contracts, to be jailed, to vote, to consume restricted goods, and to marry and procreate. Should they be free to decide whether to work or not to work if we introduce a basic income?

Some young adults will benefit a great deal from a basic income. Those who are aging out of the child welfare system without family or social support could use the basic income to set themselves up in life and to pay for job training. People with parents who have little foresight could similarly benefit. Other young people might use a basic income to travel, to write a symphony, to volunteer, to take low-paid internships, or to go to school. The children of many middle-class and wealthy parents have always had a basic income in the sense that their parents often chose to subsidize this activity for some time on the grounds that it would allow the young person to learn something about themselves and the world, and to make better labor market decisions going forward. A basic income, then, is a matter of leveling the playing field and offering similar opportunities to all young people.

Some economists, however, have a more jaundiced view of these opportunities. They argue that future wages, employment, and career paths are negatively affected by periods of unemployment, particularly at a young age (e.g., Nordstrom 2011). The theoretical basis for labor market scarring can be found in human capital theory, which suggests that the deterioration of both firm-specific and general skills during periods of unemployment can reduce future employability and wages (Becker 1994). This deterioration is compounded if potential future employers perceive periods of unemployment as indicators of lower productivity or poor work habits (Lockwood 1991; Pissarides 1994). Some researchers have explored the psychological effects of not working on subsequent job search behavior (Clark, Georgellis, and Sanfey 1991).

Some young people, and some adults, are not mature enough to make far-sighted decisions with long-term consequences. The justification for a basic income is that individuals should make their own decisions and reap the consequences. Is there an argument to be made that adults younger than some arbitrary age—say, 25—should be denied an unconditional basic income that would without doubt benefit many on the grounds that some people, because of their own lack of foresight, would be harmed by the policy?

I leave the question open: Reasonable people might have different opinions about the age at which an unconditional basic income ought to be available. For most adults, however, the benefits of an unconditional basic income far outweigh the costs.

References

Becker, G. S. 1994. *Human Capital: A Theoretical and Empirical Analysis, With Special Reference to Education*. Chicago: University of Chicago Press.

Bentham, J. 1830. "*The Rationale of Reward*, excerpted and reprinted." In *The Classical Utilitarians: Bentham and Mill*, edited by J. Troyer. Indianapolis: Hackett, 2003.

Case, A. and Deaton, A. 2017. *Morbidity and Mortality in the 21st Century*. Brookings Papers on Economic Activity. Spring.

Clark, A., Georgellis, Y. and Sanfey, P. 2001. "Scarring: The Psychological Impact of Past Unemployment." *Economica* 68(270): 221–241.

Gao, P., Kaas, H.-W., Mohr, D., and Wee, D. 2016. *Disruptive Trends That Will Transform the Auto Industry*. McKinsey & Co. September. www.mckinsey.com/industries/automotive-and-assembly/our-insights/disruptive-trends-that-will-transform-the-auto-industry

Helliwell, J., Layard, R., and Sachs, J. 2017. *World Happiness Report 2017*. New York: Sustainable Development Solutions Network.

Lee, J. 2015. "Self-Driving Cars Endanger Millions of American Jobs (and That's OK)." *Mud*, June 19. www.makeuseof.com/tag/self-driving-cars-endanger-millions-american-jobs-thats-okay/

Lockwood, B. 1991. "Information Externalities in the Labour Market and the Duration of Unemployment." *Review of Economic Studies* 58(4): 733–753.

Nordstrom, O. 2011. *Scarring Effects of the First Labor Market Experience*. Bonn: IZA Discussion Paper, No. 5565.

Nussbaum, M.C. 2011. *Creating Capabilities: The Human Development Approach*. Cambridge, MA: Harvard University Press.

Pissarides, C. 1994. "Search Unemployment With On-the-job Search." *The Review of Economic Studies* 61(3): 457–475.

Rutherford, M. 2011. *The Institutionalist Movement in American Economics, 1918–1947*. Cambridge: Cambridge University Press.

Sayers, S. 2005. "Why Work? Marxism and Human Nature." *Science and Society* 69(4): 606–616.

Smith, A. 1776. *The Wealth of Nations*. Edinburgh.

6   Work, Technology, and Inequality

Kory P. Schaff

Recent technological innovation in microchip processors, robotics, and artificial intelligence has the potential to create a perfect storm that radically transforms the structure and organization of work. In particular, the rise of "smart" machines on assembly lines, delivery drones, and self-driving vehicles are likely to eliminate many kinds of jobs in the near future.[1] The prospect of such changes raises serious concerns about the impact of technology on human values and what will happen to the welfare of millions of workers whose livelihoods are rendered obsolete. At the same time, democratic welfare states continue to struggle with inequality in many spaces, including education, gender and racial discrimination, unemployment and stagnant wages, poverty, and wealth disparity. These problems have also been intensified by technology and globalization. Despite an unprecedented expansion of access to information and communication the digital revolution has made possible, inequality in developed countries is at record levels, and the gap with developing countries grows wider (Pikkety 2014).

Given these developments, a novel proposal that is the subject of debate among both academics and policymakers is now gaining fresh momentum: Provide all citizens with a "basic income" that ensures a social minimum. The strategy of this proposal is to give all qualified individuals an unrestricted cash grant that provides them with all-purpose means that do not depend on status, wealth, or employment. Without restrictions, individuals can choose for themselves how best to utilize the grant. Some of these choices may include reducing work hours, increasing leisure time, investing in financial markets, creating small businesses, or consuming more goods. The creation of this social minimum might also alleviate some of the problems of inequality just described. For example, the automation of workplaces will mean fewer jobs in the future, so the provision of a basic income could be an efficient solution to a rather complex set of problems.

Can basic income replace work in the age of automation? More specifically, we want to know whether a basic income scheme can replace the benefits of work in an age where technology has the potential to eliminate work altogether. Work has financial and non-pecuniary benefits. While it provides individuals with an income to satisfy their needs, it also has benefits in the form of self-realization, self-respect, and community. However, work also entails various burdens in the form of low wages, overwork, and diminished autonomy. The provision of a universal cash grant can supplement the financial benefits of work by giving individuals flexible means to maximize their choices and achieve their goals. To the extent it is used to reduce work hours in favor of leisure, or expand occupational choice, basic income can improve the welfare of its beneficiaries. There is still the question whether such a grant can replace the non-pecuniary benefits of work. To answer the question, we shall investigate these overlapping areas of concern, which are the benefits and burdens of work, the effects of technology on work and welfare, the benefits of basic income, and the limits of this scheme for a social minimum.

The first section examines the benefits and burdens of work, drawing a distinction between its financial and non-pecuniary benefits in the form of self-realization, self-respect, and community. In the second section, the effects of technology on work are considered. Although innovation can improve efficiency, and has the potential to enhance welfare for this reason, the effect of this process has been the intensification of labor and, ultimately, its obsolescence. For this reason, the automation of work does have significant costs to the welfare of workers, and these ought to be weighed against its potential benefits in the future. The third section examines the arguments for a basic income that make it a philosophically attractive alternative to traditional welfare policies. One reason is that a universal cash grant avoids some classical objections to the welfare state including that of paternalism and "free riding." A basic income scheme might be a clever way of avoiding these problems, but without addressing the structure of property relations that gives rise to them, it is doubtful it can reduce inequality. Finally, the last section focuses on the question whether the benefits of basic income can replace the loss of work caused by automation and obsolescence. Even though it can augment the financial benefits of work, or supplement their loss, a cash grant by itself cannot replace its non-pecuniary benefits.

The Benefits and Burdens of Work

The value of work is defined by two recurring themes historically. The first emerges from the Reformation and has the optimistic view that work is a *good* for individuals. In his classic study of it, Max Weber argues the "protestant ethic," which is composed of hard work and deferred gratification among other things, is the "spirit" that animates modern capitalism. He claims that part of what makes this mode of production distinct from past forms of accumulation is "the rational capitalistic organization of formally free labour." In combination with "the separation of business from the household" and "rational book-keeping," capitalism allows individuals to pursue their self-interest while promoting the welfare of others (Weber 1930: xxxv). In this respect, the work ethic also fulfills a divine command to do "good works and deeds" in this life. The second theme is far older and pessimistic: Work is a burden suited for lesser men, or even punishment imposed on humans for violating divine law. The first belief figures in Greco-Roman thought, which holds that the highest good of contemplation is opposed to physical toil and justifies the hierarchy of the *polis* that is built on slave labor. The second can be found in Judeo-Christian thought from the Book of Genesis to the writings of St. Augustine and beyond. Taken together, the themes that work can be a force for good as well as burdensome alternatively figure in our own understanding of work.[2]

Let us start by considering the benefits of work. In a market economy, work *is* an activity requiring the time and labor power of individuals who receive compensation for it. Work has obvious benefits that are instrumental for this reason. With the compensation earned from work, individuals have the means to satisfy their needs and create financial stability to make future plans including retirement. The value is instrumental because work is a mere means to other ends. By providing universal means in the form of money, which can be used to buy goods or invest in their own social capital, individuals exercise their autonomy, make choices about how to prioritize needs, and satisfy their desires. One might object that work has no value in itself for this very reason. If it has instrumental value only because it provides individuals with an income, then these means have value and not work. [This raises a question about basic income and whether individuals will work if they are provided with other means that do not depend on gainful employment. We shall return to this question later, when we examine the benefits of basic income and whether they can replace work.]

There are other benefits to work that are not instrumental. These include the role it plays in the self-realization of individuals, the self-respect they gain from it, and the sense of community it fosters. What role does work play in terms of self-realization? Jon Elster defines it as "the self-externalization and self-actualizing deployment of one's powers and abilities" (Elster 1988: 66). He claims that self-realization is not only the most important work-related value, but also its most peripheral for the following reason: In market economies, production is decentralized, so there are many job opportunities for individuals to choose from. This decentralization also means "that working conditions for most people in contemporary industrial societies—capitalist and communist—do not lend themselves to fulfillment of this goal" (Elster 1988: 66). So work has the *potential* to promote individual self-realization, but this is frustrated by the fact that most work in market economies does not require much of individuals in terms of their capacities. However, the lack of fit between "self-realization" as Elster defines it, and opportunities for work that can realize it, suggests that the standard here might be set too high.[3]

What do "powers and abilities" mean in this context, and how do they realize the self? Arguably, all work involves the use of these capacities since any activity requiring the use of labor power to produce goods or provide services entails the use of at least some of these. To be sure, there are "powers and abilities" such as mathematical skills that are more complex and deliberative and that require more education. These are typically rewarded with more compensation than skills that are simple and non-deliberative. However, the difference between these skill sets is not a binary, at least where the "deployment of powers and abilities" is concerned. The difference is rather one of degree. The concepts of "complexity" and "simplicity" are continuous and admit of more or less degrees when applied to skills that are utilized for work. So making or doing something of any kind requires using "powers and abilities" whether these are more or less skilled. It seems to be a mistake, then, to claim that the value of self-realization found in work is peripheral because there are few opportunities for work that fulfills this goal. The problem with Elster's conclusion is its implicit perfectionist assumption about the "powers and abilities" that compose the self. He conceives of an ideal "self" with the potential for robust capacities, which are wasted in work that requires less knowledge and skills. The implicit ranking of skills depends on the view that all individuals should strive to realize their greatest potential in highly skilled work. Since only some can do this in market economies, that standard is self-defeating. So the self-realization that work offers should be agnostic about ranking "powers and abilities" in perfectionist terms. Instead, we should affirm a minimal but still significant sense in which work promotes self-realization, simply because in making or doing something, individuals are externalizing their capacities, whatever those happen to be.

Another benefit of work is that individuals gain self-respect from it. John Rawls claims that self-respect consists of "a person's sense of his own value" and "confidence in one's ability to fulfil one's intentions" (Rawls 1999: 386). If we take these features in combination, work should give individuals a sense of worth and confidence they can achieve their goals. Ostensibly, work does measure a sense of worth because of its compensation. From the viewpoint of the labor market, individuals literally have a value placed on them by being paid for their time and labor power. This cannot be the basis of worth described by Rawls, however. We must be careful not to imply some individuals are *worth* more than others simply on the basis of the size of their income. From the moral point of view, the lives of all individuals have equal worth, so the monetary value of work cannot be its source of worth. Instead, it must foster a sense of value that is not merely about money, but about something else.[4] Work contributes to a person's sense of worth in at least two other ways. The first is that individuals gain satisfaction from making or doing something that utilizes their labor power. Using their time and skills to produce goods and services that others require or desire can be a satisfying endeavor itself.[5] A second way that work fosters self-respect is because it is a social activity that involves cooperation with others. This is a crucial source for a sense of worth since all of our interactions with others are structured by mutual recognition. Individuals depend on one another for achieving the self-satisfaction of knowing that others regard their actions or interests as having value. This is not just a question of having a sense a worth because one feels useful to others, though as studies of workers and unemployment show, this is part of the reason why work fosters self-respect.[6] Work also entails other kinds of social interaction that support a sense of worth. These include camaraderie, friendships, water cooler gossip, teamwork, and even a sense of belonging to a community, which can also be found in different forms of association as well.

What about the second part of self-respect regarding "confidence" that individuals can achieve their goals? Work builds confidence in various ways. First, utilizing one's power and abilities to achieve a personal or common goal is essential for gaining confidence. By committing to some task and accomplishing it, individuals affirm their own capacities to achieve it. The use of their talents, skills, and education all figure in this respect. Even low-skill jobs that lack the use of deliberation require individuals to select the proper means for realizing the ends that are constitutive of the work. Moreover, research shows that on-the-job training for low-skill jobs does build confidence and develops human capital in the form of commitment, time management, responsibility, and other qualities that are useful at work and beyond.[7] Work also promotes confidence through social interaction, which is crucial for affirming our sense of how well we are doing. Since it is a form of social cooperation, confidence is shaped by feedback from employers, co-workers, clients, and customers alike. This is why modern workplaces are organized by procedures of assessment and evaluation—to ensure individuals are doing the tasks required by the job and to improve on the execution of those tasks. Taken together, the exercise of "powers and abilities" in the context of social interaction with other promotes self-respect, in terms of an individual developing her own sense of worth and the confidence she gains from it.

Finally, work has value because it fosters community. This is both an individual and collective good in the following sense. When individuals are engaged in common projects that most work entails, they commit to them as individuals *and* help to realize those projects as members of an association. If such a commitment is voluntary, then work is good for individuals in all the senses described earlier. It promotes their self-realization because they must deploy their capacities to produce some good or service, and it fosters self-respect because they gain a sense of worth and build confidence that they can realize their ends. There is competition in the labor market, of course, where individuals compete against others for positions and promotions. This does not mean, however, that competition exclusively defines work. There can be healthy competition that pushes individuals to achieve excellence or otherwise excel at whatever talents and skills they happen to have. This also benefits others who rely on their use of such talents and skills. Furthermore, the conditions of interdependence found in work signal that there is also a collective good that is achieved as well. While it does require engaging in common projects that benefit both individuals and communities, from the collective viewpoint work also promotes forms of mutual recognition such as assurance, trust, and empathy. These are essential for the stability and reproduction of the social life of a community, and they give purpose and meaning to the work that individuals do in their communities.

Now we can consider a serious objection to the idea that work has value other than providing individuals with the means to satisfy their needs and achieve their ends. Some philosophers reject the claim that work is a good in itself because that assumes an essentialist conception of work that amounts to paternalism about what is good for all individuals. Andrew Levine makes a novel argument for a right *not* to work in this respect. In a paper titled "Fairness to Idleness," he claims the liberal commitment to state neutrality regarding conceptions of the good must permit individuals to pursue their own good without favoring one particular view over another (Levine 2001). For this reason, an individual's conception of the good that eschews work must be given the same weight of consideration as an individual who prefers to work. The neutrality thesis can be construed along these lines to require the democratic state to provide individuals with basic goods so they can pursue whatever ends they adopt, even if these ends are otherwise thought to be unproductive. In effect, neutrality toward the good supports a right to leisure against the paternalist principle that it is good for individuals to work and support themselves. This means individuals can decide work is not good for them, preferring instead to "count blades of grass on the courthouse lawn" or take up surfing as a way of life (Rawls 1999: 432). Thus, work has no value in itself unless individuals determine that it is good for them.

One way to respond to this objection is to show that the benefits of work just described do not logically entail paternalism about what is good for individuals. With respect to self-realization, we have seen that that the "powers and abilities" required for work need not be deliberative and require complex skills. The conception that these capacities should be deliberative and skilled in order to realize a robust self depends on perfectionist principles that we can do without. Whether it involves highly complex skills requiring an advanced education or digging trenches for sewer lines, all individuals utilize their capacities of labor power at work. The intuition that "brain work" is better for realizing the self than "dirty work" misses the point that all work is the externalization of human capacities in the service of some end. This line of reasoning applies to self-respect and community as well. Individuals in so-called menial jobs are no less entitled to a sense of worth and confidence that they get from a job well done. Work does not impart self-respect because only the best kinds of "powers and abilities" it requires are things worthy of respect. As we have shown, much of the value that work imparts depends on taking into consideration two things: whether the work itself is done well, and whether there are others who recognize that. Indeed, the fact that work depends on social interaction is a significant reason why it fosters self-respect and community. Without the mutual recognition that gives structure to our forms of social interaction, it is hard to conceive of values like self-respect and community having any meaning at all. So it cannot be the case that work has nothing but instrumental value for individuals, because value is determined in the context of inter-subjective relations with others. The non-pecuniary value of work does not require paternalism about deciding what is good for individuals, then, only that it is a good thing for individuals to have social interaction that is a rich source of meaning for their own lives. For most individuals, work is that daily venue where this interaction takes place, though it is not and need not be the only such venue.

What about the burdens of work? These burdens include instrumentalism, exploitation and coercion, and diminished autonomy. Again, the instrumental value of work gives individuals an income that is the means to satisfy their needs and pursue their goals. This is external to the work itself and employers make provision for it. For this same reason, work can also be a burden when it fails to provide enough means for individuals to meet needs and support pursuits. The elasticity here suggests that its instrumental benefits are only as good as they are sufficient to satisfy basic needs and allow individuals to pursue their life plans. If work fails to provide enough income to do these things, it easily turns into a burden that is all-too-familiar for those working multiple jobs to make ends meet. Indeed, the costs associated with financial instability found among the working poor are serious, including the decline of health and economic indicators (Singer and Ryff 2001: Ch. 7). The double-edged nature of this instrumental value suggests that a minimum wage policy is better than no policy at all, but that something like a living wage policy might be the best way to maximize the instrumental benefits of work (Pollin and Luce 2000).

An additional burden of work is the problems of exploitation and coercion. These are concerned with the voluntariness of conditions in which agreements between employers and workers are made. From the moral point of view, exploitation occurs whenever one agent uses another merely as a means, whereas coercion involves persuading an agent to do something by using force or threats. In the nineteenth century, Bruno Bauer and Karl Marx helped to popularize the criticism that capitalism *exploits* workers (Breckman 1999). Marx's theory of exploitation is that unequal property relations between owners of the means of production and the proletariat enables the former to use the latter for the creation of profit, since they pay wages that are far less than the exchange-value of the products created by workers (Marx 1844: 324–25). More recently, philosophers have examined the problem of coercion regarding labor to determine whether employment offers count as instances of coercion. Robert Nozick argues that coercion occurs when one agent attempts to induce another to act by means of a threat (Nozick 1974). What distinguishes a threat from other kinds of offers is the allegation that there will be consequences attached to the recipient if she does not alter her course of action accordingly. On this basis, offers of employment in the labor market are not supposedly coercive, because there are no threats attached to it. If an individual does not like the offer for work, she simply moves along to consider further prospective offers. However, other philosophers argue that wage offers can still be coercive despite the absence of explicit threats. David Zimmerman claims that an offer is coercive under the following conditions: "(1) an alternative pre-proposal situation workers would strongly prefer to the actual one is technologically or economically feasible when the offer is made, and (2) capitalists prevent workers from having at least one of these feasible alternative pre-proposal situations" (Zimmerman 1981: 145). On this view, workers are still coerced to accept employment offers because they have no access to better pre-offer proposals, and property relations under capitalism give employers both material and non-material resources to restrict the availability of such alternatives.

We cannot resolve these problems by evaluating the arguments found in an extensive literature.[8] Rather, the point here is to highlight that there are conditions of "social unfreedom" relating to the value of work as a voluntary choice that must be considered (Ezorksy 2007: 9). Setting aside for the moment any substantial differences between exploitation and coercion, it is clear that work poses some constraints on autonomy. After all, without inheritance or other sources of income, most individuals are *obliged* to find (and keep) paid work in the labor market. Doing so is what gives them independence and self-sufficiency, features we typically associate with what it means to live a free life. Without work, they have to rely on others such as family, friends, churches, or the state to satisfy their needs, which is a condition of dependence that is the opposite of living a free life. Questions about whether capitalism is exploitative, or whether offers for work are coercive in the absence of threats, are narrowly tailored and can miss the broader context of these social and political relations influencing our work lives. At one level, individuals are apparently free to choose from different offers for work (assuming there are more jobs than workers looking for them). As we have pointed out, this is one set of alternatives, the structure and consequences of which tend to exclude rational consideration of the alternative *not* to work. So workers are "unfree" in a sense as well. They cannot consider that alternative because the consequences of choosing it either expose them to the harms of depravation or commit them to dependence on others. These harms are widely confirmed by studies of workers dealing with job loss, which show that they suffer from severe and chronic medical problems ranging from self-doubt and depression to loss of sex drive and suicide (Uchitelle 2006: Ch. 8).

Finally, work is also a burden because it diminishes autonomy. For almost all workers in market economies, the structure and organization of work is anti-democratic. We can illuminate this problem by summarizing the "parallel case" argument comparing the similarities of democratic states and market firms:

> [W]henever individuals cooperate together in a rule-governed common enterprise that should work to their common advantage, they all have the right to participate by way of majority-rule procedure in making the association rules, provided all have the capacity to do so. The political order and the economic firm are both common enterprises in the relevant respects, so the right to democratic citizenship applies equally in both arenas.
>
> (Arneson 1993: 139)

Since most firms are organized vertically so that decision-making is centralized under executive management, workers are prevented from participating in decisions affecting their interests. One argument in favor of this hierarchical form emphasizes its economic efficiency, citing the need for responsiveness to quickly changing market conditions and the expertise required for reading these changes. There are clearly costs associated with this form of work as well, including lack of autonomy, transparency, and accountability that come with centralized decision-making. Whether such trade-offs are justified by the alleged efficiency of such arrangements, or whether there are alternatives that can fulfill these values and maintain economic efficiency, is beyond the scope of our present concerns.[9] We cannot settle this debate here, but that is not essential for a brief review of the claim that anti-democratic work can be a burden.

There is something insightful about the "parallel case" argument. The purpose of the democratic state is to secure individuals liberty by making provisions for self-government and protecting their property rights. By contrast, the purpose of markets is to set prices on goods and services on the basis of the principles of supply and demand, and permit both producers and consumers to pursue their own ends accordingly. In the former, participation is guaranteed equally by citizenship that is protected by the right to vote, public offices that are open to all, and protection of rights to free speech and association. In the latter, there is no guarantee for equal participation because the principal entry point in the market is finding work, but there is no right to it in the form of guaranteed employment.[10] Nevertheless, having and keeping work is thought to be essential for living a free life, because without it individuals cannot satisfy their own needs and must depend on others. To the extent that work is organized on the basis of democratic values, it appears to provide more opportunities for work that can enhance these benefits. However, if it is organized exclusively on the basis of profitability and efficiency, and serves anti-democratic outcomes such as suppressing the choices of workers for better alternatives, then it clearly frustrates the values of self-realization, self-respect, and community.

Technology, Automation, and Obsolescence

Philosophers have long reflected on the relationship of technology and labor. Both Plato and Aristotle claim that "practical action" *(phrónēsis)* and "craftsmanship" *(téchne)* play substantial roles in the acquisition of knowledge, virtue, and the highest good. In the twentieth century, Martin Heidegger and Herbert Marcuse contend that modern technology objectifies the world to the detriment of human flourishing. The latter, more pessimistic, view resonated in particular among those who survived the death and destruction of both the First and Second World War. Before considering the effects of technology on work, we should pause to consider this more fundamental question of how technology itself ought to be evaluated.

There are two competing theories here—instrumentalism and substantivism. The first defends a view widely shared by governments, technocrats, and policymakers that technology is value-neutral because it is merely a means to achieve ends that are external to it. As a means, it can have no value in itself because only those agents who wield it can have values. The second claims technology "constitutes a new cultural system that restructures the entire social world as an object of control" (Feenberg 2002: 6). On this view, means and ends are deeply intertwined, so that the former inevitably embodies values that influence and shape the latter. Whether technology is value-neutral is not our focus *per se*. If it is neutral, its effects on work will be determined by the values of agents utilizing them, but if not, its effects will be determined by values it embodies in its design and implementation. The purpose of introducing these theories is that they provide different conceptual resources for evaluating the effects of technology on work. This is the case in terms of its instrumental effects, as well as the profound influence that technology has in shaping the ends of those agents who use it.

What about the effects of technology on work? First, it has significant effects on work when applied to methods of production because it utilizes resources more efficiently and increases the productivity of labor. Adam Smith made this observation a basic part of his theory of economic development:

> This great increase of the quantity of work, which, in consequence of the division of labour, the same number of people are capable of performing, is owing to three different circumstances; first, to the increase of dexterity in every particular workman; secondly, to the saving of the time which is commonly lost in passing from one species of work to another; and lastly, to the invention of a great number of machines which facilitate and abridge labour, and enable one man to do the work of many.
>
> (Smith 1776: 11)

The introduction of machines and innovation of new techniques for production helps to alleviate work comprised of physical, redundant, and dangerous tasks. This saves time for workers by reducing the need for labor power but also protects their health and longevity by mediating between them and harmful work. Technology also facilitates the specialization of labor in this regard. The increase of innovation creates new kinds of work for it in the division of labor. With this specialization arises new and expanded opportunities for the development of social capital in the form of skills, training, and education. The development of this social capital spurs further innovation and specialization, thereby completing the dynamic loop of development and wealth that supposedly "lifts all boats with the rising tide."[11] Moreover, technology can also expand opportunities for leisure. Since it creates more wealth, it can be used to improve the use of income that is earned from work. For example, with a reduction in the necessary labor time, individuals have more time to enjoy activities that do not require them to use their labor power.

The effects of technology on work are not always optimal, however. We noted in the last section that the instrumental value of work cuts both ways, so to speak, in terms of its benefits and burdens. Although work provides individuals with the benefit of an income, it is a burden if that income is not adequate to satisfy needs and pursue a life plan. Technology is similar in this respect. While its effects can improve the benefits of work, it can also exacerbate its burdens. An example of this "Catch-22" is the propensity it has to increase productivity and create overwork at the same time. In her study *The Overworked American*, the economist Juliet Schor describes the problem this way:

> Productivity measures the goods and services that result from each hour worked. When productivity rises, a worker can either produce the current output in less time, or remain at work the same number of hours and produce more. Every time productivity increases, we

are presented with the possibility of either more free time or more money. That's the productivity dividend.

(Schor 1991: 2)

She discovers a significant trend in the American economy that started in 1948 and continues today. During this time, the pace of innovation occurred steadily while productivity more than doubled, so we can now produce a 1948 standard of living with less than half the work hours needed in that year. However, nothing of that productivity dividend led to decreased work hours and increased leisure. Americans now work more and longer hours than they have at any time in the past. We might explain this trade-off in terms of instrumentalism: Technology did not cause the burden of increased work hours because it is value-neutral. To determine the cause of overwork, we would have to look closer at the actions of the agents employing the technology. The failure of workers to capitalize on this dividend by taking more leisure time might, therefore, be attributed to the values of agents and not the technology itself. For economists, this outcome merely signals that workers themselves prefer to increase income rather than take more leisure. However, a more likely explanation seems to be that weak labor laws, coupled with declining participation in unions, helped suppress the alternative choice of taking more leisure time.

To understand the imperatives that govern technology and shape the ends of agents, we need to understand that the structure of modern capitalism is composed of private ownership over the means of production, wage labor, and expansion of technology. As Weber noted, perhaps its most distinctive feature is "rationally organized labor." This rationality is instrumental because the price of wage labor is determined by the market principles of supply and demand. As a result, the structure of capitalist property relations contributes to the alienation of workers by treating them as variables in the calculation of profit. According to Marx, workers do not own either the resources they use or the commodities they produce with them and become estranged from themselves and one another as a result (Marx 1844: 63–64). Under these conditions, the productivity of labor is intensified and alternatives for leisure are suppressed. Marx observed this trade-off between productivity and leisure as well. He claims technology decisively favors the former over the latter because it embodies unequal property relations and emphasizes efficiency and exploitation:

> If machinery is the most powerful means of raising the productivity of labour, i.e. of shortening the working time needed to produce a commodity, it is also, as a *repository of capital*, the most powerful means of lengthening the working day beyond all natural limits in those industries first directly seized on by it. It creates, on the one

hand, new conditions which permit capital to give free rein to this tendency, and on the other hand, new incentives which whet its insatiable appetite for the labour of others.

(Marx 1867: 526; italics mine)

Since technology is designed and implemented to intensify productivity, labor becomes an integral part of this technical process. Accordingly, "it is animated by the drive to reduce to a minimum the resistance offered by man, that obstinate yet elastic natural barrier" (Marx 1867: 527). Insofar as labor is a commodity in this equation, it is subjected to the imperatives of this drive for improved productivity and increased profit. Such influence helps explain the outcome of the trade-off between productivity and leisure. For workers, the latter is foreclosed as a viable alternative because the system is organized by the imperatives of instrumental rationality. The conditions of work are thereby shaped by what Michel Foucault describes as "disciplines," or ever more refined modes of control, in the form of surveillance and normalization (Foucault 1975). Modern equivalents of these disciplines include unscheduled drug tests, task monitoring, and incentives for careerism that supplant preferences for leisure.

Suppose the claim of substantivism is true that technology embodies values that shape the ends of those agents using it. Under modern capitalism, these values objectify the environment and its inhabitants, subjecting it and them to increasingly instrumental modes of control. The members of the Frankfurt School developed and defended a "critical theory" along these lines, arguing that modern technology replaces the substantial values of humans conceived as social members with instrumental ones conceiving of them merely as producers and consumers.[12] In these conditions, the social relations that are the inter-subjective conditions for substantive values are replaced with the technical imperatives of efficiency and profit. These effects are not mutually exclusive with the benefits that technology seems to provide, given that its widely touted benefits could just be further modes of control. Marcuse claims these benefits are thinly disguised countervailing effects that sustain and reproduce the ideology of "one-dimensional society" (Marcuse 1964: 12). The decrease of physical labor and increase of pleasure-seeking experiences create the conditions in which autonomy is reduced to the repetition of work and consumption. Even though technology improves the efficient allocation of resources and this enhances "welfare" (defined according to such values), the process negatively affects workers by decreasing opportunities for self-realization, self-respect, and solidarity. These values are sacrificed in the short run by the imperatives of technology, because the "creative destruction" of modern capitalism sells itself on the assumption that new, better opportunities for work are always created as part of this process. That is not always the case, however, though it might be sometimes (Uchitelle 2006: Ch. 3).

Since technical innovation has immediate and significant costs to workers' welfare, these costs ought to be weighed against any potential future benefits. Yet the anti-democratic organization of work frustrates the participation of workers to help determine their own fate where innovation and obsolescence are concerned. A seemingly innocuous example of the technical intensification of labor in this respect is the use of digital communication in our daily lives. The introduction of "smart" phones and tablets, and our tendency to rely on these seamless modes of interaction, expands the productivity of work beyond normal business hours. By and large, we have accepted the invasiveness of such devices on the basis of their efficiency so that the new normal is to work everywhere and at all times. Whether that is a benefit or a burden might seem like a question that is relative to an individual's preferences, but the real issue is whether workers get a substantial voice in how such technology is used. The fact that we have assimilated their use into our culture so quickly without much personal reflection or public debate is telling in this regard.

Finally, the intensification of labor merely precedes the next and final stage in the domination of technology over human beings. The present stage increases production with more efficient means, while the industrial destruction of the environment is reframed as "progress" for humankind. It is not just the resources of nature that are viewed as raw materials to serve the ends that are dictated by this form of rationality, but also workers themselves. They are used to create the goods and services that ensure the perpetual motion of the commodity machine, until they are replaced with more efficient machines in the form of computers, algorithms, and automated systems. In the earliest stage of industrialization, G.W.F. Hegel anticipated this outcome: "The abstraction of production makes work increasingly *mechanical* so that the human being is eventually able to step aside and let a *machine* take his place" (Hegel 1821: §198). The ultimate effect of technology is obsolescence—replacing work with machines. While it raises obvious concerns about how workers will satisfy their welfare, the process does not end with the mere replacement of workers by machines. What may happen next is the subject of both dystopian science fiction and popular entertainment—the obsolescence not just of work, but also of workers themselves. In a pessimistic narrative that can be traced back to substantivism, the "rise of the machines" is the end game in which humans are either hunted down and eliminated or cultivated as batteries to power the machines. Perhaps these scenarios are merely the stuff of imagination, but serious questions remain: What will happen to humans when the level of technology that is achieved truly makes it possible to reduce the workday, or eliminate it altogether? What will happen to workers who are replaced with machines? How will they satisfy their welfare?

Basic Income and Inequality

In this section, we shall examine the benefits of a basic income scheme with an emphasis on what makes it an appealing alternative for addressing the problem of inequality. In its conception, the idea is rather simple and elegant. All qualified individuals will receive a cash grant regardless of their employment history, income, or status. The grant is universal and unrestricted since all beneficiaries will receive the same amount and all of them are free to use it however they choose.[13] In addition, basic income is often defended as viable policy for ensuring a social minimum that avoids some of the problems of traditional welfare policies. The idea of providing this social minimum in the form of a universal grant has increased in popularity in democratic welfare states for this reason.[14] This idea is appealing to both right- and left-leaning theorists and policymakers alike for the following reasons: On one the hand, libertarians argue that provision of a basic income eliminates the need for paternalistic welfare policies, enhances the buying power of consumers, and ultimately promotes economic growth. On the other hand, egalitarians claim it will address the problem of inequality by ensuring a social minimum for all regardless of contribution or status. The appeal of such a scheme across the traditional economic spectrum has also been spurred by the growth of a cottage industry advocating on its behalf, as well as political parties who have taken up its cause in the European Union and beyond.[15] As a result, dozens of states and local governments around the world from Finland to Bakersfield, CA, have created pilot programs to test the feasibility of a basic income scheme.

A basic income scheme has two major benefits when compared with traditional welfare measures. First, it promotes the value of liberty by allowing persons to choose what to do with their share of the grant. In doing so, it avoids the paternalism of traditional welfare policies, which often require the least well off to provide evidence of need by submitting their private lives to invasive state procedures. A basic income grant avoids this "means-testing" because one does not have to lack means to get it. The grant is paid to everyone regardless of means and no questions are asked about how or where it is used. This will obviously appeal to libertarians and liberals alike who reject paternalism in favor of individual liberty. Second, basic income also promotes the value of equality by subsidizing a more egalitarian distribution of resources arising from social cooperation. Rather than basing its distribution on income, in which the wealthy pay higher tax rates to provide resources that can be redistributed to the least well off, basic income provides a cash grant that all citizens are entitled to regardless of their contribution. As such, it avoids a familiar objection to the welfare state that "free riders" benefit from such policies without paying any of the costs. This objection looms large in the economics of envy and politics of resentment, fostering opposition to taxation and welfare assistance, and supporting a disturbing form of scapegoating that is currently resurgent in debates about immigration and sovereignty.[16]

For these reasons, Phillipe Van Parijs claims that a basic income scheme has the potential to reconcile the conflicting values of liberty and equality in democratic welfare states. His theory of "real-freedom-for-all" is based on the libertarian conviction that the efficiency of markets can be used to expand the liberal value of equality by providing a social minimum to all that avoids the objections just described. According to Van Parijs, the principle of "real-freedom-for-all" combines the formal freedom of negative liberty to do as one pleases (short of coercion or harm to others), with an all-purpose means for realizing the ends of positive liberty. Subsequently, he advocates granting all citizens an equal share of a bundle of resources consistent with "security" and "self-ownership" (Van Parijs 1995: 33). In effect, this libertarian approach avoids the problem of redistributing *downward* by "taking from the rich and giving to the poor" and retains the egalitarian commitment to the value of equality. All beneficiaries can use these means for whatever purpose they want. Some examples that may help reduce inequality include buying insurance against sickness or unemployment, giving the grant to charity, supplementing consumption habits, and working less to take more leisure. An obvious attraction of basic income, then, is its practical flexibility. The cash grant can be used in diverse ways, many of which will contribute to economic growth that, in turn, could increase the amount of the grant over time.

A relevant feature of Van Parijs's proposal here is that basic income can, in principle, reduce the now dominant reliance on work. He claims that one way it splits the difference, so to speak, between capitalism and socialism is it displaces work as the primary requirement for a social minimum. A problem with that displacement, however, is it does not fit neatly (not yet, anyway) with the normative principle in capitalism that reward ought to be a product of contribution. For this reason, it "differs from a social insurance scheme to the extent that its beneficiaries need not have contributed to it out of their past earnings in order to be entitled to benefit from it" (Van Parijs 1995: 34). While Van Parijs stresses the compatibility of basic income with the values of liberty and equality, the ideal of this policy does not actually fit well with a central tenet of both capitalism and socialism, namely, reciprocal contribution and reward. One relevant objection here is that individuals will opt out of working altogether as the amount of the grant increases:

> The real freedom to accept a low-paid job one would like to take, whether because of its intrinsic appeal or because of the training or experience it provides, is unambiguously increased as the level of the unconditional income goes up.
>
> (Van Parijs 1995: 37)

The more their income is supplemented by the grant, the more likely it is that individuals will opt out of full-time work and perhaps even work altogether, preferring instead to be surfers who are fed by the productive contribution of others.

The worry here is that basic income's effect on work can undermine its efficacy and success at reconciling the values of liberty and equality. Insofar as the cash grant diminishes the necessity of work and pushes its value in the direction of freely undertaken labor, it can lead to economic inefficiencies. With the right mix of incentives that larger amounts of the grant would induce, it has the potential to undercut productive contribution over time as workers leave the labor market altogether. In turn, this will decrease the total value of resources to be distributed, thereby leading to a decrease in the amount of the grant over time. One endemic feature of capitalism that makes this problem more likely is the boom-bust cycle and its relation to unemployment. When the market is booming and unemployment is low, the amount of the grant will be higher and may induce individuals to reduce their work hours for more leisure time. But when the market is a bust and unemployment is high, the amount of the grant will be lower, even though individuals will likely rely on it to make up for lost income. In this scenario, the cost of keeping the grant at pre-recession levels will increase along with the political pressure to do so, but the economics of doing so are murky and hard to predict.

There are other technical difficulties that face the success of a basic income scheme as well. For example, whether the grant is paid in full annually or provided by regular installments can change some of the complexities we have been discussing. While one or the other might be more or less efficient economically, paying the grant out in equal install-ments could lead to a paternalist effect on the choices of beneficiaries, something the proposal is supposed to avoid (Van Parijs 1995: 46–47). Another problem that faces the "universal" feature of a basic income grant is that of capabilities and disadvantage. An equal share of resources provided to all in the form of a grant cannot achieve the egalitarian aim of equalizing the net benefits accrued by it where moral luck is concerned. As Amartya Sen claims, individuals with a lower threshold of functioning require a larger share of resources to translate functioning into capabili-ties (Sen 1992). For individuals with physical disabilities, a greater share of resources is required in order to achieve the same level of capabil-ity as the able-bodied. In this respect, the "universal" feature of a basic income grant may have to be modified more to address the complexities of "difference" as a critical normative consideration of equality.[17] These problems might raise some doubts about the ethical and economic appeal that basic income offers, but they cannot be resolved here. At the very least, a basic income scheme warrants serious consideration and further research.

The Limits of a Basic Income in the Age of Automation

So far, we have established that the instrumental and non-pecuniary benefits of work are a mixed picture at best. Under cyclical market conditions, these benefits are often turned into burdens by contingent forces beyond the control of workers. The income that work provides is a good thing if it is sufficient to satisfy needs and support life plans, but if not, or there is no work available, it becomes a serious burden. These same forces also influence the benefits of self-realization, self-respect, and community that work can provide, leading to jobs that are exploitative and coercive and that diminish autonomy. When the effects of technology are added to this picture, these burdens are intensified. To be sure, the advance of science and technology has had a significant impact on life. It is has decreased injuries, disease, and death, as well as improved our understanding of the universe and our place within it. Yet the benefits of technology do not necessarily improve working conditions for everyone. The domination of instrumental rationality leads to the intensification of labor and, in many cases, exacerbates its burdensome aspects.

What happens when basic income is added to the picture we have just described? At a glance, ensuring a social minimum for all citizens seems to be an elegant solution to some serious problems facing the democratic welfare state. With the cash provided by such a grant, workers can supplement their income and enjoy greater buying power, or reduce their work hours for more leisure time. Moreover, it has the potential to offset the harms caused by job loss and remove some of the stigma attached to unemployment and welfare assistance. Although it can augment the financial benefits of work in these respects, by itself a basic income grant cannot replace self-realization, self-respect, and community. In line with Van Parijs's slogan of "real-freedom-for-all," one might object that providing individuals with these means is an optimal way to help individuals to realize their ends. A basic income guarantees a flexible form of support that can support any and all values in this respect. However, before giving up altogether on the non-pecuniary benefits that work offers, it is worth considering some limitations of basic income.

First, it seems that a basic income scheme will have little effect on reducing inequality. While it augments the income of beneficiaries, and this sounds like good policy especially for struggling low-income earners, this does not reduce inequality. One reason it will have little effect in this respect is that the grant is paid out in an equal amount to everyone, so its effects on the *distribution* of income will actually be nil. The concentration of wealth and the growing income gap is a significant problem that should give us pause. For example, the three richest individuals in the United States together own more than 50% of its income earners, which is 63% of American households, or 160 million workers (Kirsch 2018). Those numbers are staggering and suggest more needs to be done to constrain the typical unequal distribution of wealth. A basic income scheme tries to avoid the problems associated with redistributive policies, but for this reason, it is not well designed to constrain the growth of inequality. Putting a social minimum in place may improve the welfare of the least well off to be sure, but it seems inequality will remain relatively unchanged and that is concerning.

Second, the provision of a basic income grant augments the income of individuals to satisfy needs and support their life plans. In effect, it will likely be used for more consumption, which can have social and environmental consequences. One social effect of increasing consumption is that inequality will be exacerbated. As Shor notes about current debates among policymakers, there is a consensus the problem of inequality can be solved "by getting more income into more people's hands" (Schor 2000: 5–6). She takes exception to this view because the goals of redistribution and growth are insensitive to the fact that consumption is part of the problem. Schor claims that the solution of *more* income "leads to consumption practices that exacerbate and reproduce class and social inequalities, resulting in, and perhaps even worsening, an unequal distribution of income" (Schor 1991: 6). This is driven by the features of what she calls "new consumerism" that perpetuate the upscaling of lifestyle norms, spending beyond the relative means of one's income, and consuming luxury goods that are branded as status symbols. Given these trends, putting more cash in the hands of consumers will exacerbate inequalities, especially for low-income households and communities of color. Thus, basic income may unwittingly make the distribution of inequality worse off by giving individuals the freedom to spend the grant how they want. Since most individuals have shown themselves to be irrational consumers for the most part, giving them more unrestricted income will simply contribute to the problem of inequality.

Another social effect that a basic income scheme may have is a diminished sense of community. In the absence of work, and without a sense of worth that accompanies engaging with others to achieve a common purpose, a basic income will leave individuals without a major source of social interaction. There are other venues that may replace lost work in this respect, but whether these offer self-realization, self-respect, and community with a common purpose is unclear. One reason why is that these benefits depend on standing in social relations with others, while lacking work undercuts the ability of one to stand in such relations. After losing their jobs, individuals report feeling more isolated and getting less enjoyment out of their daily activities (Uchitelle 2006). It is true that work is not the only context in which social relations provide support for doing productive activities, gaining a sense of worth, or engaging with others in a common purpose. However, for most workers, it is clearly a significant form of such support. If machines replace jobs and entire industries are automated, the elimination of social relations found in workplaces will almost certainly diminish a sense of community. Whether that can be replaced by other social relations, or how quickly that process of adjustment will take, is an empirical question that cannot be answered here.

Finally, a basic income grant that increases income and consumption raises worries about the environmental limits of welfare policies that are based exclusively on economic growth. There is a serious concern among scientists that the rapid growth of industrialization over the last century, which is predicated on burning fossil fuels, has already pushed the planet past its tipping point in the direction of massive and inhospitable climate changes. We are looking at a future planet that will be significantly warmer, with more intense weather events, diminished natural resources, and significantly larger populations requiring more resources to satisfy welfare. Schor claims there can be no common solution to these problems without addressing the underlying patterns of consumption that feed them:

> [I]t is difficult to make an ethical argument that people in one of the world's richest countries need more when the global income gap is so wide, the disparity in world resource use so enormous, and the possibility that we are already consuming beyond Earth's ecological carrying capacity so likely.
>
> (Schor 2000: 7)

Under these circumstances, a basic income scheme is more likely to contribute to the problem of consuming beyond our ecological limits by providing a grant to individuals that immediately boosts their buying power as consumers. Perhaps basic income can be part of a solution to these problems by encouraging workers to reduce work hours, take more leisure time, and engage in sustainable forms of consumption. However, in an age of automation where many workers are likely replaced by machines, and where goods and services can be produced more efficiently, it is hard to predict what they would do with their time and money. If we already spend most of our time working in order to consume, as Schor ably shows, it seems that a sudden increase in unstructured time brought on by part-time work or unemployment will be filled by consuming more of those goods and services. That is not an outcome either the planet or future generations can afford.

What is to be done? The question remains an open-ended one. At the very least, the current debate about basic income and the need for a social minimum pushes us to answer the question. When we also consider the benefits and burdens of work, the effects of automation on the future of work, and the viability of basic income in this context, it is clear that democratic welfare states need to develop new strategies for resolving the problems that are endemic to them.

Notes

1. An early version of this argument is made by Rifkin (1995), and an insightful economic history of technology and obsolescence can be found in Slade (2007). A recent review of technical developments can be found in *Wired*, "A.I. and the future of work" (2018).
2. For studies of these themes in ancient Greek thought, see Meiksens Wood (1997) and Murphy (1993). The idea of work as punishment in the thought of St. Augustine is described in Kidwell (2013).
3. In its conception, the self-realization argument is a version of Marx's argument about alienated labor. He claims that the "species-being" *(Gattungswesen)* of human beings is social labor, and under capitalism the form this labor takes alienates individuals from this essential nature (Marx 1844: 58–68; Brudney 1998: Ch. 4).
4. I am not suggesting it is impossible for individuals without work to have self-respect, but as studies of the consequences of unemployment show, self-respect *suffers* from the lack of work in most contexts.
5. A critique of the skilled/unskilled distinction can be found in Crawford (2009: Ch. 2).
6. A good review of the literature on the psychological and physiological harms of unemployment and joblessness can be found in Uchitelle (2006: Ch. 8).
7. See Warren, Thompson, and Saegert (2001: Ch. 1).
8. The most comprehensive discussion of these concepts can be found in Wertheimer (1987, 1996).
9. The costs and benefits of vertical work organization are reviewed by McPherson (1983), Bowles and Gintis (1993), Schweickart (2002), Schaff (2012), and Anderson (2017).
10. For a recent defense of a right to work as fair conditions of employment, see Schaff (2017).
11. This statement is often mistakenly attributed to Adam Smith, but it is actually a slogan used by the New England Council, a regional chamber of commerce, which President John F. Kennedy appropriated and first used in a speech in 1963.
12. This is the basis of Jürgen Habermas's claim that the "life-world," which grounds the communicative action and inter-subjective relations of rational agents, is eclipsed by a "system" of instrumental and technological domination (Habermas 1985).
13. One problem that is not addressed here is the question of who qualifies for basic income. Most theorists and policymakers advocate for it on the assumption that citizenship is the proper category for the benefit, but the presence of migrant workers and undocumented immigrants in market economies, whether they contribute or not, complicates this question. For a review of this question, see Bay and Pedersen (2006).
14. There is a historical pedigree to basic income. Rawls mentions the so-called negative income tax in this respect, which was a popular topic of policy discussions in the 1970s following the Great Society programs. Ideally, this policy would involve a systematic transfer of resources through a reverse income tax that progressively pays greater compensation to the least well off (Rawls, 243).
15. Examples include Basic Income Earth Network (BIEN), US Basic Income Guarantee Network (USBIG), and Basic Income Canada Network, among many others.
16. While this phenomenon is not new historically, it has become resurgent in the form of misinformation and propaganda that led to Brexit in the United Kingdom and Trumpism in the United States.
17. See Anderson (1999) for a discussion of difference and equality in this respect.

References

Anderson, E. 1999. "What Is the Point of Equality?" *Ethics* 109(2): 287–337.

Anderson, E. 2017. *Private Government: How Employers Rule Our Lives (and Why We Don't Talk About It)*. Princeton: Princeton University Press.

Arneson, R. 1993. "Democratic Rights at the National and Workplace Level." In *The Idea of Democracy*. Cambridge: Cambridge University Press.

Bay, A. and Pedersen, A. 2006. "The Limits of Social Solidarity: Basic Income, Immigration and the Legitimacy of the Universal Welfare State." *Acta Sociologica* 49(4): 419–436.

Bowles, S. and Gintis, H. 1993. "A Political and Economic Case for the Democratic Enterprise." *Economics and Philosophy* 9: 75–100.

Breckman, W. 1999. *Marx, The Young Hegelians, and the Origins of Radical Social Theory*. Cambridge: Cambridge University Press.

Brudney, D. 1998. *Marx's Attempt to Leave Philosophy*. Cambridge, MA: Harvard University Press.

Crawford, M. 2009. *Shopclass as Soul-Craft: An Inquiry Into the Value of Work*. New York: Penguin Books.

Elster, J. 1988. "Is There (or Should There Be) a Right to Work?" In *Democracy and the Welfare State*. Princeton: Princeton University Press.

Ezorksy, G. 2007. *Freedom in the Workplace?* Ithaca, NY: Cornell University Press.

Feenberg, A. 2002. *Transforming Technology: A Critical Theory Revisited*. Oxford: Oxford University Press.

Foucault, M. 1975. *Discipline and Punish: The Birth of the Prison*. New York: Vintage.

Habermas, J. 1985. *The Theory of Communicative Action, Vol. 2: Lifeworld and System*. Boston: Beacon Press.

Hegel, G.W.F. 1821. *Elements of the Philosophy of Right*. Cambridge: Cambridge University Press.

Kidwell, J. 2013. "Labour in St. Augustine." In *Oxford Guide to the Historical Reception of Augustine*, 779–784. Oxford: Oxford University Press.

Kirsch, N. 2018. "The 3 Richest Americans Hold More Wealth Than Bottom 50% of the Country, Study Finds." *Forbes Magazine*. www.forbes.com/sites/noahkirsch/2017/11/09/the-3-richest-americans-hold-more-wealth-than-bottom-50-of-country-study-finds/#2997688c3cf8

Levine, A. 2001. "Fairness to Idleness: Is There a Right Not to Work?" In *Philosophy and the Problems of Work*. Lanham, MD: Rowman and Littlefield.

Marcuse, H. 1964. *One-Dimensional Man: Studies in the Ideology of Advanced Industrial Society*. Boston: Beacon Press.

Marx, K. 1844. "The Economic and Philosophical Manuscripts." In *Selected Writings*. Indianapolis: Hackett Publishing.

Marx, K. 1867. *Capital*, Vol. I. New York: Penguin Press.

McPherson, M. 1983. "Efficiency and Liberty in the Productive Enterprise: Recent Work in the Economics of Work Organization." *Philosophy and Public Affairs* 12(4): 354–368.

Meiksens Wood, E. 1997. *Peasant-Citizen and Slave: The Foundations of Athenian Democracy*. New York: Verso.

Murphy, J.B. 1993. *The Moral Economy of Labor: Aristotelian Themes in Economic Theory*. New Haven: Yale University Press.

Nozick, R. 1974. *Anarchy, State, and Utopia*. New York: Basic Books.

Pikkety, T. 2014. *Capital in the Twenty-First Century*. Cambridge, MA: Harvard University Press.

Pollin, R. and Luce, S. 2000. *The Living Wage: Building a Fair Economy*. New York: New Press.

Rawls, J. 1999. *A Theory of Justice* (Rev ed.). Cambridge, MA: Harvard University Press.

Rifkin, J. 1995. *The End of Work: The Decline of the Global Labor Force and the Dawn of the Post-Market Era*. New York: Putnam Publishing.

Schaff, K. 2012. "Democratic Rights in the Workplace." *Inquiry* 55(4): 386–404.

Schaff, K. 2017. "A Right to Work and Fair Conditions of Employment." In *Fair Work: Ethics, Social Policy, Globalization*. London: Rowman and Littlefield.

Schor, J. 1991. *The Overworked American: The Unexpected Decline of Leisure*. New York: Basic Books.

Schor, J. 2000. "The New Politics of Consumption." In *Do Americans Shop Too Much?* Boston: Beacon Press.

Schweickart, D. 2002. *After Capitalism*. Lanham, MD: Rowman and Littlefield.

Sen, A. 1992. *Inequality Reexamined*. Cambridge, MA: Harvard University Press.

Singer, B. and Ryff, C. 2001. "The Influence of Inequality on Health Outcomes." In *New Horizons in Health: An Integrative Approach*. Washington, DC: National Academies Press.

Slade, G. 2007. *Made to Break: Technology and Obsolescence in America*. Cambridge, MA: Harvard University Press.

Smith, A. 1776. *An Inquiry Into the Nature and Causes of the Wealth of Nations*. Chicago: University of Chicago Press.

Uchitelle, L. 2006. *The Disposable American: Layoffs and Their Consequences*. New York: Alfred Knopf Publishing.

Van Parijs, P. 1995. *Real Freedom for All: What (if Anything) Can Justify Capitalism*. Oxford: Oxford University Press.

Warren, M., Thompson, J., and Saegert, S. 2001. "The Role of Social Capital in Combatting Poverty." In *Social Capital and Poor Communities*. New York: Russell Sage Foundation.

Weber, M. 1930. *The Protestant Ethic and the Spirit of Capitalism*. New York: Routledge.

Wertheimer, A. 1987. *Coercion*. Princeton: Princeton University Press.

Wertheimer, A. 1996. *Exploitation*. Princeton: Princeton University Press.

Wired. 2018. *A.I. and the Future of Work*. www.wired.com/wiredinsider/2018/04/ai-future-work/

Zimmerman, D. 1981. "Coercive Wage Offers." *Philosophy and Public Affairs* 10(2): 122–145.

7 In Defense of the Post-Work Future

Withdrawal and the Ludic Life

John Danaher

Introduction

The Japanese word "hikkomori" translates, roughly, as "to pull inwards and be confined." It is a term now used to describe the living arrangements of approximately half a million Japanese adolescents and young adults (Jozuka 2016; Teo and Gaw 2010; Teo 2010). They are modern-day urban hermits. They withdraw from society and its demands. They live inside their digitally saturated, climate-controlled homes, subsisting on a stream of entertainment and food, all made possible by the conveniences of modern technology. Some commentators (Teo 2010) suggest that the "hikkomori syndrome" is a product of Japan's demanding educational and work culture. The demands are so strenuous that some young people cannot cope and so withdraw into a self-created cocoon. Others argue that the syndrome it is not unique to the Japanese culture, with cases being reported in other countries as well (Ovejero, Caro-Cañizares, de León-Martínez, and Baca-Garcia 2014). Whatever the case, it certainly seems to be a modern-day phenomenon, virtually unheard of before the 1970s, and with an ever-increasing incidence since then (Teo 2010).

I am not a psychologist or psychiatrist. I cannot claim any expertise in diagnosing or understanding the phenomenon of the hikkomori. I know only what I have read. Nevertheless, I use them as a jumping off point for the argument in this chapter. I do so for two reasons. First, I think they represent one *possible* symptom of an underlying malaise in modern life, a malaise that relates specifically to our culture of work and the burdens it places on our psychological well-being. The burden is so great that some people are cracking under the pressure (Frayne 2015). What's more, and as I have argued elsewhere (Danaher 2017, 2018), this burden is set only to grow as a result of increased automation. Second, and more controversially, I think the hikkomori represent a *possible* solution to this malaise. This is somewhat paradoxical, and I don't wish to trivialize what many see as a serious mental health condition, but I do want to argue that general idea of "withdrawing" from the demands of economic life is something that should be taken seriously as a pathway to human flourishing in post-work future. Indeed, I want to argue in favor of this strategy of withdrawal.

The remainder of this chapter elaborates on both of these ideas. In doing so, it differs from many of the other chapters in this book: Where they focus on how to address the income-related losses of technological unemployment, this chapter focuses on the meaning/purpose-related losses. For better or worse, many people derive meaning and self-worth from the work that they do. When work is taken away from them, or when it becomes increasingly precarious, this sense of meaning is threatened. It is theoretically easy (though perhaps practically difficult) to address the income-related losses. It is more conceptually challenging to address the meaning and purpose-related losses. This leads many people, to argue in favor of work, particularly in its more "dignified" forms. People struggle to see meaning and purpose beyond a work-saturated culture. Yet that is what this chapter tries to do. It does so by arguing (i) that our current form of work is *structurally bad* and its automation should be welcomed—hence we should welcome a genuinely post-work economy, and (ii) that in withdrawing from the "real world" we can realize a form of flourishing that satisfies our demands for meaning and purpose.

The argument develops in three parts. First, I make the case for thinking that work is structurally bad. Second, I make the case for thinking that the strategy of "withdrawal" is desirable, using three arguments to bolster my case. Third, I respond to some obvious criticisms of my proposal.

Work Is Bad and Automation Is Desirable

My first argument is that work is bad and its automation is to be welcomed. This is an argument I have defended before (Danaher 2017, 2018). What I present here is a summary and slight modification of these previous efforts. The argument starts with the premise that work is bad and that anything that hastens its demise is to be welcomed, it then notes that automation is something that can hasten its demise, and thus concludes that the automation of work is desirable. For the purposes of this chapter, I am not going to defend the claim that automation can hasten the demise of work. This is not an uncontroversial premise, but a full defense of it would require an excessive amount of time and space. It is something that has been defended by myself and others, at much greater length, in other work (Brynjolfsson and McAfee 2014; Ford 2015; Avent 2016; Frey and Osborne 2017; Danaher 2017; Danaher 2019). For the purposes of this chapter, I am asking the reader to grant, if only for the sake of argument, that automation can hasten the demise of work and to focus on the axiological premise of my argument instead. Is work really bad, and should its demise be welcomed?

For the purposes of my argument, "work" should be defined narrowly as a type of economic employment, that is, as the performance of activities and skills for the purpose of receiving (or in the hope of receiving) an economic reward (Danaher 2017). To claim that work, so defined, is a bad thing is not a new idea. There are many well-known anti-work theorists who have argued that work both immiserates and imprisons the ordinary worker (Black 1986; Gorz 1989; Frayne 2015; Anderson 2017; Graeber 2018).

The problem with such arguments, as typically presented, is that they contradict the lived experiences of many workers. Although there are, no doubt, lots of people who feel immiserated and imprisoned by the work they do (Graeber 2018), there are also, no doubt, many who see their work as a great source of satisfaction and personal fulfillment. To insist that work is bad in the face of this experience stretches credulity. It usually requires an argument to the effect that these happy workers are victims of a kind of "false consciousness." Although they might think their work is meaningful and desirable, they are wrong to think this: They have imbibed and absorbed a pro-work ideology that inures them to the true horrors of what they are doing. Although there is something to be said for this idea, I prefer not to deny the actual experiences of happy workers. I prefer to make two connected points: (i) that while certain forms of work may be quite good, and certain individual workers quite happy with what they do, their work takes place within an institutional structure that is bad and becoming worse (call this the "structural badness" thesis); and (ii) that non-work is better, that is, that a life free from the demands of economic employment would allow for a greater form of personal fulfillment and meaning (call this the "opportunity cost" thesis). Let's briefly consider both of these claims.

Let's start with the claim that work is structurally bad. The basic idea here is that work in the modern world takes place within a set of institutional structures (markets for goods and services, contract and employment law norms, social welfare and entitlement law norms etc.) that is bad and becoming worse. On a previous occasion (Danaher 2018), I suggested that the structural badness of work has the character of a collective action problem. While taking up work is often rational and beneficial from an individual's perspective, the net result of everyone doing this is an equilibrium pattern of employment that is bad (and becoming worse) for the majority of workers. The badness of this equilibrium arises from the tendency of modern employment to undermine individual freedom and subject workers to arbitrary practices of domination (Anderson 2017), from the increasingly fragmented and precarious nature of employment (Weil 2014; Standing 2011), from the growing levels of income inequality and distributive injustice in employment-related rewards (Piketty 2014; Atkinson 2015), and from the tendency for modern work to colonize our time and our mental real estate (Frayne 2015). The result is that much of what we now do is geared around ensuring our employability and proving our productivity—so much so that we aren't even given the opportunity to imagine what a world without work might be like. What's more, all of these negative structural features of work are being made worse by technology: Technology enables greater surveillance and connectivity, thereby exacerbating the tendency for work to colonize our minds and to undermine our freedom; the very same features also facilitate the fragmentation of the workplace and the precariousness of employment; and, finally, advances in automation often benefit the few, highly skilled workers, at the expense of the many.

Let's now consider the opportunity cost thesis. The idea here is that if we could exist in a world without the pressures and demands of work, then we might be able to flourish in a way that we currently cannot. This claim is essential if you are to embrace the notion that the automation of work might be a good thing. If you don't believe that non-work would be better, then a natural response to the structural badness thesis might be to try to slow the development of automating technologies and try to reform work from within. But if you believe that non-work might be better than work, you can embrace the disruptive potential of automating technologies. So is there any reason to believe this? Bertrand Russell (1935) famously argued that non-work was better than work because it would give people the opportunity to develop higher, intellectual virtues. Indeed, he went so far as to argue that the leisure classes have, historically, been responsible for all the advances of civilization. The goal should be to make everyone part of the leisure class. This smacks of a certain aristocratic elitism and suggests that the value of a non-working life should be measured in terms of its social contribution and productivity. That's not all that different from what we currently have, it just replaces economic contribution and productivity with another metric of success. A simpler argument, and one the pushes us further away from the "work ethic" paradigm, is that without the economic pressures and necessities of work, people will be free to do what they most desire to do—to pursue their own conception of the good life. Of course, this is true only if, having been freed from the pressures of work, they are not left starving and destitute. This is where proposals for the basic income, or similar schemes of welfare distribution, become essential to any case for a post-work future. But assuming they are not left starving and destitute—that they all participate fairly in the benefits of automated abundance—there is reason to hope that they will be free to pursue whatever meaning and purpose they see fit to pursue.

This argument quickly runs into a problem. The hope that people who are freed from the yoke of work will be able to pursue whatever conception of the good life they happen to prefer rests on the naive assumption that the effects of automation will be limited. To be precise, it assumes that people will be displaced from forms of work they don't enjoy and left free to pursue whatever they do enjoy. This is naive because it is unlikely that we can easily control the automation of different modes of work, and it is quite likely that advances in automating technologies will have far wider effects, particularly if those advances are sufficient to hasten the general demise of work. In a world of significant technological unemployment, automating technologies will displace humans from not only unpleasant forms of work, but also activities that are associated with high levels of meaning and satisfaction, for example, scientific discovery, or moral/charitable work aimed at alleviating the suffering of others (Danaher 2017). What's more, even if machines don't completely replace humans in the pursuit of these goods, they may assist humans in such a way that undermines or lessens the value of human achievements in those domains. They will make things too easy and sever the connection between human activity and the goods toward which that activity is directed. Humans will still be able to derive some meaning and purpose from what they do, but it will be an impoverished or lesser form. We end up with a paradox of sorts: The kind of automation we need to achieve a genuinely post-work world may be the very same kind of automation that undermines the pursuit of happiness beyond the world of work. What can be done about this paradox?

In previous work, I argued that we could solve this paradox by pursuing an *integrationist* approach to technology (Danaher 2017). In other words, instead of racing against the machines, we can race with them and become more machine-like ourselves. We can prioritize the development of technologies that enhance and augment human capacities, not technologies that replace or displace such capacities. This would enable us to continue to pursue the kinds of projects that currently bring us much meaning and happiness (e.g., discovery of new truths, benefiting our fellow humans and so on), without completely sacrificing the benefits of technology.

There are, however, some significant problems with the integrationist approach. For one thing, it is a largely conservative strategy for dealing with the automation of work and the post-work world. Its appeal lies in its capacity for maintaining the current pathways to meaning and fulfillment. The irony, then, is that if the integrationist strategy were truly successful, it may just suck us back into the world of work—the very world that I am arguing we should be glad to escape. What's more, the integrationist strategy is highly uncertain and unpredictable. We may not develop the requisite technologies in time to stop the negative effects of automation beyond the workplace, and we may not be able to develop them at all. To pursue the integrationist strategy is thus to make a bet that is highly uncertain and highly conservative.

This leads one to wonder whether there might not be an alternative strategy that would provide a more radical break from the world we currently have while being more practically feasible. This is where the strategy of "withdrawal" comes in. I now turn to the defense of that strategy.

The Strategy of Withdrawal

To start, I need to clarify what I mean by the strategy of withdrawal. I understand it to be the practice of withdrawing from the demands of the world as it is currently constituted, into a world that is largely ludic or game-like in nature. This isn't a new idea. Bob Black, a famous anarchist anti-work writer, long ago argued that work should be abolished in order to enable us to live a more play-like existence (Black 1986). And Bernard Suits, in his philosophical dialog *The Grasshopper*, argued that a perfect technological utopia (in which all productive activities have been automated) would be a world in which we do nothing but play games. My goal is to offer a more persuasive case in favor of this approach.

To do that, I have to put some shape on the idea by identifying some minimal conditions on what would count as a game-like existence. One minimal condition is that individuals who pursue a game-like existence must retreat from the world of objective, instrumental goods—such as economic productivity, scientific, and intellectual discovery, the alleviation of distributive inequalities and human suffering, and so on. These things will still be important to human flourishing, but the assumption is they can be left, largely, to the machines to bring about (who will do so in a more effective, efficient, and tireless manner than their human forebears). Individuals can then dedicate themselves to maintaining relationships with families and friends (always a core part of human life) and, most important, to game-like pursuits.

What, then, is a game-like pursuit? Bernard Suits's (2005) widely cited definition holds that a game is a set of activities aimed at an arbitrarily defined end (the prelusory goal), where those activities are pursued in an inefficient rule-bound manner (the constitutive rules), and where the people playing the game willingly accept its rule-bound inefficiencies (the lusory attitude). Put more pithily, Suits argues that a game is any voluntary triumph over unnecessary obstacles. As definitions of game-like activities go, this is pretty good. But for present purposes, I think we need to add one more ingredient in order to properly distinguish game-like activities from non-game-like activities. This additional ingredient is "triviality." That is to say, the key defining feature of a game is that it does not (and is known not to) serve a higher purpose or significance. Winning the game (if the game has a clear winning state) does not necessarily make the world a better place, improve one's economic standing, or contribute to the sum total of human knowledge. Success in the game may exemplify certain aesthetic virtues, it may develop individual or collective character, and it may make the players happy or more satisfied, but that is about it. If it does serve some additional higher purpose, this is entirely accidental or contingent upon its role is a certain social order. In short, games are things that are to be enjoyed for the performances they entail, not for the outcomes they realize.

Insisting upon this "triviality" condition helps to avoid two important errors that arise from thinking about games and the post-work future. First, it avoids Yuval Noah Harari's mistake of presuming that everything we do is a game. Harari is interested in human flourishing and meaning in a post-work economy, and he is dismissive of those who worry that in such a world we would do nothing but play sophisticated "virtual" reality games of no ultimate significance (Harari 2017). He is dismissive because he thinks this is what we already do. For example, he argues that religion is a virtual reality game in which we score points in order to progress to the next level (heaven) and that consumerism is a virtual reality game in which we score points in order to gain social status. While this reframing of current social practices as games has a delightful insouciance to it—and may appeal to someone like me who is deeply skeptical of religion and modern capitalism—it clearly does violence to those who actually live those belief systems. They don't think that what they are doing is trivial or virtual or game-like. They think it is very real and very important. Insisting on the triviality condition avoids conflating or stretching the concept of the game so far as to include these serious pursuits.

Similarly, it avoids the error of assuming that much of what the work we currently do is an elaborate (if occasionally torturous) game. Someone who has read David Graeber's critique of modern employment may be inclined to make this error (Graeber 2018).[1] Graeber argues that many of the jobs in modern service and knowledge economies are, as he bluntly puts it, "bullshit": They serve no higher purpose or need, and the people working in them are aware of this but try to ignore it or justify it. I don't deny Graeber's claims about the pointlessness of much work. I would just argue that it is a mistake to infer from this that work as currently constituted is an elaborate game. It is not. Although the tasks that make up any particular job might be trivial and pointless, having a job is not. It is economically and socially necessary. Without a job you will more than likely be left destitute and unable to thrive, and viewed as a social pariah. This makes work something that is far from a game. You would have to sever the connection between bullshit work and instrumental economic gain to make it a game. Insisting on the triviality condition avoids trivializing current forms of work.

The importance of the triviality condition should not, however, be misunderstood. To say that games and game-like activities are trivial does not mean they are "unreal" or "unimportant." The things that happen within the games might be very real indeed. You can develop real skills and capacities within a game. You can forge real friendships and alliances. You can experience real pain, joy, frustration, and satisfaction. None of this need be trivial. It's just that the game itself that serves no larger purpose.

So, to clarify, in arguing for the strategy of withdrawal I am arguing that we should retreat from the demands of the world as currently constituted, with its focus on instrumental activities and economic gains, to a world of largely game-like activities (with plenty of time for sociability, family, and friendship). I make no prescriptions about the kinds of game-like activities people will or should pursue in this post-work future. To make such prescriptions would undermine one of the benefits of escaping the world of work—the freedom to pursue that which you desire to pursue. I only make prescriptions about the abstract properties of game-like activities, properly construed.

But even if you focus on those abstract properties, I suspect you will have some questions. Why on earth would a game-like world be desirable? How could humans flourish if they knew that what they were doing was ultimately trivial? I have three arguments to offer.

(i) The Argument From Internal Goods and the Value of Craft

The first argument is that a life of game-like activities provides a forum in which people can foster the mind-set of the "craftsperson"[2] and so realize the internal goods associated with a wide variety of activities. The argument consists of four premises and a conclusion (Note: This is not intended to be a formally valid statement of the argument.):

1. The life of the craftsperson is one that sustains human flourishing.
2. The life of the craftsperson is distorted by economic and instrumental pressures; that is, the life of the craftsperson can be best sustained in a world without those pressures.
3. The game-like world is a world without these distorting pressures and is one that can sustain the life of the craftsperson.
4. Therefore, the life of the craftsperson is best sustained in the game-like world.

Let's go through each premise of this argument in more detail. The first premise is crucial because it establishes that the life of craft is one that can sustain human flourishing. This is not some novel or odd ideal. It is one with very deep roots in human society and thought (Sennett 2008). The life of the craftsperson is one that is dedicated to the skillful mastery of certain patterns of action. Think about the master chess player, who can strategically plan and execute moves in anticipation of what her opponent might do, and who has spent years learning sequences of openings and endings and the consequences they entail. Or think about the master furniture maker or blacksmith, who has dedicated his life to the skillful and artistic manipulation of wood and metal to his own ends. These "masters" are often taken to represent the pinnacle of human performance and expression. They are absorbed and dedicated to what they do. They derive tremendous satisfaction and self-worth from it. Sometimes crafts are largely physical and dedicated to producing outputs (e.g., an item of furniture or a sword), and sometimes they are more intellectual and based on skillful performances (e.g., the winning moves of the master chess-player). But even when they are output-oriented, they are never really about the instrumental gains associated with those outputs. As Richard Sennett puts it in his book about the value of craft, the craftperson's labor is purely self-contained: They do what they do for the love of it, not because it will bring them greater success or more money (Sennett 2008: 20). This dedicated performance is an important kind of human flourishing. Indeed, some authors go so far as to argue that it provides us with a secular equivalent of the sacred (Dreyfus and Kelly 2011: 197).

In addition to its intuitive and historical appeal, the notion that the life of the craftsperson can sustain human flourishing does has some additional philosophical support. Alasdair MacIntyre's famous account of the good life makes the point that the good life is not something that can be defined or determined in the abstract (MacIntyre 1981)—to be honest or courageous or virtuous, only something that can be understood or make sense relative to some activity. In other words, the "thick" sense of the good can be realized only within specific domains of activity. You can be a courageous warrior or a courageous football player; you cannot be courageous simpliciter. This makes intuitive sense. The radical aspect of MacIntyre's view is that *any activity* can take on this role of providing a forum for the realization of some virtues and goods, as long as it is pursued in a serious and dedicated fashion. There are some exceptions, of course. A completely immoral activity couldn't do the trick, since its broader consequences would corrupt any of its internal goods. For example, an honest torturer is not living the good life. Furthermore, to really count as part of the good life, the particular domain of activity would also have to have some resonance within a broader cultural tradition, otherwise the individual might question its role in his life. But neither of these constraints should concern us here. The life of the craftsperson within a world of game-like activities easily satisfies both of these demands. The triviality of game-like activities ensures that they serve no wicked or evil purpose; they are morally neutral with respect to their broader consequences. And, as noted already, the ideal of the craftsperson is something with deep cultural and historical relevance.

Moving on to the second premise, why think that the life of the craftsperson is distorted by economic and instrumental pressures? The reasoning is straightforward. The good of craft lies in the skillful dedication to performance. If the performance must also serve some instrumental end, there is a danger that this end will distract or undermine the skillful performance. Sennett (2008: 28ff) argues that the capitalistic profit motive often forces craftspeople to sacrifice art and skill for the mediocrity of mass production, and that communistic central planning often replaces skill with incompetence. Whatever the nature of the instrumental pressure, if a craftsperson is beholden to it, there is always a risk that he will have to compromise on the craft itself. He may have to compete with others for the relevant instrumental ends and become absorbed by that competition (and its economic or personal necessity) instead of the craft.

This brings us to the third premise. The argument in favor of this premise should be relatively clear from the foregoing. Games themselves provide a forum for skillful performance and, as defined and characterized, the game-like world is one in which the instrumental pressures of work have been removed. They no longer serve to distort the pursuit of the craft within the confines of the game. It is true that there could be other distorting instrumental pressures, such as a pressure to achieve social status or recognition. But these pressures are present anyway and it is probably impossible to completely eliminate them. Eliminating the major economic instrumental pressures is still valuable and still makes it more possible to realize the value craft. It would be a better mode of existence even if it is not a perfect one.

More important is whether games can, in fact, allow for the life of the craftsperson to develop. There are two reasons for thinking that they can. First, many of the activities we currently perceive as crafts, and as activities that can sustain the value of crafting, would continue to do so in the post-work world. Following Suits's definition of a game as the voluntary triumph over unnecessary obstacles, we see that many of the traditional crafts are nowadays games. Nobody needs a blacksmith to handcraft a sword, or a carpenter to handcraft a table. These things can all be done more efficiently and effectively by machines. They are quasi-game-like in the modern world; the only thing that prevents them from being games that is that many people still pursue them for economic reward. I'm just imagining a world in which these economic rewards are no longer part of the picture. In addition to this, it should be clear that games of all kinds are themselves forums in which the skillful mastery of performances is both encouraged and rewarded.

In conclusion, then, the life of the craftsperson is something that can sustain human flourishing and is something that can be realized, to a heightened degree, in the post-work, game-like world.

(ii) The Argument From Arendt

The second argument riffs off some ideas from Hannah Arendt's book *The Human Condition* (1958/98). In that book, Arendt develops a conceptually complex account of human activity. She argues that there are three basic forms of human activity—labor, work. and action. Each of these forms of activity responds to (or is contingent upon) one or more of the basic conditions of human existence. Labor is dedicated to the urgent and repetitive maintenance of the biological systems of life: We labor to eat, stave off threats to survival, and to reproduce. Work is dedicated to developing a constructed human environment, to building a world of artifacts and symbols that is stable, durable, and distinct from the natural world. Action is dedicated to sociability and spontaneity, that is, to doing new and creative things in an environment with other human beings serving as either audience or collaborators.

Arendt orders these three modes of activity into a hierarchy of value. She thinks that labor is the most base and inferior mode of activity. It is the least distinctively human as it is so tied to the biological realities of existence. Action is the most human, and therefore the most advanced form of activity. It allows for genuine creativity and novelty (what Arendt calls "natality"). Work lies somewhere in between. A natural consequence of this hierarchy is that, for Arendt, a world in which action (and to some extent work) is prioritized and allowed to flourish is better than a world in which labor dominates. One of her central claims is that technological modernity has a negative impact on human flourishing by reducing all human activity to laboring. She criticizes automating technologies in particular. So-called labor-saving devices have, she argues, increased the prominence of labor in human life. We work to produce machines that are themselves dedicated to maintaining our biological systems of life. In other words, our work now serves labor. As a result, labor has become the preeminent and most valorized mode of human activity. Action has been all but forgotten and work has been degraded to the handmaiden of labor. As Arendt puts it, there is now a relentless "instrumentalization of the world and of the earth, this limitless devaluation of everything given, this process of growing meaninglessness where every end is transformed into a means" (Arendt 1958/98: 121).

The argument I make here is that by embracing the disruptive potential of automation, and withdrawing into the game-like world, we can recapture the higher forms of activity (the purer form of work and the spontaneity of action) and save them from the relentless instrumentalization that Arendt abhors. Again, the reason for this is partly built into the characterization of the game-like world. It is a world that is free from the instrumental pressures of work as currently constituted. It is a world in which performances are all that matter. This world can allow for spontaneity—in both the discovery of new "moves" within an existing game and in the creation of new games—and it can allow for the right kind of sociability and political engagement—in the way in which the games allow for actions to take place before an audience of peers and within a collaborative space, and in the way in which freeing us from the yoke of work will allow us to dedicate more time to the political sphere of action (somewhat akin to the ancient leisured classes of Greece and Rome).

Of course, the appeal of this argument lies largely in the appeal of Arendt's conceptual framework. If you reject that framework, and the hierarchy it establishes, you may be less swayed. That's why I don't rest too much weight on it here. It is just one argument among three. Nevertheless, I think Arendt's concerns about relentless instrumentalization, and the need to develop a form of existence that frees us from this instrumentalization, are valid and provide a good reason to embrace the strategy of withdrawal. If everything we do must serve some ephemeral and seemingly urgent need, we can never truly feel satisfied with our lives. Our current world is one that fixates on ephemeral and urgent needs—the next paycheck, the promotion, the degree or qualification. Everything is pursued, achieved, and quickly forgotten (Landau 2017: Ch. 11). A more ludic life would allow us to wallow in the pleasures of the moment and the virtues of our actions in and of themselves. This is a legitimate and desirable form of flourishing.

(iii) *The Argument From Idleness*

The third argument makes a virtue out of a perceived vice. One thing that people often worry about in a post-work world, particularly one in which "withdrawal" from the instrumental demands of the world is celebrated, is that people will do nothing with their newfound freedom. They will become idle, slothful, and selfish. They will have no care for the morrow; they will become absorbed in moment-to-moment pleasures. They will have no direction or purpose or meaning. As Voltaire famously put it in *Candide*, "Work saves a man from three great evils: boredom, vice and need." If you don't have to work for a living, you won't have the discipline or focus you need to truly flourish.

This fear of idleness has been with us for a long time. As Brian O'Connor (2018) notes in his extended philosophical essay on the topic, many famous Enlightenment thinkers, including most notably Immanuel Kant, railed against the idea of idleness. Kant went so far as argue that we have a duty not to waste our talents, and that to be a truly autonomous, well-rounded individual, you have to work hard, make the most of yourself, and triumph over any tendency toward apathy (O'Connor 2018: 37ff). This is a theme taken up by several more contemporary theorists of autonomy, including Richard Arneson and Christine Korsgaard (O'Connor 2018: 177). They all advocate what O'Connor calls a "muscular autonomy" which insists on the presence of goals, targets, and other instrumental pressures to lift us out of a primitive, pre-rational, purely instinctual mode of existence. They don't want us to slip back into this pre-rational mode of life. It looks like there is a risk that we will do exactly that if we embrace the strategy of withdrawal. Indeed, I suspect this is what people worry about most when they look at the hikkomori. They see people who are not applying themselves, whose ambitions are paltry, and who can get what they want too easily and too conveniently. They are quick to pathologize this form of life, not to celebrate it.

The standard response to this fear of idleness among post-work thinkers is to argue that it is mistaken. When freed from the yoke of work, people don't succumb to the temptations of idleness. On the contrary, they often apply themselves with great industry to the pursuits they truly enjoy. This, once again, is Bertrand Russell's famous defense of idleness—that it will enable people to invest in building the great artifacts of civilization, as the leisure classes of old have always done. Whether Russell's argument would continue to hold true in world of rampant automation is, for the time being, anyone's guess (we cannot run the exact experiment just yet), but all the experiments on basic income schemes around the world to date suggest that people who receive a non-contingent income do not succumb to idleness (Van Parijs and Vanderborght 2017: 138–144; Widerquist 2005). They invest in improving themselves and their families. The assumption and hope is that they will continue to do this in a post-work future.

But there is another way of looking at it. As O'Connor argues in his essay, idleness is not necessarily a vice. On the contrary, looked at in the right way, idleness may be exactly what we need in order to live truly free and autonomous lives (O'Connor 2018: 179–186). O'Connor develops this argument in three ways, each of which applies quite well to the post-work world. First, he argues that most accounts of what it means to be a free and autonomous individual insist on *authenticity*, that is, that the person lives a life of her own choosing, not one that conforms to the expectations and demands of others. A world of idle withdrawal is more conducive to this than the world in which we currently live. In a world in which we must work out of economic necessity, we cannot be fully authentic (or if we can be, it is largely a matter of luck): We must conform to the demands of the market, our clients, our employers and our economic dependents. If we remove the economic necessity of work, we can be more authentic. Second, he argues that most accounts of autonomy insist on an *independence* condition, that is, that an individual is not subject to manipulation, coercion, or indoctrination by others. Again, a world of idle withdrawal and game-like activities is more conducive to this than the world in which we currently live. The demands of the market economy and its associated work ethic mean that we are easily manipulated into doing things out of some genuine or perceived need for money, status, or employment. These manipulating forces dissipate in idleness. We are free to adopt reasons for action that are desired in and of themselves, not ones that are forced upon us by others. Third, and finally, although some people worry that idleness is without its own ethic (its own sense of the good life), this is not the case. To live an idle life is to embrace a clear conception of the good life, one that prioritizes freedom from external demands, and non-instrumentalism in activity. Again, these are goods that can flourish in the post-work world, particularly in the world of games with its focus on performance over outcome.

In sum, to the extent that we value freedom and autonomy, we should try to create a mode of existence that celebrates idleness over industriousness. The strategy of withdrawal into game-like activities does exactly that.

Final Criticisms and Concerns

I will conclude by considering some general criticisms and concerns about the argument developed over the preceding sections. To briefly recap, that argument has come in two parts. First, I argued that work is structurally bad and that its automation is something to be desired. I then noted that this argument runs into the paradox of desirable automation: The kinds of automation we need to hasten the demise of work are likely to impact on human flourishing in other ways. This led us to the second part of the argument—the strategy of withdrawal. I argued that by withdrawing from the world as currently constituted, we can resolve the paradox of automation and realize a genuine and desirable form of human flourishing. Far from this being something to fear and lament, it is something to desire and hasten.

I appreciate that this argument may be tough to swallow. The most obvious criticism is that the vision of the good life being imagined here is somewhat impoverished. Even if it is true that withdrawal satisfies *some* of our demands for meaning and purpose, it does not satisfy them *all*. Ceding the pursuit of the classic objective goods (like the pursuit of knowledge and the alleviation of suffering) to machines must surely result in a "lesser" existence for us humans? We would much rather participate in the pursuit of those goods.

There are three responses to this criticism. First, it's not clear that this is an impoverished form of flourishing. The human good is pluralistic and multi-faceted: different modes of existence help us to realize different mixtures of goods. It's hard to say that these modes of existence can be ordered into a clear hierarchy of "betterness" or "worseness"—pursuing one objective good often comes at a cost to other goods (e.g., friends and family). What's more, on some plausible theories, a mode of existence in which we do nothing but play games and pursue trivialities really does represent the best hope for humankind. This is Suits's famous argument for the "utopia of games" (Suits 2005). He suggests that if we live in a world in which do nothing but play games all the time, it must be because we have achieved a level of technical mastery over the world that eliminates the basic forms of human suffering and want from life. Surely that is as close to the best of all possible worlds as we can hope to get? Second, even if there is something less desirable about a world in which humans pursue trivialities and machines pursue objective goods, we may, ironically, have a moral obligation to prefer that world over the alternative. This would be the case if the machines are able to realize those goods in a more efficient and effective way, and if humans actually impede or hinder the pursuit of those goods. We already see some reason to suspect that we face this choice. Consider the debate around the merits of self-driving cars. These merits are often expressed in terms of the safety benefits for humans. Suppose these benefits are real. Would it be right for a human to insist upon driving when they know that this poses a greater risk to their fellow humans? Clearly not. The same logic could take hold in many other domains of activity, thus ethically requiring us to prefer withdrawal over continued engagement. Third, I suspect that any lingering insistence on the "lesser" virtues of withdrawal stem from the suspicion that the benefits of this mode of existence are somehow surreal or unreal. For example, someone might argue that success in a game is not "real" success because it lacks real stakes. I hope it is clear from what was said earlier that this is a misconception about what life in a game-like world would be like. There is nothing surreal or unreal about what happens in such a world. The skills and virtues we develop are real, they just happen to be tied to a particular set of performances that are ultimately trivial. If we follow MacIntyre, this is all we can ever hope for when it comes to skills and virtues: They only ever make sense relative to some defined domain of activity. It is only when they are embedded in such a domain that they become "real."

Another criticism people are likely to have is that the world being imagined is one that lends itself to isolation, selfishness, and narcissistic pleasure-seeking. If we don't have to work for a living, and if we don't have to strive to produce objective goods for the rest of humanity, then we lose the outward, other-facing domain of life. We will become inward-looking and self-focused. This is part of the fear that surrounds the hikkomori in Japan. They are seen as a group of people who have turned inward and lost the will to communicate, engage, and be held accountable to others.

There are two responses to this criticism. First, although I did use them as a jumping-off point for the argument in this chapter, the argument I have developed should not be mistaken for endorsing the hikkomori way of life. My understanding of what it means to withdraw from the pressures of life is slightly different from theirs and is wholly consistent with a flourishing social and family life. In fact, I would argue that it is work and its insatiable demands that takes us away from these outward-looking and other f-acing activities. Withdrawing from the world of work makes it possible to engage with them with greater vigor. Second, even though I make this distinction, I suspect some of the concern and indignation around isolation and selfishness makes sense only in a world of instrumental pressures. If you have to work to survive and thrive, and to ensure that others survive and thrive, any desire to withdraw from work will seem overly selfish and narcissistic. You will not be making your contribution to collective economic well-being, you will be living off the backs of others. In a world without those instrumental pressures, the withdrawal from work will seem a lot less selfish and narcissistic. It will seem like a reasonable choice.

This brings us to another potential criticism—that I am overselling the difference between what would happen in the game-like world and what happens in our world now. The claim I'm advancing is that in the game-like world, the distorting effects of instrumental pressures would be removed from human activity. But surely this is naive? Even if we succeed in removing economic pressures, or the pressure to do some objective good, it is likely that other instrumental pressures will step in to take their place. For example, people will want fame and social status, and they may use games as a stepping-stone to such ends. These new instrumental ends are just as likely to corrupt or undermine the value of withdrawal.

There are two responses to this criticism. First, as hinted at previously, we shouldn't make the perfect an enemy of the better when it comes to the elimination of instrumental pressures. Our current world is one in which our activities are distorted by a wide range of instrumental pressures, including the need for money and the desire for fame and social status. Eliminating some of the major instrumental pressures from the mix will make for a better, and less distorted, mode of existence, one in which the virtues of craft, action, and idleness have more space to breathe. In this regard, I think it is especially important not to understate the negative impact that the pressures of work have on life as currently lived. Eliminating its instrumental pressures would be a major improvement. Second, notwithstanding this point, there is reason to hope that instrumental pressures such as the desire for fame or social status will hold less sway in a post-work world. For one thing, the desire for fame and social status is currently catalyzed by the desire for economic security and success—the latter strengthens the former. In a world of automated abundance, this strengthening effect will be lessened. Furthermore, we already have ample evidence to suggest that the possibility of fame and status does not distort or undermine the conviction with which people play games. The leagues of amateur sportspeople, hobbyists, and gamers, who show up week-in-week-out for the love of what they do, and not for fame or glory, is testament to this. It suggests, at the very least, that a large majority of people can flourish in playing games without worrying about other instrumental ends those games may serve.

Finally, there is the criticism that the strategy of withdrawal is impractical. Remember, I originally sold the idea of withdrawal on the grounds that it was more practical (and more radical) than the integrationist strategy that I favored in earlier work. The integrationist strategy may help to conserve much of what we currently value, but it is technically uncertain and potentially impossible. The strategy of withdrawal is, on the face of it, much more tractable. But maybe this is not quite right? Maybe to truly embrace the ludic life, we would have undergo a major cultural revolution[3] that would be just as impractical and uncertain as the technical obstacles facing the integrationist strategy.

I think this criticism is a bit of a stretch, but, nevertheless, there are two responses to it. First, if it does require a major cultural revolution, this is a revolution that may be forced upon us anyway as a result of technological change and the effects it has on the mechanics of capitalism.

If advances in automation result in significant increases in the "surplus population" (i.e., the people who are not needed for the productive work of capitalism), then we will have to come up with some conception of the good life that is attainable and meaningful to them (and, to be clear, this is not an "us vs them" issue—I include myself within their potential ranks). Second, I think what I have said in the preceding sections should make it clear that this strategy of withdrawal and the pursuit of ludic pleasures, is not completely alien to human society. It has a long cultural and philosophical pedigree. It is just that the institutional structure of modern capitalism has blocked us from fully realizing it. As those institutional structures start to fray, it becomes both tangible and realizable. It wouldn't require a major cultural revolution, just a cultural reprioritization.

Notes

1. I don't suggest here that Graeber himself makes this mistake.
2. I say "person" to be gender neutral. The more common term in the literature is "craftsman." This is the title of Sennett's book on the topic.
3. I appreciate the historical resonances of this term and call upon them deliberately in order to make a strong case for the prosecution.

Bibliography

Anderson, E. 2017. *Private Government: How Employers Rule Our Lives (And Why We Don't Talk About It)*. Princeton: Princeton University Press.

Arendt, H. 1998. *The Human Condition*. Chicago: University of Chicago Press—originally published 1958.

Atkinson, A. 2015. *Inequality: What Is to Be Done?* Cambridge, MA: Harvard University Press.

Avent, R. 2016. *The Wealth of Humans: Work, Power and Status in the 21st Century*. New York: St Martin's Press.

Black, B. 1986. *The Abolition of Work and Other Essays*. Port Townshend, Washington: Loompanics Unlimited.

Brynjolfsson, E. and McAfee, A. 2014. *The Second Machine Age*. New York: W.W. Norton and Co.

Danaher, J. 2017. "Will Life Be Worth Living in a World Without Work? Technological Unemployment and the Meaning of Life." *Science and Engineering Ethics* 23(1): 44–64.

Danaher, J. 2018. "The Case Against Work." *The Philosophers' Magazine* 81: 90–94.

Danaher, J. 2019. *Automation and Utopia: Human Flourishing in a World Without Work*. Cambridge, MA: Harvard University Press.

Dreyfus, H. and Dorrance Kelly, S. 2011. *All Things Shining: Reading the Western Classics to Find Meaning in a Secular Age*. New York: Free Press.

Eberstadt, N. 2016. *Men Without Work*. West Conshohocken, PA: Templeton Press.

Ford, M. 2015. *The Rise of the Robots: Technology and the Threat of Mass Unemployment*. New York: Basic Books.

Frey, C.B. and Osborne, M.A. 2017. "The Future of Employment: How Susceptible Are Jobs to Automation?" *Technological Forecasting and Social Change* 114: 254–280.

Frayne, D. 2015. *The Refusal of Work*. London: ZED Books.

Gorz, A. 1989. *Critique of Economic Reason*. London: Verso.

Graeber, D. 2018. *Bullshit Jobs*. New York: Simon and Schuster.

Harari, Y.N. 2017. "The Meaning of Life in a World Without Work." *The Guardian*, 8 May 2017.

Hurka, T. 2006. "Games and the Good." *Proceedings of the Aristotelian Society* 106(1): 217–235.

Jozuka, E. 2016. "Why Won't 541,000 Young Japanese Leave the House?" *CNN*, 12 September 2016. https://edition.cnn.com/2016/09/11/asia/japanese-millen nials-hikikomori-social-recluse/index.html.

Landau, I. 2017. *Finding Meaning in an Imperfect World*. Oxford: Oxford University Press.

MacIntyre, A. 1981. *After Virtue: An Essay in Moral Theory*. South Bend: University of Notre Dame Press.

McNamee, M. 2008. *Sports, Virtues and Vices: Morality Plays*. London: Routledge.

Ovejero, S., Caro-Cañizares, I., de León-Martínez, V., and Baca-Garcia, E. 2014. "Prolonged Social Withdrawal Disorder: A Hikikomori Case in Spain." *International Journal of Social Psychiatry* 60(6): 562–565.

O'Connor, B. 2018. *Idleness: A Philosophical Essay*. Princeton: Princeton University Press

Piketty, T. 2014. *Capital in the 21st Century*. Cambridge, MA: Harvard University Press.

Russell, B. 1935. *In Praise of Idleness and Other Essays*. London: Routledge.

Sennett, R. 2008. *The Craftsman*. London: Penguin.

Standing, G. 2011. *The Precariat: The New Dangerous Class*. London: Bloomsbury.

Standing, G. 2016. *The Corruption of Capitalism: Why Rentiers Thrive and Work Does Not Pay*. London: Biteback Publishing.

Suits, B. 2005. *The Grasshopper: Games, Life and Utopia*. Calgary: Broadview Press—originally published in 1978.

Teo, A.R. 2010. "A New Form of Social Withdrawal in Japan: A Review of Hikikomori." *International Journal of Social Psychiatry* 56(2): 178–185.

Teo, A.R. and Gaw, A. 2010. "Hikikomori, a Japanese Culture-Bound Syndrome of Social Withdrawal? A Proposal for DSM-V." *Journal of Nervous and Mental Disorders* 198(6): 444–449.

Van Parijs, P. and Vanderborght, Y. 2017. *Basic Income: A Radical Proposal for a Free Society and a Sane Economy*. Cambridge, MA: Harvard University Press.

Weil, A. 2014. *The Fissured Workplace: How Work Became So Bad for So Many and What Can Be Done About It*. Cambridge, MA: Harvard University Press.

Widerquist, K. 2005. "A Failure to Communicate: What (If Anything) Can We Learn From the Negative Income Tax Experiments?" *Journal of Socio-Economics* 34(1): 49–81.

8 Universal Basic Income and the Good of Work

Andrea Veltman

Proponents of a universal basic income argue that, regardless of work and other income, every adult citizen should receive a modest, unconditional income that he or she can augment as he or she chooses.[1] Universal basic income is a bold and unconventional idea with an implicit ethical premise that the lives of all people are valuable in themselves and, if people are to live well, people need an income, a primary means of living. The ideal level of universal income would be sufficient for subsistence, but proponents are generally willing to start with smaller sums that would ameliorate oppression and poverty that persist even in the midst of affluent nations. Notably, apportioning all citizens or permanent residents an income does not entail abolishing private property, labor markets, or inequalities in income or wealth, but it may remove the conditions of desperation from which many people now seek gainful employment. In this chapter, I join others in defending proposals for a universal basic income. As I am a philosopher of work, I look at these proposals particularly with respect to how they intersect with working life, and I seek to defend them against two primary concerns: (1) universal basic would undermine motivation to work, and (2) providing a universal basic income conflicts with a social duty to work. First, I would like to review the many advantages of a universal basic income, and second to look at outstanding issues concerning work, including lingering issues of who will do the bad work that is integral in social functioning, if everyone enjoys an income that is not conditional upon willingness to work.

Advantages of a Universal Basic Income

The primary argument for a universal basic income rests on norms of justice and freedom. The argument is not that justice requires everyone have the same income, but that everyone should have some income—ideally enough for subsistence—which anyone can choose to boost through work, investments, or entrepreneurship.[2] A basic income for all would thus not eliminate higher and lower incomes, but it would temper the extreme economic inequalities that characterize our current order. Two of the leading contemporary proponents of universal basic income, Philippe Van Parijs and Yannick Vanderborght, call the economic security of universal basic income an instrument of real freedom for all.[3] Basic income provides a means of pursuing life goals, and proponents believe that all people, rather than just the well-to-do, should enjoy this concrete freedom. Moreover, it is important to proponents that a political community[4] pay money to all its members at regular intervals, rather than providing food stamps or housing grants, for money increases freedom, whereas goods such as food stamps are inherently restrictive in their purchasing power.

This argument draws implicitly on the concept of positive freedom, which is the ability to do what we desire, rather than simply freedom from the interferences or restrictions imposed by others. Using a positive conception of freedom, we might say that people cannot be truly free if they have no material means of pursuing their life goals, or if they are chronically struggling with hunger or homelessness, or if they are compelled to work for whatever meager wages employers offer. In his foreword to *What's Wrong With a Free Lunch?* Robert Solow captures this sense of positive freedom in conveying the primary goal of a universal basic income: "People should have not only the abstract right to choose the lifestyle that suits them but also the economic wherewithal to convert that right into lived reality."[5] In essence, a basic income secures the material conditions of freedom: The idea is that the worth of our freedoms depends on the resources people have at hand to make use of formal freedoms, and having an income is primary among these resources.[6]

Notably, in his book 1967 book, *Where Do We Go From Here: Chaos or Community?* Martin Luther King, Jr. also advocates a guaranteed income on grounds of justice and liberation. In discussing ways of abolishing poverty, King argues that improving education, job opportunity, and housing are all indirect measures that ultimately fail to attack poverty successfully. He writes, "The simplest approach will prove to be the most effective—the solution to poverty is to abolish it directly by a now widely discussed measure: the guaranteed income."[7] A guaranteed income would transform the lives of those living in poverty and inspire the sort of work that improves the progress of human civilization. It will also help the United States to overcome a tendency to "compress our abundance into the overfed mouths of the middle and upper classes until they gag with superfluity."[8] King suggests that a guaranteed income is major a step toward justice that secures individual dignity:

> The dignity of the individual will flourish when the decisions concerning his life are in his own hands, when he has the assurance that his income is stable and certain, and when he knows that he has the means to seek self-improvement.[9]

As proponents highlight, a basic income would not only ameliorate problems of poverty and hunger that persist even amid affluence, but also lessen social problems that are consequent to poverty, such as ill health, exploitation, violence, and lack of real opportunity for education. It would enhance democracy and endow the weakest citizens with bargaining power, such as by providing a stronger position from which to negotiate terms of employment or by allowing citizens to refuse desperation jobs. It would provide support for those who are unemployed, underemployed, or precariously employed. It would provide a subsidy of sorts that allows employees—or potential employees—to accept jobs with shorter hours or even lower wages, which some may seek if the work is sufficiently attractive in virtue of, for instance, the training it provides (as in a teaching assistantship) or the creativity it allows (as in an artist residency). Even more, universal basic income would advance the autonomy of women, such as by allowing women to leave abusive relationships or tyrannical husbands. As Van Parijs writes:

> It is not only against the tyranny of bosses that a UBI supplies some protection, but also against the tyranny of husbands and bureaucrats. It provides a modest but secure basis on which the more vulnerable can stand, as marriages collapse or administrative discretion is misused.[10]

A universal basic income would also facilitate taking a break from paid employment and experimentation with different kinds of lives. It would support a choice to be a full-time caregiver in the home or a full-time adult student. It would promote a culture of free citizenship, send a message that the lives of all citizens have inherent value, and free us from interminable debates, social stigmas, and bureaucratic intrusiveness that surround government welfare systems. In fact, one way of arguing for the feasibility of a universal basic income is to advocate replacing administratively costly and intrusive welfare systems with a simpler and streamlined universal basic income, which has no means-test and no bureaucratically enforceable requirement that beneficiaries be willing to accept jobs or training if they are able to work. A universal basic income includes both rich and poor, and both the industrious and the idle.

What About Work?

A question inevitably arises in response to basic income proposals: What about work? Work is ordinarily the means by which people try to earn a living, and if people no longer must work to earn a living, will many people abjure work for a life of idleness? This question invites several replies at the start. First, one could point out that empirical studies show the answer to this question is "no." Over the last several decades, research on the work ethic has consistently shown that a majority of people report they would continue to work even if they won the lottery and faced no economic need for work.[11] Most of those who are, in fact, quite wealthy, enjoying lives of economic freedom unimaginable to the rest of us, also do choose to work.[12] Cynics may believe that the wealthy work primarily to retain their wealth or obtain more money, or that ordinary people report a desire to work to provide a socially acceptable answer to inquiring researchers, but the fact is that a work ethic runs deep, and it does so because people perceive the many personal and social benefits of work. Productive employment is a foundation of individual and social prosperity, and psychologically healthy people find pleasure in activity, including many kinds of work. Many people have a basic desire to contribute to the world and to make something of themselves through work. Work is a source of pride and self-respect, and it is the primary way of making oneself useful in the world through the exercise of one's skills.

Second, although a fear that many people will go for a life of idleness is unfounded, we cannot take for granted that promoting idleness is an objectionable consequence of proposals for a universal basic income. Some thinkers embrace idleness as an idyllic form of a good life for human beings; such a perspective welcomes universal basic income as a means of promoting a good life for more people. In his classic essay "In Praise of Idleness," Bertrand Russell, for instance, expresses hope for a future world in which modern technology makes possible a four-hour workday and happier and more leisurely life for all people.[13] Relatedly, nowadays some thinkers position universal basic income as an answer to a possibility that technologically advanced societies will face work shortages in the foreseeable future. For instance, in *Rise of the Robots*, Martin Ford forecasts that developments in information technology, artificial intelligence, and automated machines in workplaces will bring a markedly diminished need for work, even in unexpected and far-reaching sectors of the economy.[14] A universal basic income, which Ford supports, answers the inevitable question, "How will many people obtain money without work?" From this point of view, we do face an existential question of what we will do with ourselves when freed from a life centered on work, but it is an advantage—rather than a concerning issue—of universal basic income that it enables a population to live without work.

Fans of idleness aside, many are concerned about the impact of a universal basic income on working life precisely because a little reflection shows that social functioning relies on the labor of people, and likely always will. Technological advancements can ease our burdens, but robots and machines cannot entirely replace the social need for human labor. Consider, for instance, the most technologically advanced society that creative minds have envisioned—the society of the starship Enterprise on *Star Trek*. Even here, functioning communities require countless workers, including commanders, administrators, engineers, information technologists, science officers, stellar cartographers, tactical officers, communications experts, exploration teams, helmsmen, bartenders, musicians, doctors, counselors, childcare workers, barbers, and so on. In the world as we know it, likewise communities rely on innumerable workers for many goods and services: We need, for instance, doctors, dentists, and teachers to care for our health, our teeth, and the development of our children's minds, respectively. We need people to build and maintain the world in all its complex aspects. Even in a world increasingly infused with technologies, many of us appreciate not having to interface only with computers; we want human beings to listen and respond to our needs, and we certainly don't want robots or machines, by themselves, teaching our children or repairing our teeth.

Consider also that caring, for instance, is a basic form of human work involving communication, human touching, empathetic interaction, and assistance to someone in need. Caring meets a need that is born out of the fragility and dependency of life itself: Many people cannot help but rely on others to maintain their lives, including young children, the elderly, the very sick, and those with disabilities. A society that would outsource childrearing and caring of sick, aged, or persons with disabilities to fully automated institutions would be a dystopia and, as one author writes, "an abandonment of people to machines."[15] The presence, judgment, and caring of a human person is irreplaceable in caring occupations and many others, although to be sure professionals who fill these occupations use all kinds of newfangled technologies to aid their work.

In *The Human Condition*, Hannah Arendt offers a similar insight that labor and work are basic conditions under which human life exists. Before we can do anything else, we must meet the daily needs we have as living embodied beings in labor that maintains life—cleaning, cooking, and perhaps bureaucratic paper pushing exemplify labor in the Arendtian sense. Arendt distinguishes labor from work, in that "work" goes beyond the labor of maintaining life to build the enduring artifice of the world or produce artifacts such as buildings, furniture, or works of art. Tools and technologies can alleviate but not eliminate labor and work from our lives: "A hundred gadgets in the kitchen and half a dozen robots in the cellar"[16] cannot replace the labor of human beings, for someone must operate these technologies, which are not always time saving and which cannot perform all drudgeries. For Arendt, the burden of laboring to maintain life can be eliminated for some only by the use of servants, and on this point I think she is right.

As work is an indelible part of life, I believe we should not answer the question "what about work" with an appeal to pleasures of leisure, or with a prognostication that technology will eliminate most work from the human condition, or with a denigration of the work ethic or the desire to work. Rather, the best defense of universal basic income will show that a universal basic income is entirely compatible with the good of work and with a work ethic. Thus, in the remainder of this chapter, I labor to show that, even with the real freedom of a basic income, people have ample reason for working, as work has a central place in a flourishing life. Furthermore, insofar as the functioning of communities relies on the labor of people, a modest work ethic reflects an enduring moral truth that we ought to contribute our time and talents to our communities, but this moral truth does not entail that the state (or the entity that bestows a basic income) should enforce a compulsion to work. A duty to work, like a duty to be honest, faithful, or charitable, is a poor subject for state oversight, and definitions of "work" employed by the state are unduly exclusionary. For these reasons, a basic income given unconditionally represents a better ideal for a well-ordered society than a government system of means-tested welfare benefits.

Universal Basic Income and Motivation for Work

Proponents of a universal basic income do face the question of how communities will motivate people to work, if people enjoy an income sufficient for a decent life. The brief answer is that the benefits of work are plentiful. First, we can reasonably expect that many people will be motivated to work by the extrinsic incentive of pay. Recall that proponents of a universal basic income do not argue for equality in income or wealth, nor do they argue for abolishing labor markets, in which people sell their labor for pay. A universal basic income is a starting floor, and people will be at liberty to work for money that augments their basic income. Furthermore, as now, some people will likely earn more than others, for various reasons. As many people desire not merely to subsist but to enjoy a life with a number of amenities, and as the expenses of a nice life add up quickly, many people will continue to have good reason to work for pay. What will change with a universal basic income is not the familiar fact of working for money but the premise that people must work or starve—and the many forms of labor exploitation that treat people as cheap, expendable resources.

Second, many forms of work have intrinsic benefits that draw people to want to contribute to communities, and these benefits are not to be forgotten among appeals to the incentive of money.[17] More than a means to a paycheck, work enables people to exercise skills, earn esteem, and serve a purpose within the world. Work is a source of pride, peer recognition, and self-respect. A strong work ethic reflects a range of virtues including willingness to contribute, self-discipline, dependability, cooperativeness, and industriousness. Work provides a satisfying outlet for our energies, a way of being useful, and a sense of accomplishment that comes from a job well done. It is at work that we hone our distinctive capabilities and skills, including job-specific skills and general problem-solving skills, social skills, and decision-making skills that help us thrive both within and outside of work. I could go on in extolling the virtues of work, but as I already labored to establish the centrality of meaningful work in a good life in *Meaningful Work*, allow me move on to another pressing question: What about work that must be done but that lacks intrinsic rewards? If a universal basic income brings real freedom for masses of people, will no one do the sort of bad work that, at present, people do only because they cannot turn down a live option for work?

First, let us pause to appreciate that the question of motivating certain kinds of undesirable work under basic income schemes is revealing in itself. It exposes something about our social orders that people ordinarily prefer not to dwell upon—the lack of freedom with respect to work that lies at the core of the lives of the majority of people. This heteronomy is easy to miss, first in the respect that a liberal democracy inclines toward celebrating the freedoms we do have in life and in work. In principle, we chose our occupations; many young people with a solid educational foundation can grow up to realize their dreams in their chosen occupations, and even adults can develop new skills and change occupations, or at least change workplaces or positions throughout life. But heteronomy envelops working life not only in that, at present, most people *must* work or fail to acquire a means of living, but also in that many people labor for much of their lives at hard, grueling work that is inherently unchoiceworthy. In his discussion of work in *Spheres of Justice*, Michael Walzer speaks of hard work as work that is harsh and difficult to endure—work that is like a hard winter or prison-sentence in that people would not choose such work if they faced even minimally attractive alternatives.[18] Hard work is entrenched in social systems of production and distribution, and it seems unlikely that advancements in technology will realize an old dream of eliminating hard, grueling, dangerous, dirty work from the human condition.

Now, one may retort to the complaint that we lack freedom in relation to work that, precisely as I argued earlier, we cannot eliminate labor and work from the human condition: Life itself thrusts upon us the need for labor and work, and there are limits to what technologies can do in lifting these burdens. Human beings—and even non-human animals—need to move matter around because what we need and want for our existence is not miraculously self-actualizing. If a compulsion to work springs from the conditions of life, some political philosophers may see the question of freedom in relation to work as something of a category mistake: Freedom does not obtain in our relations to nature but in relations among persons.[19] I say in response that, at the same time that work is an indelible part of the human condition, communities do face moral and political choices concerning work, including choices about what we produce, how much we produce, how we organize and assign production, and how we distribute the benefits of production to benefit some people but not others. Universal basic income also animates additional choices in relation to work, because it raises the possibility that people can turn down work they rather not perform, including the heaps of superfluous work that now run through our culture.

The heteronomy that covers the world of work is also easy to miss because, as Elizabeth Anderson writes in *Private Government*, we see surprisingly little discussion of power relations in the workplace even among thinkers concerned with freedom. Anderson presents a striking analogy between communist dictatorships and everyday workplaces, in which, standardly, nearly everyone operates under surveillance and has a superior they must obey. The orders of this superior may be arbitrary and subject to change at any time, and those of lower ranks "may have their bodily movements and speech minutely regulated for most of the day."[20] Superiors are not accountable to those they order around and, without question, routinely monitor the communications of the inferior ranks, and even claim authority to regulate workers' off-duty lives, as when workplaces effectively prohibit use of recreational drugs and enforce this prohibition through routine or random drug testing. If one doubts things are really so bad in average contemporary workplaces, one should consider the factual examples Anderson presents at the start of her treatise. Walmart employees cannot talk casually among one another, lest they be charged with time theft; Apple employees lose unpaid time every day as they wait for supervisors to search their personal belongings; Tyson employees are not allowed to use the restroom while on duty, with the result that some "urinate on themselves while their supervisors mock them."[21] Anyone in doubt of oppressive workplace realities should also read some of the many empirical and journalistic exposés of everyday working conditions, such as Christian Fuchs's *Digital Labor and Karl Marx*, Robin Nagel's *Picking Up*, Barbara Ehrenreich's *Nickel and Dimed*, or Ruth Cavendish's *Women on the Line*.[22]

One of the greatest advantages of a universal basic income is that it would revolutionize the world of work by granting unpresented bargaining power to workers and potential workers. Workers would have an income to fall back on in case they decide to say to their employer, "take this job and shove it." People with an income sufficient for subsistence still have ample reasons for participating in the working world (as argued earlier), but they also have real freedom to exit workplaces, or to exit the workforce altogether. Resultantly, most bosses will be unable to get away with being difficult to work for, and employers will not get away with paying paltry wages to people who cannot turn down work or foisting grueling workers conditions on people. To recruit and retain employees, employers will need to make work attractive by, for example, offering good pay, increasing opportunities for advancements and development of skills, improving the quality of working conditions, creating pleasant workspaces, and generally eliminating "lousy, degrading, dead-end jobs."[23] Social and economic institutions ranging from universities to factories will no longer be able treat some classes of people as wage slaves, and the production of commodities created by workers who are treated cheaply will probably disappear or diminish markedly, at least within the borders of the political community that bestows a basic income.

I admit that the consequences of putting real freedom in the hands of the workforce are potentially far-reaching and hard to envision. But I invite the reader to consider that, over time, workplaces in many parts of the world achieve significant measures of moral progress that would be hard to envision at historical moments in which many are mired in severely oppressive work. It is now commonplace to maintain as ideals— and to instantiate in practice in varying degrees—rational and fair hiring processes, non-discriminatory and harassment-free workplaces, equitable wages, and freedom from threats, abuse, and profanity while on the job. According to historian Sanford Jacoby, not one of these ideals was in place roughly a century ago, when the dominant mode of commodities production in the United States was a factory drive system in which foremen used close supervision, abuse, profanity, and threats to motivate faster and harder work, and in which work was highly insecure, poorly paid, fraught with pay inequities and ethnic discrimination, and not uncommonly secured through nepotism, favoritism, and bribery.[24] Some of us already live in workplace utopias in comparison with the factories of the late 1800s, at which time it would have been difficult to see possibilities for the sort of change that is now a reality. Taking a broad historical perspective, we ought not to say that work simply is what it is, or take it as given that many workplaces are lousy unpleasant places to be. Appreciating moral progress achieved in workplaces over past centuries highlights the abilities of human communities to transcend and reinvent given workplace structures and should lead us to a position of open-mindedness. Let us welcome further possibilities for transforming workplaces that stifle human development or undermine human dignity.

Universal Basic Income and the Duty to Work

Let us move on to another way in which issues surrounding work trouble proposals for a universal basic income. A feminist proponent of basic income, Kathi Weeks writes in her book *The Problem With Work* that the primary point of contention from those who oppose a universal basic income is not cost-feasibility: It is a moral ideal of social reciprocity reflected in the idea that work is a social duty.[25] Proposals for basic income are seen as maligning a work ethic according to which work is virtuous, and doing one's part, if one is able, in contributing to a community is carrying a share of a social burden that justifies partaking of the benefits of social cooperation. None other than Elizabeth Anderson, whose compelling work on heteronomous work I mentioned earlier, argues against a universal basic income because taking without giving is wrong; it represents freedom without responsibility. She writes:

> The UBI promotes freedom without responsibility, and thereby offends and undermines the ideal of social obligation that undergirds the welfare state. A UBI would not only inspire a segment of the able population—largely young, healthy, unattached adults—to abjure work for a life of idle fun. It would also depress the willingness to produce and pay taxes of those who resent having to support them.[26]

The idea is that work is not only a social duty but also a way to *earn* a living: It seems wrong to permit many people lives of leisure while others toil away at the many forms of work necessary for society to survive and thrive.

In various forms, the idea that work is a social duty through which a person earns her daily bread enjoys wide support: The Christian epistles to the Thessalonians include the command that "If anyone will not work, let him not eat" (3:10). This often-cited command does not seem entirely in keeping with the Christian spirit of charitable giving, but let's let that pass. In the twentieth century, none other than John Rawls observes a basic unfairness in gaining from "the cooperative labors of others without doing our fair share," such as in living a life of leisure on the state's dollar.[27] Igniting a critical motif of free-riding Malibu surfers, which now appears widely as the Malibu surfer problem in the literature in political philosophy, Rawls writes in a footnote in later paper: "Those who surf all day off Malibu must find a way to support themselves and would not be entitled to public funds."[28] The possibility that citizens who can, in principle, contribute labor to the common good defect from duties of contributing is thought to engender such resentment on the part of workers, and exploitation of the industrious on the part of the idle, that proposals for a universal basic income will fail on account of perceptions of fundamental unfairness.[29] Of course, it is interesting that a fair amount of ire surrounds the likelihood that non-working persons will free ride on the productive efforts of others, for present economic systems permit considerable free riding on the part of the idle rich, who receive abundant shares of social products without contributing as much in return. The public mind still has plenty of ire for "welfare moms," but none for Paris Hilton.

Is there really a social duty to work? Before endorsing the idea, let us consider a long-standing socialist skepticism about the work ethic. Among others, Bertrand Russell and William Morris would suggest we be suspicious of flowery praise of work, for such praise serves the interests of the wealthy and infuses a fabric of economic injustices. In something of a Thrasymachean perspective about the virtue of hard work, Russell writes that the whole gospel of work issues from "the rich and their sycophants," in order that the working classes will accept a notion that it is their duty to work, all the while supporting others in idleness.[30] For Russell, the idea that work is virtuous is positively harmful; it impedes progress toward a world in which everyone can, through the advent of modern technology, work much less and cultivate a life of educated but playful happiness. In "Useful Work vs. Useless Toil," William Morris also observes:

> Most of those who are well-to-do cheer on the happy worker with congratulations and praises. . . . It has become an article of the creed of modern morality that all labor is good in itself—a convenient belief to those who live on the labor of others. But to those on whom they live, I recommend them not to take it on trust, but to look into the matter a little deeper.[31]

Morris grants that nature does not grant us our livelihood for free; we earn our living through work, which can be pleasant under the right conditions. But working without an end in sight to produce items that are not truly useful is a curse, not a pleasure or an excellence, and the rich use hypocritical praise of all labor to thrust endless, useless toil upon the working classes for their own privilege and profit.[32]

Notably, philosopher Michael Cholbi carries forward something of this long-standing socialist criticism of the work ethic in a recent argument that the desire for work can be seen as an adaptive preference—the sort of preference that policymakers can question in facing cultural and economic trends toward a post-work future.[33] Cholbi points out that, like all adaptive preferences, the desire to work has been formed under unjust conditions in which we develop a dislike for what we cannot possess: In this case, a life of greater leisure. Even today, workers are often not fairly remunerated for their efforts, endure personal and financial costs through the long reach of jobs on our lives, and remain subject to many infringements of liberties in workplaces that feel entitled to control employees considerably.[34] Rather than crafting policies that satisfy a desire for work, he suggests policymakers facing a post-work future would do better to "acclimatise individuals to a society in which work is more peripheral."[35] Changing our common view of education as a process of job training, lowering retirement ages, lessening hours spent at work, and praising rather than shaming adolescents who choose self-exploration over work are all ways of supporting a shift in culturally entrenched attitudes about work, Cholbi suggests.[36]

There are elements of truth in these concerns over the work ethic: We should be entirely suspicious of an ethic that serves the interests of the wealthy, and ingrained social practices can create malformed desires about work. If people who have imbibed the norms of our culture feel they ought to work at least 40 hours a week, lest they be lazy leeches, they have a particular form of a desire to work that we should question as we move into a future with a diminished need for work. Standard to us now, the 40-hour workweek is not, in fact, a universal given, a rational Archimedean starting point for structuring working life; it is a historically contingent norm that arose following considerable struggle on the part of labor movements in the early twentieth century.[37] We now have good reason to accept a social norm of shorter working hours, particularly as advancements in technology appear to lead us in the direction of a lesser need for work. Many thinkers now champion shortening the working day or the workweek on grounds that shorter hours will permit a welcomed increase in leisure, allow more time for family and community participation, boost productivity during working hours, ameliorate problems of unemployment (by spreading around the limited good of good work), reduce worker fatigue and burnout, and permit us time to "re-learn some of the arts of living."[38] I myself would join this chorus and add that it is certainly not the case that the good of work should be maximized, as though the more work we have, the better off we are. Minimizing hours spent at work would allow people to enjoy a plurality of other goods, which is precisely the idea of human flourishing, and in a well-ordered society, and in the absence of emergencies, working a few hours a day or a few days a week may suffice to meet social and personal needs for work.

However, as work remains integral in the functioning of communities, a social duty to work appears justifiable. I would frame it as a contingent and limited moral obligation that, like most moral obligations, individuals realize in diverse ways. A social duty to work is dependent in the first place on the existence of a genuine social need for a critical mass of people working at a range of occupations—and the extent of this social need is clearly subject to rise or fall as history unfolds. If a society needs people (rather than machines) to produce goods and services that all people use in daily life, it does appear reasonable to believe that all people who benefit from the cooperative efforts of others and who are able to work themselves have some obligation to contribute to social functioning and flourishing. Someone who lives on the productive efforts of others and who chooses not to work herself, though she has the ability to do so and work is available for her, says, in effect, "others should sacrifice their time and energy for me, but I have no need to sacrifice time and energy for them."[39] Such a statement does not appear morally defensible, and in this way an obligation to work if one is able derives from an ethical principle of reciprocity and from an ethical repugnance to freeloading.

It is important to recognize that affirming a social duty to work does not entail a political compulsion to work. Not all social duties should be enforceable by the state: Some social duties are better framed as moral rather than political duties, and instruments of esteem, moral judgment, and social opinion are better suited to motivate and regulate these duties than the carrots and sticks imposed through law. John Stuart Mill articulates essentially this point in the first chapter of *On Liberty*, where he distinguishes political control from the force of social opinion: Both forms of power have a legitimate place in regulating behavior in a free society, although both can become overbearing, he believes.[40] In a society that values individual liberty, duties of honesty, fidelity, or generosity, for instance, are not usually enforced by the state; these are expressions of individual conscience and personal character, although they affect the social fabric and invite the brunt of moral judgment from a community. Putting a kind of moral accountancy for work in the hands of the state— which seems to be the underlying idea of workfare and all welfare systems in which receiving benefits depends on working, training for work, or being willing to work—is highly imperfect, expensive, and bureaucratically clunky. It is also intrusive and antithetical to the personal freedom that basic income seeks to promote.

Moreover, if it falls to the state to ensure that able-bodied citizens are dutifully working, then the state needs a definition of work, and the common political definition of work as paid employment is woefully inadequate in capturing the range of ways in which people give their time, develop their talents and contribute to communities. In fact, work is a concept that eludes clean conceptual analysis, and for this reason alone state bureaucrats trying to enforce an imperative to work are doomed to gross moral imperfections. We should certainly reject as under-inclusive (and sexist) any definition of work that restricts work to paid employment. Quite a bit of what should count as "work" is not paid, including caring for children; caring for relatives who are elderly, sick, or have a disability; work around the house, including housecleaning and home repairs; work at family businesses that carries no paycheck; volunteer work; work on articles, books, art, or crafts that never brings income; commissioned work that unsatisfied customers refuse to pay for; subsistence farming; work done by slaves; and even homework done by students. Work transcends paid employment, and proponents of basic income are correct to try to wrest away from the state the power to enforce a moral duty to work centered on the paradigm of paid employment.

It is also important to recognize that communities can flourish with a more minimal level of work than the 9-to-5, five-day-a-week routine that is standard at this place and time. Indeed, examining the history of work turns up a surprising array of examples in which peoples worked far less than 40 hours per week, which disconfirms a common belief that advancements in technology have already engendered unprecedented amounts of leisure for citizens in contemporary Western societies.[41] Clearly, it is also possible for communities to suffer from pervasive problems of overwork, in which workers work longer and harder than truly necessary and in which a work ethic has run afoul. In the respect that problems of overwork pervade contemporary American society,[42] we would be well advised to jettison any belief that we *ought* to be working diligently several hours a day, several days a week, in favor of a much more modest ethos regarding how much we work. As I suggested earlier, the fact that work is a good for human beings does not mean the more of it we have, the better off we are. A modest social duty to work should be balanced among other components of a flourishing life, and it should be paired with a broad and inclusive conception of work that includes unpaid work.

The Lingering Issue of Bad Work

In this final section, let us return to an issue concerning the heteronomy of work: In the world as we know it, massive amounts of work depend on compulsion and probably will not happen in a new era of radical freedom for workers. With a basic income sufficient for subsistence, who will do the grueling work of slaughterhouse assembly-line workers, or the tedious work of, say, data entry or manufacturing massive amounts of clothing? Who will slave away at the factories making the latest technologies and other gadgets, or take on the unpleasant work of dealing with angry customers or messes made by others, whether at call centers, fast food restaurants, or other places visited by the public? If the answer is that hardly anyone will, then one imagines society will go to the dogs, and universal basic income therein appears unfeasible. If the answer is that political outsiders or alien insiders will perform most of this work (as now), then proponents of basic income face further issues of injustice: Laborers who are not citizens of the political community that bestows a basic income are people too, and for this reason, exploiting them is wrong. If the answer is that such bad work will fade away with the right moral and technological progress, then proponents of basic income appear hopelessly utopian, as these and many other forms of bad work remain entrenched in widespread practices of production and consumption for the foreseeable future.

Some may also single out sanitation work as an outstanding concern: Who will be the janitor, or the city sanitation worker, or the rodent control specialist, or the person who picks up roadkill for the city, if everyone enjoys a basic income? This question actually strikes me as mistaken in that clean-up work is, often enough, both socially necessary and freely performed. My father, for instance, is a retiree who enjoys a basic income as a pensioner, but he continues to work part-time as a janitor, both for extra money and for the satisfaction that comes from being useful. Janitorial work and other clean-up work are sources of pride, as this work serves a vital function for communities and therein has an element of meaningfulness. I would even say that cleaning and tidying are more essential to a university community than, say, the activities of an associate dean, as the fundamental work of teaching and learning can carry on without the contributions of associate deans, but we cannot carry on without the contributions of our housecleaning staff. Moreover, not everyone chooses to contribute to a community through the exercise of an impressive skill or knowledge; unskilled routine work can be a freely chosen source of pride, satisfaction, and income. Still, the general point raised earlier remains: much work that is integral to society as we know it is heteronomous and supervenes on oppression. Progressive theorists may welcome the downfall of many types of socially eliminable bad work, such as the grueling work of slaughterhouse assembly-line workers, which persists because masses of people (the reserve army of laborers, in Marx's terms) lack significant freedom in relation to work. But in an unjust meantime, people who are fairly powerless and vulnerable to exploitation are found to do the bad work, and they suffer accordingly.

The problem of bad work raises unpleasant truths and moral quagmires for communities, and to be fair to proponents of basic income, the problem of bad work extends beyond the provision of basic income. Bad work is an intractable problem for any community, and in all its diversity, it probably has no singular solution. The problem itself sheds light on an enduring dark side of human social life, namely that our comfortable and pleasant lives depend on the toil of workers whose suffering is ordinarily shielded from our view in, for instance, the misery of the maquiladoras or in sweatshops around the globe.[43] These forms of work undermine the health of workers, imposing mind-numbing repetition and physical strain upon people who toil for extremely low pay amid noxious chemicals while stuck at workstations, sometimes unable to get up and move about freely. Consumers have a tendency to ignore this dark underbelly of their purchases and, as Russell Muirhead writes in *Just Work*, "to wish away the bad work we make necessary, and to turn away from those who do such jobs."[44] Cultivating awareness of the suffering of those whose work is bad is an important first step in envisioning and implementing a diverse handful of solutions to problems of bad work that can include, first, precisely the sort of technological progress in the workplace that motivates some to propose schemes for universal basic income.

Although it is doubtful that machines can eliminate bad work from the human condition, technological advancements do promise to free us from substantial amounts of drudgery and toil, if robots continue to replace human workers in factories, laboratories, food industries, and other service sectors. In the present day, many understandably worry about the consequences of robots taking paying jobs from those willing to work: corporate concerns with cost-savings function in effect to deprive people of the means of living. What are people to do? Answers for the here and now are unclear, but answers for the long-term include moving to a just society with a universal basic income, giving all people greater opportunities for self-development, and accepting that, from a moral point of view, it is fitting that work that wears out a person should be performed by a non-person, namely a machine. Interestingly, if capitalist impulses for higher profits now fuel the large-scale replacement of people with robots, a universal basic income that will make this replacement a welcomed change certainly requires rejecting the premise, which Karl Marx sees embedded in capitalism, that a worker "is allowed to live only insofar as the interests of the ruling class requires it."[45] The ethical premise of universal basic income is quite the opposite: working people are not merely means to increasing productivity or corporate profit but are ends-in-themselves. Ironically, the capitalist replacement of people with machines also realizes an old socialist dream that dispiriting and dreary work will be done by machines. As Oscar Wilde hopes in *The Soul of Man Under Socialism*:

> All unintellectual labor, all monotonous, dull labor, all labor that deals with dreadful things, and involves unpleasant conditions, must be done by machinery. Machinery must work for us in coal mines and do all sanitary services, and be the stoker of steamers, and clean the streets, and run messages on wet days and do anything that is tedious or distressing.[46]

Apart from employing machines for automated work, we can reduce the amount of bad work that people perform through moral cognizance that moves us to (1) consider the impacts of our practices upon workers, (2) clean up after ourselves, rather than leaving messes for others to clean, and (3) generally purchase less. In discussing heteronomous work, John White asserts the basic point that "the case for reducing unpleasant work—work which is mechanical, exhausting, dangerous or boring—in the interest of personal well-being is overwhelming," and he points in particular to the temptations of consumerism: "The wastefulness of our consumer society heaps up behind it a quite unnecessary mountain of heteronomous work."[47] From this viewpoint, obvious solutions to problems of bad work include rejecting the excesses of consumerism—and the maximizing economic philosophies that support these excesses—and embracing values such as simpler living and "enoughness."[48] In addition to reducing bad work through better moral values and technological progress, communities concerned with problems of bad work can also share or rotate some forms of bad work, amply remunerate bad work, recognize the value of unglamorous work that sustains social functioning, increase opportunities for occupational mobility and skill training, and limit the hours of the working day. Even if these measures cannot guarantee that no one toils crushingly at bad work, taken collectively, they can bring us considerably close to ideals of worker freedom and flourishing.

In brief, I believe a just society can embrace a universal basic income without undermining either (1) motivation to work or (2) an ethos of contributing to the world through work. By endowing workers with greater bargaining power, a universal basic income stands to radically undermine footholds of exploitation by providing people with basic material resources and greater autonomy over whether, where and under what conditions to work. More broadly, it also stands to improve conditions of life, especially for those who live hand to mouth and who are vulnerable to harms of poverty and oppression in nations that are advanced in productivity and wealth.

Notes

1. Among academic political theorists, those who argue in favor of basic income include, for example, Philippe Van Parijs and Yannick Vanderborght, *Basic Income: A Radical Proposal for a Free Society and a Sane Economy* (Cambridge, MA: Harvard University Press, 2017); Philippe Van Parijs, *Real Freedom for All: What (If Anything) Can Justify Capitalism?* (New York: Oxford University Press, 2003); Philippe Van Parijs, "A Basic Income for All," in *What's Wrong With a Free Lunch?* ed. Joel Rogers, Joshua Cohen, and Philippe Van Parijs (Boston: Beacon Press, 2001). Among the contributing authors in *What's Wrong With a Free Lunch?* Anne Alstott, Brian Berry, Ronald Dore, and Robert E. Goodin also argue in favor of a universal basic income. Also Guy Standing, *Basic Income: A Guide for the Open-Minded* (New Haven: Yale University Press, 2017); Mark Walker, *Free Money for All* (Hampshire, England: Palgrave Macmillan, 2016); Carole Pateman, "Democratizing Citizenship: Some Advantages of a Basic Income," in *Redesigning Distribution*, ed. Bruce Ackerman, Anne Alstott, and Philippe Van Parijs (London: Verso, 2006); Erik Olin Wright, "Basic Income, Stakeholder Grants, and Class Analysis," in *Redesigning Distribution*; Kathi Weeks, *The Problem With Work: Feminism, Marxism, Anitwork Politics, and Postwork Imaginaries* (Durham: Duke University Press, 2011); Brian Berry, "Real Freedom and Basic Income," *The Journal of Political Philosophy* 4, no. 3 (September 1996): 242–276; Berry, "The Attractions of Basic Income," in *Equality*, ed. Jane Franklin (London: Institute for Public Policy Research, 1997); Trudy Govier, "The Right to Eat and the Duty to Work," *Philosophy of the Social Sciences* 5, no. 2 (June 1975): 125–143; and Andre Gorz, *Paths to Paradise: On the Liberation From Work* (Boston: South End Press, 1985).
2. Notably, the idea that inequality is not itself objectionable but that no one should fall below a certain threshold is the primary thread of argument of Harry Frankfurt's short treatise *On Inequality*. Frankfurt does not argue for a universal basic income but expresses a principle that underlies arguments for a basic income. He calls the principle "the doctrine of sufficiency": "What is morally important is that each should have *enough*. If everyone had enough money, it would be of no special or deliberate concern whether some people had more money than others." Frankfurt, *On Inequality* (Princeton: Princeton University Press, 2015), 7, emphasis in original.
3. Philippe Van Parijs and Yannick Vanderborght, *Basic Income: A Radical Proposal for a Free Society and a Sane Economy* (Cambridge, MA: Harvard University Press, 2017), see especially p. 4.
4. Philippe Van Parijs defines a universal basic income as paid by a political community, but he notes that his definition of basic income as "an income paid by a political community to all its members on an individual basis, without means test or work requirement" does not fit all uses of the term

"basic income" (Van Parijs, "Basic Income: A Simple and Powerful Idea for the Twenty-First Century," in *Redesigning Distribution*, 4–5). One recent campaign for basic income, run by the international charitable organization GiveDirectly (https://givedirectly.org/basic-income), works to improve the lives of African villagers living in extreme poverty through direct cash transfers of modest sums. This is an example of a basic income initiative that is not funded by a government for its own people, but a common model for a basic income in which a state funds basic income through taxation.

5. Robert Solow, "Foreword," in *What's Wrong With a Free Lunch?* xi. Solow is Emeritus Professor of Economics at the Massachusetts Institute of Technology and won the Nobel Prize in Economics in 1987.

6. Philippe Van Parijs makes this argument using Rawls's phrase "the worth of liberty"; see for instance Van Parijs, "A Basic Income for All," in *What's Wrong With a Free Lunch?* 14.

7. Martin Luther King, Jr., *Where Do We Go From Here: Chaos or Community?* [1967] (Boston: Beacon Press, 2010), 171.

8. King, *Where Do We Go From Here*, 174.

9. King, *Where Do We Go From Here*, 173.

10. Philippe Van Parijs, "A Basic Income for All," in *What's Wrong With a Free Lunch?* 20.

11. A classic study on this question is Nancy Morse and Robert Weiss, "The Function and Meaning of Work," *American Sociological Review* 20, no. 2 (1955): 191–198. For a discussion of this study and subsequent similar studies, see Al R. Gini and T. Sullivan, "Work: The Process and the Person," *Journal of Business Ethics* 6 (1987): 649–655. For a more recent survey, see Scott Highhouse, Michael J. Zickar, and Maya Yankelevich, "Would You Work If You Won the Lottery? Tracking Changes in the American Work Ethic," *Journal of Applied Psychology* 95, no. 2 (2010): 349–357.

12. Theorist of work Russell Muirhead writes that the wealthy "see their advantage more in finding good work than in escaping the world of work. More than 90 percent of those with a net worth of more than 2.5 million dollars continue to work and earn; riches, it appears, do not put an end to work." Muirhead, *Just Work* (Cambridge, MA: Harvard University Press, 2004), 47–48 and 189.

13. Bertrand Russell, "In Praise of Idleness" (1935) in Bertrand Russell, *In Praise of Idleness and Other Essays* (New York: Routledge, 2004). To be sure, idleness is different from leisure. Idleness carries connotations of doing nothing and, in large doses, it appears as a vice or an affliction. A life of leisure, in contrast, connotes the possibility of many non-working activities, or even (in an Aristotelian sense) a privileged life devoted to higher activities, such as contemplation of the eternal truths. In "In Praise of Idleness," Russell occasionally implicitly appeals to an Aristotelian ideal of leisure: "The wise use of leisure," he writes, "is a product of civilization and education," and enables a person to indulge curiosities for knowledge (8, 14). He also stresses that, after four hours of work a day, people should be able to use their leisure as they see fit (12). In any case, the point remains that, in response to proposals for a universal basic income, some people would welcome freedom from work, whether they plan to spend their days doing very little or whether they plan to take up activities such as contemplation, reading, gardening, tennis, or surfing, for example.

14. Martin Ford, *Rise of the Robots: Technology and the Threat of a Jobless Future* (New York: Basic Books, 2015).

15. Diemut Grace Bubeck, "Justice and the Labor of Care," in *The Subject of Care: Feminist Perspectives on Dependency*, ed. Eva Feder Kittay and Ellen K. Feder (Lanham: Rowman & Littlefield, 2002), 162.

16. Hannah Arendt, *The Human Condition* (Chicago: University of Chicago Press, 1958), 122.
17. Andrea Veltman, *Meaningful Work* (New York: Oxford University Press, 2016).
18. Michael Walzer, *Spheres of Justice: A Defense of Pluralism and Equality* (Oxford: Basil Blackwell, 1983), 165.
19. Libertarian political philosophers, who think extensively about the meanings of freedom, are prone to clarify that freedom is a relation among persons, not a relation between humanity and nature. John Hospers, for instance, argues that rights and liberties on the part of one person entail only duties of forbearance on the part of others, and "[t]he non-violation of these rights [to life, liberty, and property] will not guarantee you protection against natural catastrophes such as floods and earthquakes, but it will protect you against the aggressive activities *of other men*. And rights, after all, have to do with one's relation to other human beings, not with one's relations to physical nature." Hospers, "What Libertarianism Is," in *Social and Political Philosophy: Classic and Contemporary Readings*, ed. Andrea Veltman (Toronto: Oxford University Press, 2008), 324.
20. Elizabeth Anderson, *Private Government: How Employers Rule Our Lives (And Why We Don't Talk About It)* (Princeton: Princeton University Press, 2017), 37.
21. Anderson, *Private Government*, xix.
22. Christian Fuchs, *Digital Labor and Karl Marx* (New York: Routledge, 2014); Robin Nagel, *Picking Up* (New York: Farrar, Straus & Giroux, 2013); Barbara Ehrenreich, *Nickel and Dimed: On (Not) Getting by in America* (New York: Henry Holt & Co., 2001); Ruth Cavendish, *Women on the Line* (London: Routledge & Keegan Paul, 1982).
23. This phrase is from Philippe Van Parijs, "Basic Income," in *Redesigning Distribution*, 14.
24. Sanford Jacoby, "The Way It Was: Factory Labor Before 1915," in *Employing Bureaucracy: Managers, Unions, and the Transformation of Work in the 20th Century*, revised ed. (New York: Columbia University Press, 2004).
25. Weeks, *Problem With Work*, 146. See also, for example, William Galston, "What About Reciprocity?" in *What's Wrong With a Free Lunch?* and Amy Gutman and Dennis Thompson, *Democracy and Disagreement* (Cambridge, MA: Harvard University Press, 1996), 227–229. Philippe Van Parijs and Yannick Vanderborght also highlight objections concerning the work ethic as being "more emotional, more principled, and more decisive in the eyes of many," in comparison to other objections. Van Parijs and Vanderborght, *Basic Income*, 99.
26. Elizabeth Anderson, "Optional Freedoms," in *What's Wrong With a Free Lunch?* 72.
27. John Rawls, *A Theory of Justice* (Cambridge, MA: Harvard University Press, 1971), 112 (section 18, paragraph 5).
28. John Rawls, "The Priority of Right and Ideas of the Good," in *Collected Papers*, ed. Samuel Freeman (Cambridge, MA: Harvard University Press, 2000), 455 note 7.
29. John Elster, *Solomonic Judgments* (Cambridge: Cambridge University Press, 1989), 215.
30. Russell, "In Praise of Idleness," 9.
31. William Morris, "Useful Work Versus Useless Toil" [1885] in *William Morris on Art and Socialism*, ed. Norman Kelvin (Mineola: Dover Publications, 1999), 128.
32. Morris, "Useful Work Versus Useless Toil," 128–130.
33. Michael Cholbi, "The Desire for Work as an Adaptive Preference," *Autonomy* 4 (July 2018): 2–17.

34. Cholbi, "The Desire for Work as an Adaptive Preference," 9–10.
35. Cholbi, "The Desire for Work as an Adaptive Preference," 14.
36. Cholbi, "The Desire for Work as an Adaptive Preference," 14.
37. Benjamin Kline Hunnicutt, *Work Without End* (Philadelphia: Temple University Press, 1988). See also Benjamin Hunnicutt, *Free Time: The Forgotten American Dream* (Philadelphia: Temple University Press, 2013), in which Hunnicutt traces the U.S. history of worker movements for shorter hours, linking these movements to visions of higher progress for humanity.
38. Edward P. Thompson, "Time, Work-Discipline and Industrial Capitalism," in *Customs in Common*, ed. E.P. Thompson (London: Merlin, 1991), 401. For a discussion of reasons in favor of shortening the working week, see Hunnicutt, *Work Without End*; Weeks, *Problem With Work*, especially Chapter 4: "'Hours for What We Will': Work, Family, and the Demand for Shorter Hours," or Stanley Aronowitz, et al., "The Post-Work Manifesto" in *Post-Work: The Wages of Cybernation*, ed. Stanley Aronowitz and Jonathan Cutler (New York: Routledge, 1998).
39. Govier, "The Right to Eat and the Duty to Work," 131.
40. John Stuart Mill, *On Liberty and Other Essays*, ed. with an Introduction by John Gray (Oxford: Oxford University Press, 1991), 9. Here, Mill writes, "All that makes existence valuable to anyone depends on the enforcement of restraints upon the actions of other people. Some rule of conduct, therefore, must be imposed, by law in the first place, and by opinion on many things which are not fit subjects for the operation of law."
41. See Juliet B. Schor, *The Overworked American: The Unexpected Decline of Leisure* (New York: Basic Books, 1991), Chapter 3; Al Gini, *My Job My Self: Work and the Creation of the Modern Individual* (New York and London: Routledge, 2000), 75–77.
42. See, for example, Schor, *Overworked American*.
43. See, for instance, Todd Chretien and Jessie Muldoon, "Misery of the maquiladoras" at socialistworker.org, published November 18, 2011, or Robert J.S. Ross, *Slaves to Fashion* (Ann Arbor: University of Michigan Press, 2004).
44. Muirhead, *Just Work*, 173.
45. Karl Marx, *The Communist Manifesto* in *Karl Marx: Selected Writings*, 2nd ed., ed. David McLellan (Oxford: Oxford University Press, 2000), 257.
46. Oscar Wilde, "The Soul of Man Under Socialism" (1891) in *The Collected Works of Oscar Wilde*, Vol. 8, ed. Robert Ross (London: Routledge, 1993), 298.
47. John White, "Education, Work and Well-being," *Journal of Philosophy of Education* 31, no. 2 (1997): 233–247, 242.
48. On the value of enoughness (which essentially means being satisfied with having enough), and on the failures of optimizing economic philosophies, see Michael Slote, *Beyond Optimizing* (Cambridge, MA: Harvard University Press, 1989) or E.F. Schumacher, *Small Is Beautiful: Economics as If People Mattered* (New York: Harper & Row, 1973).

9 What Difference Does It Make?
UBI and the Problem of Bad Work

Frauke Schmode

Introduction

> "The fact is that civilization requires slaves. The Greeks were quite right there. Unless there are slaves to do the ugly, horrible, uninteresting work, culture and contemplation become almost impossible."
>
> Oscar Wilde

Every society has depended on people who had no choice but to perform *bad work*—or as Oscar Wilde put it: "the ugly, horrible, uninteresting work." Many of these forms of work entail severe harms for the workers. Just think about the gruesome working conditions of workers in the global supply chains of major companies like H&M, GAP or Walmart. The collapse of the Rana Plaza in Bangladesh in 2013 revealed how much we *really* pay for cheap clothes. And this is just the tip of the iceberg with lots of forms of bad work going unnoticed. Every year, thousands of workers become injured or die because of their work.[1]

But throughout history, most societies have disregarded the value certain forms of bad work had for society.[2] Take ancient Egypt, for example: Slaves were forced to build the pyramids with incredible skills, efforts, and exertions. Yet the achievement and glory are attributed to the pharaohs, who it is safe to assume did not lift a finger themselves but ordered others to perform the actual work. Bertolt Brecht hints at this disputable ascription of glory in his poem "Questions From a Worker Who Reads": "Who built Thebes of the 7 gates? In the books you will read the names of kings. Did the kings haul up the lumps of rock?"[3]. In addition, many societies have obscured those performing bad work with social exclusion and stigma. While the extent to which this has happens varies, the most severe cases of occupational stigmatization result in workers becoming "untouchable" by ordinary citizens.[4]

Now, one could argue that it is only just if those contributing most to society are valued most and that those not doing their part to contribute deserve to be treated respectfully. But even if we agree to this reasoning, it bears to question whether this is really the case. After all, many forms

of bad work are *socially necessary*, that is, without someone performing it, society would not function properly. Just think about bus drivers, kindergarten teachers, garbage collectors, or construction workers:
If they strike, it really strikes a nerve. Moreover, bad work is distributed
quite unequally. The most dangerous and dirty work is still being left for
the worst off in society: To slaves, to the (global) poor, to immigrants,
to prisoners, to women, and to those not keeping up at school—it "is
distributed to degraded people. Citizens are set free."[5] Thus, bad work is
often done by those most desperate and already disadvantaged. The low
compensation and low social prestige they receive in return for doing bad
work only deepens the pre-existing inequalities. We, therefore, need to
ask whether the current distribution of bad work and society's treatment
of it is just. And if not, if *the market alone* is able to bring about a just
distribution of it. Because as

> long as there is a reserve, a class of degraded men and women driven
> by their poverty and their impoverished sense of their own value, the
> market will never be effective. Under such conditions, the hardest
> work is also the lowest paid, even though nobody wants to do it.[6]

As we have seen, this reasoning applied to the distribution of bad work
throughout most of our history.

Unconditional Basic Income and the Problem of Bad Work

But the world of work is changing rapidly. Technological advancements
are (albeit slowly) transforming the nature of work itself as well as the
working conditions. Many forms of bad work might be automated
or improved. Some people even dream of (or dread) a future without
work. While this is still a long way off, the formerly utopian idea of an
unconditional basic income (UBI) is now considered a real possibility.
The idea of a basic income, introduced as a means to reduce poverty, is
steadily rising in popularity worldwide. Regardless of the model that is
chosen—a (partial) basic income or a negative income tax—past experiments with basic income have resulted in positive economic, social, and
psychological effects such as a reduction of poverty, improved health, or
a better work-life balance.[7] However, the introduction of a basic income
could not only radically change the current social security system, but
also it might even have more far-reaching impacts on the labor market.
Charles Fourier, for example, imagined a basic income that would value
unpaid work (such as housework) and volunteerism. He, as well as modern advocates of a basic income, think it would strengthen the workers'
position in the labor market: As a UBI would ultimately free people from
their dependency on paid labor, their bargaining power would increase.
Moreover, as every citizen would get a basic income regardless of his

or her employment status, the "stain" of unemployment is also likely to lessen. A basic income could thus constitute a real *exit option*.[8] If it does, it might "remove the conditions of desperation from which many people now seek gainful employment."[9] Something which in turn has the potential to change the distribution pattern of bad work *drastically*—if and how much so, is the question I want to explore in this chapter.

What difference would a UBI make? Assuming an unconditional basic income that constitutes an exit option were to be introduced, how would bad work be affected? When *would* workers choose to opt out? Which jobs are so bad that we might have a serious problem finding people willing to do them? And what if these jobs are nonetheless socially necessary? Just think about the precarious working conditions of construction workers—low pay, low job security, and a high risk of health endangerment. Nevertheless, the work is vital for our infrastructure and thus the proper functioning of our society. In a world with basic income, who will still be willing or rather desperate enough to perform our "dirty work"? To discuss these questions, we first need a comprehensive account of bad work. Thus, I will start by clarifying my notion of work to then introduce a two-dimensional account of bad work. I then differentiate between four forms of bad work: low job satisfaction, bad employment conditions, bad job design, and essentially bad work. Afterwards, I will elaborate on the idea of basic income as an exit option from the labor market and will subsequently analyze how the different forms of bad work will be affected. I argue that we can make out three trends: (i) People will have more autonomy in choosing their career and its development. (ii) Working conditions will assimilate as bad work will be rewarded with higher incentives than "decent" work. (iii) In the case of extremely bad work that imposes permanent and irreversible harms, fair schemes of compensation are out of the question. This might result in certain work being left undone which could pose serious problems for the functioning of society if the work is socially necessary—unless society agrees upon fair ways of sharing it. By way of doing this, I aim at two things: (i) to discuss potential effects the introduction of a UBI might have on bad work and its distribution in a given society. Moreover, the possible scenario of having socially necessary bad work left undone should instigate a debate about fairer ways of distributing bad work equally among all members of a society—which, in turn, should (ii) call attention to the problem of bad work and the injustice that surrounds it also in the here and now.

A Two-Dimensional Account of Bad Work

When I talk about work, I refer to *a physical or mental activity done in order to change a current state of affairs or a condition in the world that is experienced as unsatisfactory or defective.* We produce clothing to fend off the cold or the heat. Likewise, we produce food in order to appease our hunger and create opportunities to entertain ourselves to dispel boredom. Thus, through work we intentionally mould our world and our existence in a way deemed appropriate.[10] Yet work is by nature Janus-faced: While it produces something of value, it also requires effort. While this holds true for all forms of work, some kinds of work seem to be particularly arduous, even gruesome. The question is: At which point do we consider work to be bad work? While there are a number of accounts of good work, philosophy has had until now very little to say about bad work. The current philosophical (and political) debate about work revolves around how best to improve working conditions with regard to the economic, social, and psychological dimensions of work, such as income, working environments, and job satisfaction. So far, there are many discourses on *particular aspects* of bad work, but these debates are not interconnected.[11] Hence, there are neither comprehensive accounts of bad work nor general debates about what constitutes bad work. To fill this desideratum, I propose a two-dimensional account of bad work that allows us to differentiate between subjective and objective criteria of bad work. After all, there are (at least) two perspectives from which one can evaluate work. First, we can look at the *worker* and judge work in relation to his or her needs, preferences, or abilities. I call this the *subjective dimension* of work. Second, we can consider the different features of the *work itself*. I will call this the *objective dimension*. The latter can be divided into three sub-dimensions: (i) the employment conditions, (ii) job design and (iii) the nature of work.

Subjectively Bad Work

The *subjective dimension* measures the degree of job satisfaction. Work is subjectively bad if the worker finds little or no pleasure in the work he or she is doing—which often is a result of a mismatch between the worker and his or her work. This is the case if the work involves tasks for which the worker is unfit, has no affinity for whatsoever, or which the worker experiences as meaningless or even morally wrong. A reporter who takes no interest in sports would be unhappy being responsible for covering the sports news, for example. Similarly, a journalist who aims at unveiling the truth of the matter and performs in-depth investigative journalism is likely to disapprove of the tactics and methods of the yellow press. Often, another worker might find this work enjoyable—an avid football fan would probably rejoice at the opportunity to work as a sports journalist, just as a career-oriented person would prefer a well-paid position at a prestigious yellow paper over work at a small-scale local newspaper. Similarly, job satisfaction is likely to be low if the work does not fit because it is not in accordance with one's capacities (someone with low stamina and physical strength doing physical labor), one's personal preferences (someone who wants to work as a football player, but has to work as a joiner), or because the work runs counter to one's personal convictions and values (a vegetarian working in a slaughterhouse).[12]

Taking into consideration the worker's individual preferences, abilities, and personal circumstances, we can determine the degree of job satisfaction by evaluating the degree of experienced meaningfulness, the degree of conformity to moral convictions, and the degree of congruence.[13] Subjectively bad work, on the one hand, affects the job performance and thus diminishes the overall efficiency.[14] But more importantly, there are indications that workers have an almost existential need to engage in meaningful endeavours[15]—so much so, that workers actively go out to see meaning in what they are doing.[16] This is not surprising since the sphere of work is a "pervasive life domain and a salient source of meaning and self-definition."[17] Individuals attach meanings to themselves in relation to their participation in work activities or membership in an occupational group.[18] A positive work identity is often seen as important for workers to maintain their self-worth.[19] Thus, subjectively bad work can, on the other hand, undermine workers' self-respect and challenge their identity.[20]

While the subjective dimension of work is an important point of reference when evaluating work, relying on subjective criteria alone is problematic. Not the least because it discloses only the attitude of the worker towards her work, but nothing about the work itself. Hence, the subjective dimension can have negative parameter values simply because someone made the wrong career choice. Moreover, due to, for example, cognitive biases, the reverse is just as likely: People might be content with their work even though it is objectively bad. As has been mentioned before, studies indicate that people actively go about searching for meaning in their work because of an almost existential need to spend their time in a meaningful way.[21] Moreover, some people are content with their work because they consider it to be the best possible option available to them: "The cleaner in the university may be satisfied with her work, as might her employer, but should she be?"[22] This question bears even more weight in the case of extremely harmful work. After all, "we can desire and be pleased by things which are bad for us, from a cigarette to a disastrous marriage."[23] Thus, the subjective dimension alone gives us very little about the work itself, despite the subjective dimension playing an important role as well. Objectively bad work, however, *always* implies the risk of impairing workers' mental or physical functioning, self-respect, or well-being.

Objectively Bad Work

The *objective dimension* evaluates the work itself and its effects on the worker. It refers to objective features of the employment situation itself, the job design, and the nature of work. Consequently, we can distinguish between three sub-categories of objectively bad work: (i) bad employment conditions, (ii) bad job design, and (iii) essentially bad work. I will start with discussing *the employment conditions* which describe the conditions under which work is performed, usually defined by one's employer. I focus on three aspects that enable us to sketch a coherent picture of the respective working conditions: the degree to which employment offers financial security, the work-life balance, and the opportunities for socializing. Bad employment conditions can have severe consequences for workers which already been discussed at length: Precarious work results in people feeling vulnerable, insecure, and unable to follow their life goals.[24] A job that leaves little to no discretionary time and hinders one's personal development can impair one's social life and lead to exhaustion and stress-related diseases. Similarly, solitary work severely limits one's opportunity to form social relationships, especially if it offers little free time or few material means to engage in other activities where one can socialize.

Second, when looking at the *job design*, one looks at the arrangement of the work itself. Bad job design prevails when the level of self-directedness or social prestige is low or if the degree of complexity does not match the worker's abilities or level of competence. Non–self-directed work can have severe impacts on the worker's autonomy, leaving her unable to live an autonomous life even outside of work. First, because the individual capacities to lead a self-directed life are not fully developed or undermined by his work. Such work "*fails to develop* cognitive complexity and a sense of personal competence, intellectually demanding uses of leisure time, liberal democratic ideology. . . , moral responsibility, receptivity to change, self-confidence, self-esteem, and protections against anxiety."[25] Second, because experiencing "work as undignified obviously amounts to not feeling respected as an autonomous person."[26] The worker feels powerless, as "an object manipulated and controlled by other people or by some impersonal system, such as technology."[27] On the other hand, work that is too complex for the worker can entail excessive demands towards him, who might exhaust himself trying to accomplish his tasks. Ultimately, he might even start doubting his abilities in light of constant failures. Yet there are very few examples of this kind of work (e.g., the work of highly specialized theoretical physicists). Yet, in praxis, work with too low a job complexity seems to be the much more pressing problem—which is probably the reason why researchers have been focused on the problems surrounding trivial and repetitive work. Workers at a production line, for example, often feel like nothing more than a "self-conscious appendage to machinery,"[28] as they perform work that has been reduced to "the most minute and repetitious tasks."[29] Often, these workers also suffer from the low social prestige of their work which can lead them to being socially degraded, stigmatized, shunned, or even isolated. Work with a low social prestige can have an extremely negative impact on an individual's life and feelings of self-worth. Moreover, his or her future prospects and social life can be affected. To put it in a nutshell: Bad job design can have negative formative effects on the worker and can negatively impact a worker's mental capacities, abilities, personality, self-worth, social life, and overall well-being.

This final category looks at *the nature of work*, that is, at intrinsic aspects of the work itself, such as work goals or tasks and their effects on the worker. I will consider the degree of repulsiveness and the degree of harmfulness as such essential features that, if scored high, the nature of work can be considered bad. Let us first take a look at repulsive work: Certain kinds of work have almost always been (and probably always will be) undesirable because they require the worker to fulfill certain tasks that the vast majority of people find "simply physically disgusting."[30] Certainly, people differ in the degree they find handling certain tasks repulsive, which is why this category overlaps to some extent with the subjective dimension. However,

> a set of activities having to do with dirt, waste, and garbage has been the object of disdain and avoidance in just about every human society. . . . The precise list will vary from one time and place to another, but the set is more or less common.[31]

While highly repulsive work might not imply severe physical or mental harms, it can nevertheless be considered a form of essentially bad work due to the degree of disgust, nausea, and hideousness involved. Another case of essentially bad work is harmful work. Such work has harmful effects on workers, other members of society, other living beings, or the environment. Mining, for example, can be considered a form of bad work because it is extremely hard, noxious, and hazardous work that can severely impair the worker's physical and mental well-being. The life prospects and the opportunity range of a former miner suffering from a miner's lung or slowly dying from tuberculosis or lung cancer are permanently and irrevocably reduced. Apart from that, the extraction and usage of coal (or other natural resources) can be considered harmful toward other people as well, namely those whose health suffers due to bad air quality. It also imposes (nowadays unnecessary) risks and harms on the environment.

Even though there might be certain overlaps, this category has to be clearly distinguished from the former category that looked at the arrangement of work tasks: The work of a mechanic is not essentially bad since it is neither particularly harmful nor repulsive. Yet, the way the work is arranged, that is, the way it is divided into small tasks each of which are rather trivial and repetitive, results in bad working conditions. Essentially bad work implies severe physical or mental discomfort, distress, and harms that endanger workers' overall well-being, their functioning, and their capabilities. Since these features are often at the very core of a certain form of work and as such almost inseparably connected with its related tasks, it is often extremely difficult to change such work for the better. Thus, one of the potential tasks of a soldier is to kill members of the adverse party if necessary. And regardless of the conditions under which work is performed, that is, whether a soldier kills in a close combat fight or by maneuvering a drone, the harmful effects on the soldier remain.[32]

Measuring Bad Work

So far, I have argued that work can be bad in four respects: because of low job satisfaction, bad employment conditions, bad job design, and/or essentially bad work. But when exactly can we classify work as bad? In general, work can be considered bad if one parameter value falls below a certain, acceptable threshold for an extended period of time. So, if work is generally interesting and sufficiently complex, having to perform a few meaningless tasks does not result in it being considered a form of bad work since the level of complexity remains above a certain threshold. But if the majority of tasks are utterly boring and trivial and in no regard match the level of skills of the worker, we have grounds to consider it a form of bad work.

But how is this acceptable threshold determined? One way to determine this threshold is to refer to the standards guaranteed by law, for example, concerning minimum wages, maximum working hours, and safety regulations. Yet the law does not regulate all aspects of work and thus can provide only guidelines for certain categories. For example, labor laws usually say nothing about the level of complexity a work should offer or the degree to which workers should be able to autonomously decide on their work routine. Moreover, what is considered to be "acceptable working conditions" by law is often insufficient to guarantee the well-being of the worker. The minimum wage many countries have introduced often does not provide people with adequate means to sustain their livelihood. Instead, one might refer to the general consensus as a more demanding guideline for what is deemed acceptable (which often overlaps at some point in time with the general law). Thus, in many countries with minimum wages, scientists, labor unionists, and employees agree that the current level of minimum wage is insufficient to provide a decent wage and propose a much higher one—which, if referred to instead, would provide a much higher threshold to be met in order for work to provide financial security.[33]

Basic Income As an Exit Option From the Labor Market

While bad work is not necessarily unjust in itself, it is a negative good— that is, something everyone prefers to have less off, rather than more. It can thus be regarded as a social burden the distribution of which ought to be of concern from the perspective of distributive justice. Currently, the distribution of bad work is extremely unequal. Often those less privileged are the ones most likely to perform bad work due to economic hardships. And, as long as people have to depend on their employment status to secure for the provision of their most basic needs, the worst off in society are likely to remain as "'the reserve army of the proletariat.' Once they have alternatives, they will rally and say no."[34] A UBI could offer such an alternative by separating survival from employment and production.[35] However, whether it can provide a real exit option depends on the monthly payment to which the UBI would amount to. To have a real exit option, it would have to cover all *existential* needs. But this sum would not be high enough to satisfy *all* needs or expensive preferences. The wages people earn through their employment would be a surplus to their guaranteed UBI. Hence, I assume that most people will keep working because they consider working a necessity, in order to reach a higher (or uphold) their social position or to continue their lifestyle, or simply because they like their work.

But what difference would the introduction of a UBI make? How would bad work and its distribution be affected? I will discuss this question with reference to three trends that are likely to follow from the introduction of a UBI: (i) more autonomy for workers to choose their career and its development, (ii) an assimilation of working conditions, and (iii) shortage of workers for specific forms of bad work.

More Autonomy in One's Career Choice and Development

The introduction of a basic income directly affects only one sphere of work: the *economic* sphere. Without a basic income, most people have to work in order to survive and to take care of their family. Under those conditions, we are "defenseless against our employers' petty abuse or their power to arbitrarily dismiss us."[36] The introduction of certain legal restrictions or the formation of unions protect workers, but only to a certain extent, since employers will still retain the upper hand. If people have to worry about being able to secure a sufficient income (e.g., because the economy is down or the unemployment rate is high), being "picky" with their potential source of income is a luxury many cannot afford and competition will be fierce for any job regardless of its nature.

The introduction of a basic income potentially could alter this situation drastically, since workers would no longer have to fear unemployment as much. In a situation such as this, people will become much more autonomous in deciding their career choice and development. First, it is much more likely that people at the beginning of their working life will be more encouraged to spend their working life with something they *want to do* (e.g., working for an NGO or as an artist), without being influenced as much by their current or prospective economic standing that often pressures people into choosing career that "pay off" (e.g., working as a corporate consultant or joining the army just in order to be able to study later on). Similarly, people already active in the labor market might aim to improve their situation by looking for new and more satisfying work.

However, whether people are willing to do this will be highly dependent on the degree of job satisfaction. Even though people in general will be far more prone to rethink their occupational choices after the introduction of an unconditional basic income, it might still be hard for people to quit their work and everything that comes with it (colleagues, income, social prestige, etc). But the worse the job and the degree of job satisfaction, the more likely people will quit their work to look for more fitting work. The introduction of a UBI might thus create a situation where people have the time and opportunity to think about which work is in accordance with their personal needs and preferences—and where they can also *re*think their choice and change their profession if these factors change. The overall congruence between work and worker and hence the degree of job satisfaction might then rise significantly.

People will be not only in a better position to choose a fitting career, but also better able to influence the way their career develops. In general, the progress of one's career is often linked to one's working time, with full-time employment, overwork, and constant availability often being a necessary precondition for successfully climbing the career ladder. What is worse, often just *keeping* the job requires employees to work (unpaid) overtime. Now, in a situation where a UBI takes away much of the economic pressure on the side of the employees and reduces the leverage of their employers, people might be less afraid to reduce their working time to spend more time with friends and family, engage in hobbies, and so forth. Many people might, therefore, be less willing to compete with other employees for the longest working hours and choose to opt out (to some extent) of the working-time rat race. For many, the work-life balance might increase drastically.

Assimilation of Working Conditions

Yet while the introduction of a UBI promises significant improvements for workers by enabling them to have more say in the choice and development of their working life, unexpected and possibly unwanted developments may also arise. For example, being able to follow "one's calling" often makes people vulnerable to exploitation. Already, people sacrifice economic gains or prestige to work in jobs they consider meaningful and important.[37] This tendency might "worsen" considerably if people are no longer dependent on a decent income. As has been discussed earlier, knowing that one's basic needs are covered, many people might cease to pursue a career out of economic considerations and might instead take jobs that are poorly paid but meaningful or enjoyable. More people might also be willing to dedicate themselves to unpaid work, for example, spending more time at home, doing housework or taking care of their children. Long-term and full-time employment are likely to decrease while some might even prefer the increased flexibility in light of their newly gained economic security—more people might prefer working for Uber and decide on their work routine freely instead of working for a taxi company with fixed rights and working hours. And with the work-life balance likely improving, workers will have more time to engage in hobbies and social activities to form social relations outside of the workplace. Thus, employment conditions might actually worsen for many forms of work.[38]

This seems to contradict two commonly hold assumptions about the effects the introduction a UBI supposedly has on the labor market, namely (i) that it will lead to a severe shift in the power relationship between employers and employees in favor of the latter, and therefore (ii) workers can demand higher wages, better working conditions, or both. It does indeed seem likely that the bargaining power of workers increases insofar as leaving the labor market is a real option which reduces the leverage employers have on their employees. Having an "exit option" would significantly enhance the bargaining position of workers. But as Gourevitch points out, a UBI might just as well lead to a further deterioration of the workers' bargaining position: If a UBI substitutes for collective self-organization by workers, it might undermine the workers' position in the long run.[39]

I think both predictions are accurate but apply to different forms of work. Thus, it seems likely that the bargaining position of workers in decent jobs decrease as economic security loses its importance and the tendency to sacrifice certain economic or social gains in exchange for meaningful work is likely to increase. If people remain willing to work in these jobs regardless of the working conditions, their bargaining position is weakened—especially so if workers' self-organization diminishes as well. The employment conditions might even grow "worse." Yet quite the opposite tendency can be assumed for most—if not all—forms of bad work. As has been mentioned before, it can be assumed that people are more likely to leave their job or refrain from paid employment the worse their work is. This is likely to result in a reverse of the quality of the work and its pay. After all, as Friedman and Friedman said:

> If Red Adair's income would be the same whether or not he performs the dangerous task of capping a runaway oil well, why should he undertake the dangerous task? He might do so once, for the excitement. But would he make it his major activity? If your income will be the same whether you work hard or not, why should you work hard?[40]

Thus, in a society with a sufficiently high UBI, the market might finally be able to create a better trade-off for those doing bad work by linking the reward of work to the quality and nature of the work. Trivial, non–self-directed, repulsive, or harmful work as well as work with low social prestige might then be rewarded with high benefits. On the flipside, decent or meaningful work would be but poorly paid. In many cases, higher (monetary) incentives might suffice to attract workers to perform bad work—a radical improvement of bad job design is thus not to be expected. Thus, a student might not mind cleaning offices if this enables him to pay the university fees for the next semester. A couple who wants to spend a few weeks at a luxury retreat on the Caribbean might not bother working on an assembly line for a while to earn the necessary money.[41] This, in turn, could alter the distribution of bad work drastically: While bad work currently is mainly done by those worst off who have no other choice but to do it, higher incentives could attract people from various social positions.

Shortage of Labor for Certain Forms of Bad Work

However, while the market might be able to create a better "trade-off" for workers performing certain forms of bad work by reversing the relationship between the quality of the work and its pay, the market might fail to distribute *all* forms of bad work. The harms of certain forms of work are so severe that the incentives offered by the market to perform the work are unable to compensate for them. If an exit option exists, people would not be willing to endure these harms regardless of the remuneration offered. To see this, let us first consider which forms of work can be properly compensated for.

Every job demands of the worker to bear with a certain amount of disutility such as commuting to the workplace several days a week, spending several hours in a way he or she cannot decide upon autonomously, performing certain unpleasant tasks, and so forth. In cases such as this, it is usually assumed that the disutility of labor, that is, "the discomfort, uneasiness, inconvenience or pain inherent in human effort" can be compensated for with (monetary) benefits.[42] And often, there seem to be fair schemes of compensation available. We might not know the exact amount of money (or of other benefits) necessary to compensate the burdens of work, but we can have a pretty good idea how a fair rewarding system could look like. One could, for example, argue with Nozick that even though we do not know what a fair compensation would look like, x (e.g., money) compensates for y (e.g., less free time due to the time necessary to commute to work) if it provides the same degree of preference satisfaction.[43]

But does this also apply to bad work? I mentioned before that, in principle, one negative parameter value in any of the categories of bad work is sufficient to objectively consider work as bad. The reason being that the implications of one negative parameter value already imposes severe strains on a worker's mental or physical health, well-being, self-esteem and/or personal development. But in many cases, a negative parameter value in one category can be leveled out by a sufficiently positive parameter value of another category. A lonely truck driver could be compensated for having to work in solitude by having to work less and being paid more. While it would not change the fact that the work is socially isolating, he could use the additional time and money to, for example, join a sports club where he can meet other people. In many cases, the harms of bad work are reversible and can thus be compensated in exchange for other benefits. Then the aforementioned mechanism sets in: If an exit option from the labor market were to be installed in the form of the UBI, these forms of bad work would be compensated better and working conditions would improve which should suffice to attract workers.

However, this reasoning does not hold true for all forms of bad work. Consider the case of the "radium girls": These girls, most of them in their early twenties or younger, worked as dial painters with self-luminous paint made with radium. At first, the only harm done was the shining aura surrounding them which let them shine like angels in the dark. Yet, later on, they suffered from anemia, bone fractures, and a radium jaw followed by an untimely and incredibly painful death resulting from radium poisoning.[44] It is difficult to believe that anyone would think that these harms can be properly compensated for. You might consider this to be a rather extreme example, yet many people have to face high risks every day when going to work—just think about soldiers, NGO workers in war zones, astronauts, professional athletes, race drivers, and so forth. Even in a country with relatively high safety standards like the United States, more than 14 people die on the job *every day*.[45] Certain burdens of work involve such high and severe disutilities that they cannot be compensated for and are thus incommensurable with benefits. Bad work is incommensurable if it entails *permanent and irreversible harms* that negatively and severely affect the workers' life, mental and physical functioning, or their self-respect. In such instances, the damage and suffering brought upon the worker (and her relatives) are so inconceivable and irreparable that no amount of money or other resources could possibly suffice to compensate for them. This is most often the case for harmful work and repulsive work or work with low social prestige. Positive parameter values can make negative parameter values in other categories "more bearable," but they can't level out the harmful effects. Rewarding those performing bad work with high wages, good employment conditions, and high social prestige, then, is necessary, but not sufficient, to compensate them for their disutility.[46]

Hence, in the case of incommensurable bad work that imposes permanent and irreversible harms, a drastic shortage of workers is to be expected if a reasonable exit option, such as the UBI, exists. This might have severe consequences for society if the work is *socially necessary*, that is, if it is necessary to sustain the institutions guaranteeing basic rights and liberties of a given society. The exact boundaries between socially necessary and unnecessary work depend on the given society and are likely to change over time. Yet we can get a rough idea of social necessity if we ask ourselves what were to happen if an entire class of workers would simply disappear: What would happen if no one were willing to work as a construction worker or a soldier any longer? It's "obvious that were they to vanish in a puff of smoke, the results would be immediate and catastrophic."[47]

If people really would "rally and say no" to certain forms of bad work once they have the option to do so, it urges us to rethink our current handling of bad work. Two complementary paths are then available[48]: Certainly, the first step to take would be to improve forms of socially necessary, incommensurable bad work if possible, as much as reasonably possible. While this might help improving bad work to a certain extent and minimize the harms involved, some forms of work are likely to remain incommensurable. Construction work, for example, is among the occupations with the highest work-related death rate due to falls from buildings, electrocutions, and so forth. If safety measures were improved, the rates of accidents and deaths might decrease significantly. Yet not all risks and dangers can ever be prevented completely. One second of carelessness when operating heavy machinery and the worker might still be losing body parts, or his or her life. If improvement or automation is impossible,[49] society might think twice about whether the work really is socially necessary. For example, not finding workers willing to work in mines might facilitate the transition from coal to green energy. But this is not always an option. Then, sharing work fairly among members of society would be the most obvious and just solution. Over the centuries, many forms of sharing socially necessary bad work have developed. Nineteenth-century France, for example, briefly revived the corvée system: In order to vote, every able-bodied man had to work three days for the public service (e.g., to maintain public roads). Countries such as Israel or South Korea still have a compulsory conscription service to share the burden of national defence more evenly among members of society. In Germany, men could decide between joining the army or doing social work and taking care of the sick or the elderly, for example. These systems of sharing socially necessary bad work acknowledge something that seems to be forgotten in many market driven societies—that socially necessary bad work is a social burden that should be shared fairly among all members in a society of equals. The introduction of a UBI could help to revive the notion of civic responsibility once more.

Conclusion

The introduction of an unconditional basic income (or similar measures) could create a situation where everyone has the financial means to live a decent life, *independent* of his or her contribution to the labor market. Given such an exit option existed, how would it influence bad work and its distribution? What difference would it make? First, some forms of bad work would improve: Subjectively bad work would decrease as workers would gain more autonomy in their career choice and its development. The employment conditions are likely to improve insofar, as working times might become much more flexible which would reduce the significance of having the opportunity to form social relationships at work. Socially isolating work might thus cease to be a criteria of bad work altogether. Similarly, the degree to which work provides economic security might cease to be important when evaluating employment conditions, as the UBI already provides this to a certain extent. Second, it is likely that the remuneration and the overall working conditions will be linked to the quality and nature of work—with bad work offering the highest incentives for workers. This might lead to an overall assimilation of working conditions: The working conditions for bad work are likely to level up, whereas those for comparably decent work are likely to decrease. However, drastic changes in job design and the social division of labor are not to be expected. Last, a UBI might affect the distribution of bad work in two ways: First, commensurable bad work would be spread more equally among all members of society thanks to the linking of remuneration to the quality of work. Second, incommensurable bad work that inflicts permanent and irreversible harms might be left undone—which would pose a serious problem if the work is socially necessary. Therefore, the introduction of a UBI is no *solution* for the problem of bad work. But thinking about an unconditional basic income and its effects on bad work urges us to reflect on the way society currently deals with socially necessary bad work. Can we continue to pretend that nothing is wrong with society practically forcing an entire class of people (or countries) to do the dirty work simply because they do not (yet) have a real exit option? If not, we need to start thinking about other, fairer ways of distributing socially necessary bad work.

Notes

1. Friedrich-Ebert-Foundation (2017).
2. Except maybe in socialist countries (such as the GDR) and communities (as in the Kibbutz).
3. Brecht (1990), *Fragen eines lesenden Arbeiters*; Translated from German.
4. One example are the Burakumin, whose fault it is to have ancestors with occupations considered impure or tainted, such as butchers, executioners, undertakers, or tanners. A stigma their descendants still bear today: they are excluded from society, are often denied access to religious temples, live in secluded communities, and suffer from marriage and employment discrimination. In addition, the remuneration is often as poor as its social prestige.
5. Walzer (1983: 165).
6. Walzer (1983: 177).
7. cf. e.g., Raventós (2016).

8. cf. e.g., Standing (2011), Widerquist (2013).
9. Veltman (2016: 95).
10. cf. Füllsack (2009: 8f); Work does not necessarily have to involve pay. After all, if we replace housework by hiring a cook or a babysitter we do consider those replacements to be workers (cf. Hall 1986: 11). Consequently, someone who stays at home and cleans and takes care of his or her children *works*, even though he or she might not have a *job* (cf. Clark 2017: 62). Therefore, we can distinguish between *work* that is not necessarily paid and an *occupation* or a *job* which can be understood as activities that produce earnings (cf. Kalleberg 2000: 2).
11. See, for example, the discourses on precarious work (e.g., Kalleberg 2008/2011; Standing 2011), work with low job quality (Carré et al. 2012; Tangian 2007), harmful work (Walzer 1983), formative work (Arnold 2012; Clark 2017), dirty work (Hughes 1962), or meaningless work (Arneson 2009; Bailey and Madden 2016; Graeber 2013; Veltman 2016; Yeoman 2014).
12. Michaelson et al. (2014: 79), Rosso (2010: 130).
13. The degree of job satisfaction is partly influenced by the parameter value of the objective dimension, since negative parameter values are likely to influence the degree of job satisfaction as well. Thus, even if my work suits me and even if I consider it to be meaningful, my job satisfaction most certainly diminishes if I have to work under exploitive working conditions or if the work is harmful to my personal well-being. However, while the parameter values of the objective dimension can affect the level of job satisfaction, if and if so, which parameter serves as a sources of discontent and the extent to which it does varies (cf. Kalleberg 1977: 126).
14. Fried and Ferris (1987), Geldenhuys, Laba, and Venter (2014), van Dick (2003).
15. Yeoman (2014).
16. Bailey and Madden (2016: 58), Dutton, Roberts, and Bednar (2010) describe similar findings: "For example, chefs describe their roles using rhetorical narratives—like artist, business person, or professional—that imbue their self-definitions with worth; . . . and hospital cleaners pick and choose from their interactions with nurses, doctors, and patients to construct self-definitions that foster a sense of value and meaning in doing cleaning work" (265).
17. Dutton, Roberts, and Bednar (2010: 265).
18. Dutton, Roberts, and Bednar (2010: 266).
19. Dutton, Roberts, and Bednar (2010), Hsieh (2008).
20. Labatut et al. (2016), Dutton, Roberts, and Bednar (2010).
21. Bailey and Madden (2016).
22. Beadle and Knight (2012: 436).
23. Clark (2017: 63).
24. McGovern, Smeaton, and Hill (2004), Kalleberg (2000), Standing (2011).
25. Lane (1991: 259).
26. Roessler (2012: 87).
27. Hall (1986: 105).
28. Marx (1990: 436); Translated from German.
29. Garson (2014: xiii).
30. Hughes (1951: 319).
31. Walzer (1983: 174).
32. For an overview of various studies on this topic cf. Dao (2013).
33. Yet this also shows that there is no universally valid threshold; rather, it is contingent upon time and place. A look at the working conditions of the last century alone demonstrates how fast the "acceptable threshold" can change.

Similarly, what counts as acceptable working standards and conditions varies among societies. Even the ILO declares that "(I)n a developing country, for example, one cannot expect to have access to the same type of social security on a daily basis as in a developed country" (Somavia 2004). Hence, the acceptable threshold is likely to differ between, let's say, Sweden and Bolivia. Thus, even though the threshold concept is based to some extent on objectively measurable criteria as defined by law or scientific research, a wide range of what counts as acceptable is determined by other (social) factors such as the economic prosperity of one's society, one's personal economic standing, one's expectation for the future, and so forth.

34. Walzer (1983: 167).
35. Prochazka (2016); There are reasons to doubt that a UBI could ever offer such an exit option (cf. e.g., Birnbaum and De Wispelaere 2016). In this chapter, I simply assume it would since it provides the framework of the thought experiment envisioning the effects of an UBI on bad work *if it were to provide such an exit option*. This allows us to consider the problem of bad work and its distribution as a problem of justice, regardless of whether an UBI is introduced and regardless of whether the UBI could offer an exit option.
36. Pettit (2007: 5).
37. Bunderson and Thompson (2009).
38. Whether they indeed worsen or whether the provision of economic security simply ceases to be of importance when evaluating employment conditions is difficult to decide beforehand.
39. Gourevitch (2016).
40. Friedman and Friedman (1980: 23).
41. Arguably, one of the huge improvements that comes with the introduction of a UBI is that the situation of society's worst off is likely to improve. Without the pressing economic need to engage in meaningful work, those who engage in bad work only out of sheer desperation will have the option to say "no." But there might as well arise a new, vicious circle of path dependencies: some people might be less able to get by with the amount the UBI provides than others and thus again become dependent on generating a high income quickly. Some might spend their UBI carelessly (out of a false sense of security maybe). Some might have higher costs or expenditures, while others might have aggravating circumstances (e.g., people suffering from gambling addiction or people with debts). Thus, certain disadvantaged groups might again be prone to do the bad work *despite* an UBI.
42. Von Mises (2007: 612).
43. Nozick (1974: 57); Yet there are several problems with this approach related to the disruption of preferences formation or the perception of preference satisfaction due to biases or irrationality. It seems more promising to rely on scientific research to estimate at which point certain conditions become harmful. The acceptable level of risks and harms again being predetermined by social consensus (and thus, e.g., in light of the current economic possibilities).
44. Moore (2017).
45. United States Department of Labor (n.n.).
46. As Stanczyk (2012) points out, high incentives often are insufficient to attract workers. Thus, some rural areas in the United States have trouble providing medical care as they fail to attract enough physicians—despite support offered to finance the studies as well as a median annual pay that is in the 96th percentile of the national distribution of household income (154f).
47. Graeber (2013).

48. This reasoning, of course, holds true only in a very virtuous society, in a closed society, or in a world where every country offers a sufficiently high UBI. Otherwise, societies might simply "export" bad work to other, poorer countries—the *global* reserve army of labor. This can already be observed in many highly industrialized countries.
49. Or, arguably, if the costs for automation are too unreasonable.

Bibliography

Arneson, R.J. 2009. "Meaningful Work and Market Socialism Revisited." *Analyse & Kritik* 31(1). doi:10.1515/auk-2009-0109.

Arnold, S. 2012. "The Difference Principle at Work." *The Journal of Political Philosophy* 20(1): 94–118.

Bailey, C. and Madden, A. 2016. "What Makes Work Meaningful: Or Meaningless." *MIT Sloan Management Review*: 53–61.

Beadle, R. and Knight, K. 2012. "Virtue and Meaningful Work." *Business Ethics Quarterly* 22(2): 433–450.

Birnbaum, S. and De Wispelaere, J. 2016. "Basic Income in the Capitalist Economy: The Mirage of 'Exit' From Employment." *Basic Income Studies* 11(1): 61–74.

Brecht, B. 1990. *Werkausgabe*, Vol. 9, Reprint of the 1967 edition. Frankfurt/Main: Edition Suhrkamp.

Bunderson, S. and Thompson, J. 2009. "The Call of the Wild: Zookeepers, Callings, and the Double-Edged Sword of Deeply Meaningful Work." *Administrative Science Quarterly* 54(1): 1–50.

Carré, F. et al. 2012. "Job Quality: Issues and Developments." In: *Are Bad Jobs Inevitable? Trends, Determinants and Responses to Job Quality in the Twenty-First Century: Critical Perspectives on Work and Employment*, 1st ed., edited by F. Carré, P. Findlay, C. Warhurst and C. Tilly, 1–24. Basingstoke: Palgrave Macmillan.

Clark, S. 2017. "Good Work." *Journal of Applied Philosophy* 34(1): 61–73.

Dao, J. 2013. "Drone Pilots Are Found to Get Stress Disorders Much as Those in Combat." *New York Times*, 22 February 2013. http://www.nytimes.com/2013/02/23/us/drone-pilots-found-to-get-stress-disorders-much-as-those-in-combat-do.html?_r=0.

Dutton, J., Roberts, L., and Bednar, J. 2010. "Pathways for Positive Identity Construction at Work: Four Types of Positive Identity and the Building of Social Resources." *Academy of Management Review* 35(2): 265–293.

Fried, Y. and Ferris, G.R. 1987. "The Validity of the Job Characteristic Model: A Review and Meta-Analysis." *Personnel Psychology* 40(2): 287–322.

Friedman, M. and Friedman, R. 1980. *Free to Choose: A Personal Statement*. New York: Harcourt Brace Jovanovich.

Friedrich-Ebert-Foundation. 2017. "Workers in the Global Economy and Trade Policy." *FES Connect*. www.fes-connect.org/monthly-focus/detail/april-workers-in-the-global-economy-and-trade-policy/ [Accessed 17 March 2017].

Füllsack, M. 2009. *Arbeit*. utb Profile 3235. Stuttgart: UTB GmbH.

Garson, B. 2014. *Down the Up Escalator: How the 99 Percent Live*. New York: Anchor Books.

Geldenhuys, M., Laba, K., and Venter, C.M. 2014. "Meaningful Work, Work Engagement and Organisational Commitment." *SA Journal of Industrial Psychology* 40(1): 1–10.

Gourevitch, A. 2016. "The Limits of a Basic Income: Means and Ends of Workplace Democracy." *Basic Income Studies* 11(1): 17–28.

Graeber, D. 2013. "On the Phenomenon of Bullshit Jobs." [Online] *STRIKE! Magazine.* http://strikemag.org/bullshit-jobs/ [Accessed 11 March 2017].

Hall, R.H. 1986. *Dimensions of Work.* Beverly Hills: Sage Publication.

Hsieh, N.-H. 2008. "Survey Article: Justice in Production." *Journal of Political Philosophy* 16(1): 72–100.

Hughes, E.C. 1951. "Work and Self." In *Social Psychology at the Crossroads,* edited by J. H. Rohrer and M. Sherif, 313–323. New York: Harper & Row.

Hughes, E.C. 1962. "Good People and Dirty Work." *Social Problems* 10(1): 3–11.

Kalleberg, A.L. 1977. "Work Values and Job Rewards: A Theory of Job Satisfaction." *American Sociological Review* 42(1): 124–143.

Kalleberg, A.L. 2000. "Nonstandard Employment Relations: Part-Time, Temporary and Contract Work." *Annual Review of Sociology* 26: 341–365.

Kalleberg, A.L. 2008. *Precarious Work, Insecure Workers: Employment Relations in Transition.* Presidential Address at the University of North Carolina at Chapel Hill.

Labatut, J. et al. 2016. "Routinized Killing of Animals. Going Beyond Dirty Work and Prestige to Understand the Well-Being of Slaughterhouse Workers." *Organization* 23(3): 351–369.

Lane, R.E. 1991. *The Market Experience.* Cambridge: Cambridge University Press.

Marx, K. 1890/1990. Das Kapital: Kritik der politischen Ökonomie. In *Collected Works of Karl Marx and Friedrich Engels,* Vol. 10, 1st ed., edited by the International Marx-Engels-Foundation. Berlin: Dietz Verlag.

McGovern, P., Smeaton, D., and Hill, S. 2004. "Bad Jobs in Britain: Nonstandard Employment and Job Quality." *Work and Occupations* 31(2): 225–249.

Michaelson, C., Pratt, M., Grant, A., and Dunn, C. 2014. "Meaningful Work: Connecting Business Ethics and Organization Studies." *Journal of Bus Ethics* 121(1): S. 77–90. doi:10.1007/s10551-013-1675-5.

Moore, K. 2017. *Radium Girls: The Dark Story of America's Shining Women.* Naperville: Sourcebooks.

Nozick, R. 1974. *Anarchy, State, and Utopia.* Cambridge, MA: Harvard University Press.

Pettit, P. 2007. "A Republican Right to Basic Income?" *An International Journal of Basic Income Research* 2(2): 1–8.

Pratt, M.G., Pradies, C., and Lepisto, D.A. 2013. "Doing Well, Doing Good, and Doing With: Organizational Practices for Effectively Cultivating Meaningful Work." In *Purpose and Meaning in the Workplace,* edited by B.J. Dik, Z.S. Byrne and M.F. Steger, 173–196. Washington, DC: American Psychological Association.

Prochazka, T. 2016. "UK's Social Security Needs a 'Fundamental Rethink'." Interview with Stewart Lansley. *Basic Income Earth Network.* http://basicincome.org/news/2016/07/interview-uks-social-security-needs-a-fundamental-rethink/ [Accessed 24 March 2017].

Raventós, S. 2016. *Socioeconomic Inequality and Mental Health: The Proposal of a Basic Income as a Means to Protect and Promote Mental Health.* PhD. diss. Barcelona: Autonomous University of Barcelona.

Roessler, B. 2012. "Meaningful Work: Arguments From Autonomy." *Journal of Political Philosophy* 20(1): 71–93.

Rosso, B., Dekas, K., and Wrzesniewski, A. 2010. "On the Meaning of Work: A Theoretical Integration and Review." *Research in Organizational Behavior* 30: 91–127. doi:10.1016/j.riob.2010.09.001.

Somavia, J. 2004. "The ILO Decent Work Agenda as the Aspiration of People: The Insertion of Values and Ethics in the Global Economy." In *Philosophical and Spiritual Perspectives on Decent Work*, edited by D. Peccoud, 3–11. Geneva: International Labour Office.

Stanczyk, L. 2012. "Productive Justice." *Philosophy and Public Affairs* 40(2): 144–164.

Standing, G. 2011. *The Precariat: The New Dangerous Class*. London: Bloomsbury Academic.

Tangian, A. 2007. *Is Work in Europe Decent? A Study Based on the 4th European Survey of Working Conditions in the Year 2005*. WSI-Diskussionspapier 157. Düsseldorf: Hans-Böckler-Stiftung.

United States Department of Labour. n.n. *Commonly Used Statistics of the Occupational Safety and Health Administration*. Data for the year 2016. https://www.osha.gov/oshstats/commonstats.html [Accessed 11 November 2018].

Van Dick, R. 2003. "My Job Is My Castle: Identification in Organizational Contexts." In *International Review of Industrial and Organizational Psychology*, edited by C.L. Cooper und I.T. Robertson, 171–203. Chichester: John Wiley & Sons, Ltd.

Veltman, A. 2016. *Meaningful Work*. Oxford: Oxford University Press.

Von Mises, L. 2007. *Human Action: A Treatise on Economics*, Vol. 4, edited by B.B. Greaves. Indianapolis: Liberty Fund.

Walzer, M. 1983. *Spheres of Justice: A Defense of Pluralism and Equality*. New York: Basic Books.

Widerquist, K. 2013. *Independence, Propertylessness and Basic Income*. New York: Palgrave Macmillan.

Wilde, O. 1915. *The Soul of Man Under Socialism*. New York: Max. N. Maisel.

Yeoman, R. 2014. "Conceptualizing Meaningful Work as a Fundamental Human Need." *Journal of Business Ethics* 125(2): 235–251.

10 Basic Income and Intimate Labor

Vida Panitch

An unconditional basic income (UBI) has begun to garner political support from both sides of the ideological spectrum. On the one hand, a UBI promises to be less paternalistic and less costly to administer than traditional in-kind welfare programs, while placing greater emphasis on preference satisfaction and individual responsibility. On the other hand, a UBI promises to liberate recipients from labor market dependency at a time of increasing job insecurity and to foster a sense of social belonging and solidarity not contingent on labor market participation. What I want to explore in this chapter is whether a UBI might also appeal to both sides of a political and ideological dispute concerning a particular kind of labor market, namely, markets in intimate labor. What I hope to show is that a UBI has the potential to resolve a long-standing debate regarding the permissibility of sales involving intimate labor, including not only sex work, but with developments in reproductive technology, commercial surrogacy, and paid egg donation as well.

Liberal and communitarian theorists have long been embroiled in a dispute over the appropriate criminal law response to intimate labor. According to theorists in the liberal tradition, intimate labor is morally worrisome to the extent that it represents a desperate choice. But the criminalization of intimate labor only serves to further constrain autonomy, on their view, because to whatever extent it may protect some from making a desperate choice, it prevents others who genuinely enjoy the work from making an autonomous choice. According to theorists in the communitarian tradition, sex work and commercial reproduction should be criminalized to protect their social value. Intimacy and motherhood, it is argued, should not be turned into another form of waged labor, as they constitute meaningful relations only to the extent that they are undertaken from fellow-feeling, and not from the bare self-interest supposedly characteristic of market exchanges.

I will argue that a UBI could better respond to the worries raised by both liberals and communitarians on this issue. More to the point, I will show that neither party's concerns are, in fact, resolved by the criminal law response each favors, and that the efforts of both liberal and communitarian theorists alike would be better devoted to arguing for a UBI. I will make this argument in three stages. I will begin, in the first section, "Intimate Labor and Criminal Law," by articulating the liberal's argument for the decriminalization of intimate labor, and the communitarian's argument, conversely, for criminalization. I will go on to show in the second section, "Autonomy, Community, an Basic Income," and the third section, "Intimate Labor and Basic Income," that both of these arguments run entirely parallel to the liberal and communitarian cases for a UBI, and that a UBI has more potential to address the concerns with intimate labor raised by both sets of theorists better than their preferred criminal law response.

Of course, a UBI is not, and should not be viewed as, a problem-free solution to any of the practical or ideological conundrums its diverse proponents are increasingly expecting it to address. The level of the income should be high enough to constitute a real alternative to working, at least in trades that one might only otherwise choose out of desperation. And yet, if set too high, the income could become unsustainable precisely because it would constitute an alternative to working, thus depriving itself of a tax base. The breadth of the income is equally relevant, because if a UBI is meant to replace rather than to supplement existing welfare programs, it matters from the point of view of promoting both liberal and communitarian aims which programs these are and to what extent they will be phased out. In the fourth section, "Institutionalizing Basic Income," I will, therefore, argue that whether a UBI might actually succeed in addressing the liberal's and the communitarian's respective concerns regarding intimate labor depends greatly on both the income's level and breadth.

Part 1: Intimate Labor and Criminal Law

By intimate labor, I have in mind work that is done primarily by women with intimate parts of their bodies or their intimate physical capacities in exchange for money, favors, or goods. This includes prostitution, which involves the sale of sexual services, broadly defined. It also includes commercial surrogacy, which involves the insemination, gestation, and delivery of a (typically non-genetically related child) for a fee earned by a gestational mother and paid by the intended parents. It also includes egg sales, involving the paid extraction of a woman's reproductive gametes for the purposes of creating an embryo to be inseminated in a separate intended or gestational mother. In Canada, commercial surrogacy and egg sales are both against the law, and although the sale of sex is legal, its purchase is heavily regulated.[1] In the United States, egg sales are legally permissible (although until recently, they were subject to wage caps), whereas commercial surrogacy is illegal in six states and heavily regulated in many others, and prostitution is illegal everywhere but a few counties in Nevada.[2]

The diversity in criminal regulation surrounding intimate labor suggests that we have not made up our minds as to its moral and legal acceptability. Perhaps because there is actually room for social impact here, theorists and activists alike have tended to frame their arguments for and against intimate labor in terms of whether it should be banned. Their arguments have highlighted an interesting feature of intimate labor, which is that it belongs to a unique category of practices that are not only permissible, but laudatory, provided *money* isn't involved. Sexual relations among intimates, altruistic surrogacy, and egg donation are not only morally permissible, but also morally praised. This makes intimate labor unlike other contested commodities, such as votes, which we cannot sell but which we are not also encouraged to away for free. It also makes it unlike other controversial social practices for which a criminal law response is often sought. Pornography, for example, would not be any more defensible to those who would like to see it banned were it made and distributed for free. The criminal law debate is thus not about whether we should be allowed to engage in non-intimate sex, act as a gestational surrogate, or donate our eggs, but only whether we should be allowed to accept *payment* for doing so.

According to theorists in the liberal tradition, the correct criminal law response to the question of intimate labor is decriminalization. Their concern is ultimately to protect individual autonomy.[3] The liberal worries, of course, that women in the sex and reproductive trades often go into this work not because they authentically prefer it, but because they have no other choice. In a society marked by income inequalities, which often track gender and racial lines, disadvantaged women can find themselves with no alternative but to enter the intimate trades. Intimate labor can, therefore, be said, along perfectly liberal lines, to have as its source a kind of one-sided vulnerability, characteristic of desperate, or even exploitative exchanges. This, however, is not a solid foundation on which to justify a criminal ban, on the liberal view.[4]

Exploitation can be mutually advantageous—unfair transactions can nonetheless be very much to the benefit of the vulnerable party. What matters in assessing whether the liberal state is justified in interfering in mutually beneficial exploitative transactions, as Alan Wertheimer has argued, is less about the fairness of the shares that each party walks away with, and more about how each comes to the arrangement in the first place.[5] Wrongful, albeit mutually advantageous, exploitative transactions are ones that depend on impairments of autonomy, characterized by misinformation, coercion, or incapacity to consent. Misinformation explains what is problematic about some surrogacy arrangements, if we allow that women who have never before given up a child cannot understand what they are agreeing to.[6] Incapacity to consent also certainly explains what's wrong with underage prostitution, whereas a lack of consent accounts for the key difference between sex work and sex trafficking. Coercion can occur at times in the form of a literal gun to the head, since physical violence so often operates in the background of sex work. It can also come in the form of internal or external manipulations exerted by a father, a partner, a pimp, or an addiction.[7] But where misinformation, incapacity, or coercion occur, they explain the wrongfulness of a *single transaction*, not an entire practice.

To say that an *entire practice* is always wrongful, on the liberal account, would depend on showing that consent to such a practice is theoretically impossible. But why should it be possible to consent to having sex for free but impossible to consent to having sex for money? Cash might serve as a kind of undue inducement to perform work one would not otherwise choose. But if so, a great deal of waged labor must also be unduly induced. And although we might concede that there are some cases, such as slavery, to which consent is indeed impossible, the impossibility does not depend on the exchange of cash.[8] We can no more agree to be traded for another slave than for money, or to be enslaved for free, because it is the enslavement itself, not the purchase, to which consent cannot presumably be given. Of course, the claim that an entire practice is always wrongful could depend on showing instead that although not theoretically impossible, consent is nonetheless lacking in every actual case. But this claim is unsustainable in light of the fact that the most vocal advocates of sex work, commercial surrogacy, and paid egg donation are women who defend the work as rewarding, empowering, therapeutic, and preferable to a wide range of alternatives.[9] We cannot conveniently invalidate this fact by insisting that all of these women must have adapted preferences or suffer from false consciousness.

To say that intimate labor as a practice is inevitably wrongful on the grounds that consent is impossible, absent, or adapted is to deny the experiences and impugn the agency of many women in the trade. A criminal sanction, on the liberal view, not only prevents empowered women from exercising a choice consistent with their conception of the good life but also disputes their very capacity for autonomy. The liberal, therefore, cannot justify castigating the wholesale practice of intimate labor, and her commitment to autonomy necessitates that she concludes in favor of decriminalization. But this conclusion does not allow her to address very legitimate worries about the desperation and vulnerability that underscore a good many individual transactions. Some liberal theorists who defend decriminalization, therefore, do so begrudgingly, acknowledging that this solution does not address the very worries that motivated their moral inquiry into intimate labor in the first place.[10]

Theorists in the communitarian tradition contend that the liberal cannot but arrive at this begrudging or even paradoxical conclusion. In order to figure out what's wrong with intimate labor, according to the communitarian, we need to focus less on transactional exploitation and more on systemic commodification.[11] What's wrong with the wholesale practice of intimate labor, rather than just with particular instances thereof, lies for the communitarian in the assignment price values to sex, gestation, and ova. The commodification of these goods, it is said, corrupts or crowds out the altruism in accordance with which, or with an eye to the promotion of which, they should be properly shared and enjoyed.[12] The competitive norms of the marketplace, including self-interest, bargaining, and ability to pay are not the right norms to govern the distribution of goods so important to the foundation of personal relationships.[13] These norms turn social relations into relations of capital. This threatens our ability to flourish not only as individuals for whom the good life depends on the enjoyment of close personal relationships, but also as citizens for whom civic flourishing depends on relations of solidarity rather than those of competition and self-interest.[14]

According to Elizabeth Anderson, sex retains its proper value only to the extent that it is exchanged between persons who seek to reciprocally promote one another's well-being through intimacy. The true value of sexual unions is threatened, on her view, by their subjection to the competitive and self-interested norms that exemplify market relations.[15] Similarly, pregnancy is a means to the forging of the mother-child bond, to which the properly altruistic goods of motherhood are tied. Introducing the norms of self-interest and bargaining into pregnancy is to corrupt the altruism and beneficence at the core of motherhood itself.[16] Anderson argues that we cannot appreciate the true value of intimacy and motherhood if these practices come to be governed by the principles of market exchanges, because their true value lies in their having an essentially beneficent nature. She argues further that the encroachment of market norms threatens not only our personal relations, but also the civic relations essential to our lives as citizens. As competitive market relations spread, they replace both the altruism on which intimate relations depend and the solidarism on which civic relations depend.[17]

Arguments of this variety have been advanced by a number of theorists who conclude in favor of criminalizing intimate labor.[18] The problem, however, is that criminal bans don't necessarily resolve the communitarian worry. Margaret Radin cautions that as much as we may want them to, in the non-ideal world in which we find ourselves, criminal sanctions do not so much protect the value of intimacy and motherhood as remove what counts for many women as their last best option, or worse, push them into the shadow economy.[19] As we know, black markets in sex, gestation, and ova are notoriously bad for women's health and well-being.[20] But what the very existence of a thriving underground economy should make equally plain is that criminal bans don't protect intimate relations from the corruptive norms of the marketplace. Black markets are markets after all, no less characterized by the norms of bargaining, competition, and self-interest. The criminal law solution communitarians favor simply turns white markets black and is, therefore, no solution at all.

It looks as though, in offering an autonomy argument for the decriminalization of intimate labor, the liberal is forced to silence her own legitimate worries about the role of desperation and vulnerability in exploitative exchanges. And that the communitarian, in offering a relational or solidaristic argument in favor of criminalization, is confronted with the fact that black markets are not only more dangerous, but also no less characterized than white markets by the competitive norms of the marketplace, and thereby just as inimical to the types of social relationships criminalization is called for to protect. If theorists in neither camp are satisfied (or should be) with their own preferred criminal law solution, one wonders what the value is of debating a criminal law response to intimate labor. To what better end might they devote their collective efforts?

Part 2: Autonomy, Community, and Basic Income

What I want to argue now is that both liberal and communitarian concerns regarding intimate labor would be better addressed by a UBI. I aim to show that the arguments of both liberal and communitarian theorists for or against the criminalization of intimate labor line up directly with two leading arguments for basic income. To this end, I will show, in this section, that the liberal argument from autonomy and the communitarian argument from solidarity constitute the two leading cases for a UBI. And, in the next part of the chapter, that a UBI can respond to both the liberal's and the communitarian's concerns regarding intimate labor better than the criminal law. While their respective aims may not be fully realizable through a UBI, I will argue that neither can they be achieved without one.

The liberal case for a basic income depends on appreciating the relationship between autonomy and freedom, whereby the freedom to live autonomously depends not only on the guarantee of formal rights and liberties but also on the material opportunity to be and do whatever one chooses.[21] Freedom of choice is hollow if it consists in formal guarantees alone because the freedom to be and do whatever one chooses requires, as a matter of fact, some control over the material preconditions of choice-making. It cannot be said, according to Philippe Van Parijs, that the abject wage laborer is free in a meaningful sense. Although he may own himself formally—in accordance with the scheme of rights and liberties to which he is entitled—he still cannot make use of himself in any real way since he lacks the opportunity, or the exclusive control of external objects, to do or be whatever he might choose. He is not autonomous in the Van Parijsian sense because he is not *really free*:

> Real freedom asserts that security and self-ownership, though necessary to freedom, are not sufficient for it, because doing anything requires the use of external objects which security and self-ownership

alone cannot guarantee . . . the term *real freedom* . . . refer[s] to a notion of freedom that incorporates all three components—security, self-ownership, and opportunity—in contrast to *formal freedom*, which only incorporates the first two.[22]

Real freedom is best guaranteed, Van Parijs continues, through an unconditionally guaranteed income. The absence of conditions ensures that no particular set of choices will be penalized or prioritized, and cash makes no presuppositions about the kinds or amount of goods that individuals may require in pursuit of their distinct projects. The point of the basic income, as Van Parijs puts it, is to guarantee the material security that underlies real freedom, or the freedom to choose among the various lives one might wish to lead, including the choice "to live as unconventionally as one might fancy."[23] One unconventional life choice may involve surfing off Malibu, but others might include artistry, caregiving, scholarship, or volunteerism, all of which go unacknowledged and unsupported by the conditioned transfers typical of the liberal welfare state. And in providing citizens with the freedom to live unconventionally, it simultaneously provides them the freedom not to; for those who would otherwise be drawn into marginalizing, stigmatizing, or exploitative jobs, a UBI could provide a genuine alternative.

The liberal argument for a UBI, however, faces the following objection:

> In granting a basic income that is not conditioned on the willingness of the able to work, the UBI promotes freedom without responsibility, and thereby both offends and undermines the ideal of social obligation that undergirds the welfare state . . . The social insurance programs that form the foundation of modern welfare states constitute the terms of a great social contract. Like any insurance, they purchase a right to provision from others conditional on a willingness to provide for others, if one is able . . . It is hard to see how such a contract can be sustained by a system that advertises as one of its virtues that it would free the able to live in idleness.[24]

The claim here is that the social contract depends on reciprocity, according to which one's entitlement to a share of the social product must depend on one's willingness to contribute to it, so long as one is able. The "exploitation" objection, as Stuart White calls it (because the lazy are supposedly exploiting the labor of the productive), poses a considerable challenge to basic income.[25] The best response to this challenge lies, however, not in mining liberal doctrine for a loophole to reciprocity, but in appreciating that a UBI has a second, and distinct underlying rationale.

A basic income is defensible not only on the liberal grounds that it provides the material freedom to do and be whatever one chooses, but also on the more relational, or communitarian grounds that it vests social entitlements not on labor market participation, but in group member-ship.[26] A basic income does not restrict social entitlements to the sup-posedly "deserving," understood as those who are willing but incapable of making a productive contribution to the economy. Rather, it ensures that all citizens are provided with a genuine alternative they would not otherwise have under a capitalist economic system, namely an alternative to the market alienation of their labor power.[27] And it does so as a matter of social right.[28] The only legitimate conditionality is that of citizenship or group membership. From this perspective, the foundational idea of the basic income is not to encourage idleness and free riding, but to satisfy the social rights of citizens, including the right to not turn one's labor power into a marketable commodity.

Van Parijs states that this defense of a UBI reflects "a key component of the old critique of capitalism by 'scientific' and 'utopian' socialism alike: the revolt against proletarian subjection to the wage relationship, and hence to the capitalists' rule."[29] On this account, a UBI is defen-sible because it de-commodifies labor, and therein fosters both per-sonal freedom and social solidarity. As Gosta Esping-Andersen explains it, de-commodification occurs when a service is rendered as a matter of right, so that a person can maintain a livelihood without reliance on the market.[30] He states: "Commodification is the condition under which workers abandon control over their work in return for wages . . . under which their dependence on the market is affirmed." He contin-ues: "Schemes that permit employees to be paid while pursuing activi-ties other than working, be they child-rearing, family responsibilities, re-education, organizational activities, or even leisure . . . are, in spirit, truly de-commodifying."[31]

The argument here is that we shouldn't have to commodify our labor power to earn an entitlement to social support and the satisfaction of our social rights. Otherwise, we are all faced with the same choice as the abject wage laborer—to work or starve. And like the abject wage laborer, when we are forced to work, we aren't really free. But real free-dom is not all that the de-commodification of labor protects. When we are forced to sell our labor power in exchange for a share of the social product, we are thereby forced into competitive relations—of buy-ing and selling, owning and laboring—governed by the self-interested norms of the marketplace. To be forced to commodify our labor power is thus to be forced into competitive market relationships in which our own interests are inevitably in tension with the interests of others. We are thereby deprived of the opportunity to relate to others on non-competitive terms.[32] And what is thereby put at risk are social relations of solidarity. A UBI, in rendering the choice to commodify one's labor power precisely that, protects not only individual freedom, but soli-daristic social relations.[33] And it does this not by *criminalizing* waged labor, but by guaranteeing an *alternative*.

Part 3: Intimate Labor and Basic Income

The liberal argument for the decriminalization of intimate labor derives, unsurprisingly, from the same normative source as the liberal case for a basic income. What matters is autonomous choice-making. It is not up to the state to decide—either through conditional welfare policy or through criminal sanctions—what kinds of things citizens should be free to do with their lives. But the criminal law response to intimate labor ends the discussion there: Sanctions impose limits on what we can choose to do and be, and their removal is thus to be preferred. But neither sanctions nor their removal does anything to actually improve the conditions of choice-making. The liberal case for a basic income depends on appreciating that without the material preconditions of autonomous choice-making, citizens may be formally free but not *really* free to do and be whatever they choose.

The decriminalization of intimate labor certainly makes women formally free to choose whether to work in the sex or reproductive trades. But income disparity, compounded by racial and gender inequalities, creates a vulnerable underclass of women for whom the choice to pursue sex or reproductive work is not much more of a choice than the one faced by the abject wage laborer forced to work or starve. For the wage laborer to be really free, as opposed to just formally free, he requires guaranteed control over a share of social resources adequate for him to choose neither exploitation nor starvation. So too does the sex worker, the surrogate, and the egg donor. In the interests of protecting their freedom to do and be whatever they choose, criminal bans are not the solution. Yet neither is decriminalization if we do not also go further to address the conditions of desperation from which so many women enter the intimate trades. What they require are the material opportunities to choose something other than intimate work, guaranteed in such a way that the formal opportunities of women in general to pursue the occupation of their choice are not thereby foreclosed.

The communitarian case against intimate labor and in favor of a basic income also share a normative foundation. The underlying imperative is to prevent social relations from becoming relations of capital, or rather, to prevent solidaristic relations from becoming competitive ones. The communitarian argument in favor of sanctioning intimate labor, however, encounters the difficulty that bans turn white markets black, and that these are no less characterized by the norms of competition, bargaining, and self-interest. Bans do not thereby have the desired effect of protecting solidarity relations from the competitive norms of the marketplace, nor stemming the tide of market encroachment into intimate and civic spheres of human life. What the communitarian case for a UBI offers is a means by which solidaristic social relations might be preserved without the introduction of criminal sanctions.

We need not ban intimate labor to de-commodify it, any more than we need to ban labor in general to de-commodify it; rather, we need to guarantee a meaningful alternative as a matter of social right. In other words, we don't have to prevent people from entering into relations of capital, we just have to ensure that doing so is not their only option. To the extent that a UBI would de-commodify wage labor more generally by making it non-mandatory, it could be expected to do the same with respect to intimate labor specifically. It could also be expected to ensure that all those who perform intimate labor do not do so strictly from pecuniary motives.[34] That is, that the women who go into the field do so at least in part because they have an interest the work, and possibly in helping others in a unique way, rather than simply an interest in profiting from intimacy. A UBI might also be expected to reduce the number and frequency of intimate transactions, since all those who currently choose it from pure desperation would no longer need to do so. In all of these respects, the communitarian and relational theorist concerned with intimate labor should endorse a UBI.

Those nonetheless committed to defending criminal bans might be tempted to reply that although a UBI could be expected to bolster beneficent motives while decreasing the number of intimate relations that become relations of capital, this wouldn't, in fact, satisfy a more central worry. The communitarian or relational theorist might argue that her main worry is neither motivational, nor consequentialist, but expressivist. On the expressivist account, bans represent a collective articulation of the belief that certain activities, and the relationships they define, should be valued in particular ways. A UBI might well decrease the number and frequency of intimate transactions, but it would not allow us to express our collective belief that motherhood and sexuality should not be valued in accordance with the market price they command. We need laws against selling intimate labor, on this interpretation, because laws function to articulate social values, and what we should want to express about sex and motherhood is that they are valuable beyond price.

But expressivist arguments have two possible solutions. One is to ensure that our laws enshrine our values. The other is to change our values. The expressivist argument as such is indifferent between these two solutions.[35] And there are strong egalitarian reasons for thinking we ought to consider embracing the latter solution over the former. To see this, we must ask why, if we're worried about market encroachment into altruistic spheres of human relations, we insist on banning only *intimate* labor? What is it about sex and motherhood that make them distinct from other kinds of relations in which we would also prefer that market norms not be present, such that their non-market value must be uniquely protected through law?

What makes sex work, surrogacy, and egg sales special is that they are done almost entirely by women (and almost entirely, or at least in part, for men).[36] This suggests that one explanation for why we seek to express our collective disdain for these particular commercial practices through the law is that they derive from the patriarchal expectation of *gendered altruism*. Accordingly, women are presumed to be better suited and more amenable to altruism and beneficence, and thereby expected to occupy social roles in which they might express these values. This expectation has long defined, and constrained, women's lives. Why should we continue to lay the burden of preserving beneficence and solidarity in our communities on the backs of women? If indeed the law serves an expressive function, we should be very wary of what it expresses where women's bodies and social roles are concerned. The patriarchal foundations of gendered altruism should give us good reason to *refuse* to express through law values that would reflect and perpetuate an oppressive social structure.[37]

Consider further that inherent to gender inequality is the view that women's work is of lesser value. This is often demonstrated by the payment of lower wages, or in the case of domestic and much care labor, no wages whatsoever. In the case of intimate labor, it appears to be demonstrated by the criminalization of wages. Failing to acknowledge the value of women's work by refusing to pay them fairly, or refusing to pay them at all, is discriminatory. And there is good reason for thinking that a citizen's wage could best ensure that much of women's unrecognized labor is properly remunerated.[38] Insisting instead on criminal bans to express a belief according to which it is women's duty to bear the burdens of altruism, from this perspective, looks like an injustice of a profound order. Although the expressivist argument is indifferent as to whether we should encode our values in law or simply change them, we have egalitarian reasons to favor the latter response, and to embrace social policies that allow us to demonstrate a commitment to solidarism without foreclosing women's choices and policing their bodies.

Part 4: Institutionalizing Basic Income

That participants to the criminal law debate regarding intimate labor should instead endorse a UBI may come as no surprise to supporters of a basic income. The autonomy-based argument against banning intimate labor is firmly rooted in a conception of liberal egalitarianism, and the anti-commodification argument in favor of banning it is firmly rooted in a conception of communitarianism, or relational egalitarianism. Each theoretical framework ultimately aims to provide grounds not for a body of criminal law, but for a system of social insurance, and for market regulation as required to support this system. I hope so far to have offered both parties to the criminal law debate grounds, consistent with their own normative commitments, for thinking that a UBI would better address their central concerns, and thus provide a mutually satisfying resolution to their ongoing debate.

But we have to be careful not to see a UBI as a problem-free solution to any of the practical or ideological issues it is increasingly being asked to address, markets in intimate labor among them. As Brian Barry has put it, "Asking about the pros and cons of basic income as such is rather like asking about the pros and cons of keeping a feline as a pet without distinguishing between a tiger and a tabby."[39] A basic income will have very different characteristics and potentialities depending on both its level and its breadth. Whether a basic income would indeed promote autonomy and solidarity depends considerably on whether it would be high enough to constitute a genuine alternative to working, and whether it would replace or supplement in-kind social transfers and insurance programs.

In order to realize its ideological goals on both the liberal and the communitarian front, a UBI would have to be set at a level high enough to constitute a genuine alternative to working. Otherwise, it could be expected neither to provide its recipients with the freedom to do and be whatever they might choose, nor to separate social entitlement from labor market participation. However, if set too high, the income may disincentivize labor market participation altogether, rendering it unsustainable. This is a notoriously difficult balance to strike. But for our present purposes, it suffices to say that the income need only be high enough to provide *an alternative to working in industries that one would only otherwise choose out of desperation.* The purpose—from the point of view of addressing concerns with intimate labor—is not that persons should be freed from having to work altogether, but that they should be freed from having to commodify their intimate capacities if they do not want to do so.

In general, sex workers enter the field in a piecemeal fashion, to cover incidental costs when they arise. Most sex workers don't self-identify as such until they have begun doing the work full-time, which can take many years.[40] This is important because it means that a basic income need not be unsustainably high to make all the difference in terms of whether sex workers enter the field in the first place. Here, the monthly grant levels of recent basic income experiments are instructive: €560 in Finland (equivalent to $640 USD), $1,000 USD in California, and $1,400 CAD (or $1,060 USD) in Ontario.[41] Taking the average of these in USD as a point of departure, $900 per month could well be high enough to provide an alternative to the sex work done sporadically by many women over the course of several years before they begin to do it full-time and come to self-identify as such. It would provide an important and reliable source of revenue for women unable to cover occasional costs and may thereby significantly alter the path along which many women become sex workers who would otherwise prefer not to.

And the same could be said with respect to egg donors and surrogates. Many egg donors in the United States are looking to pay their tuition or student loans.[42] They receive payments averaging $4,200 USD per donation, and cannot donate more than six times, although most donate fewer than two times.[43] Regular monthly payments of $900 USD (or $10,800 annually) that could be counted on year after year would provide a very real alternative. Similarly, most American surrogates see it as an opportunity to bring in extra needed income while they are studying or raising their own families, and not as a long-term career choice.[44] While a basic income of $900 a month would not come close to the earnings of an American surrogate over a nine-month period, that this income would be guaranteed annually over the course of a life means that it would provide much more for educational or child-rearing purposes over time than the amount earned for a single pregnancy. For egg donors, commercial surrogates, and sex workers, although a basic income at this level may not provide an alternative to their working altogether, it could cover the kinds of costs that initially induct them into the intimate industries in the first place.

The second issue to consider has to do with the breadth of the grant, or whether it would supplement or replace existing welfare programs on which women in the intimate industries rely. Whether a UBI replaces existing conditional cash programs is an altogether different story to whether it replaces an existing network of in-kind provisions, such as health care, education, the shelter system, or subsidized housing. It matters that the UBI would not replace such in-kind provisions where they exist, and that it should be implemented along with such programs where they are lacking. There are higher rates of prostitution among young women who do not graduate high school.[45] If public education were to be replaced with a UBI, such that school fees had to be paid out of the grant, this would defeat one of its most significant potentialities, namely bolstering high school completion rates.[46] And because the intimate industries are closely linked with sexual and reproductive health care needs, the costs of health care or insurance for women in these industries might be higher than those of other grant recipients; were the cash grant to replace health care or health insurance where they are provided, this would be unfair. Finally, because women trying to leave the sex trade rely at times on social housing and the shelter system, it matters that this system should be adequately subsidized.

In-kind provisions are consistent with both the liberal and the communitarian arguments for a basic income. Such provisions may look more problematic on the liberal view because their lack of fungibility is arguably an affront to the autonomy and neutrality supposedly enhanced by cash transfers. But the in-kind goods and services provided by the welfare state could be seen to constitute the *preconditions* of autonomous choice-making and cash transfers to enable the *exercise* thereof. (For how could we identify what it is we'd like to do and be, and rationally decide how best to spend our income in furtherance of our goals, if we're uneducated, feverish, or overly consumed with the need to find nourishment or shelter?) And second, people are bad with money, at least at first. Managing liquidity is not an easy thing to do, given a tendency even the financially literate have of prioritizing inferior present goods over superior future goods. In-kind provisions are, therefore, something we have rational reasons to endorse in many instances as self-biding mechanisms, and thus something we can defend on perfectly liberal grounds.[47] Finally, certain public in-kind provisions are also preferable on liberal grounds where inefficiencies are generated by private markets, health insurance being a prime example.[48]

A broad package of in-kind support to which the grant would be supplemental is also consistent with the communitarian case for basic income. For some, this is because certain goods are necessarily public, in that they cannot be enjoyed unless they are communally provided. According to Bill Jordan, this is why a basic income could be expected to give rise to a just communitarian society only if it is paired with "an equally determined policy commitment to communal resources."[49] For others, the public provision of in-kind goods and social services is necessary to ensure de-commodification and the social relations that depend on it.[50] Since the aim of the grant, on communitarian grounds, is to de-commodify labor so as to prevent all social relations from becoming market relations, replacing public goods and services with a single cash transfer would have the counter-productive effect of forcing citizens into the market to satisfy all their basic needs.[51] The need for an income can be met only with cash; many other basic needs, however, are best met directly if the aim is to prevent the proliferation of market transactions and thereby market relations.

The purpose of this final section has been to show that a UBI would only achieve the goals identified by liberal and communitarian theorists and provide them both with a more satisfying response to the question of intimate labor than the criminal law to the extent that its level is adequate, and its breadth constrained. For the liberal, the level of the grant is crucial to promoting the real freedom of women in the intimate industries to do other things with their lives. The level of the UBI should, therefore, be at least high enough to enable women who might otherwise find themselves entering the intimate trades out of desperation to do something else instead. And the liberal should prefer that the a UBI be implemented alongside a broad network of social supports for reasons of efficiency and fairness, along with reasons of autonomy. For the communitarian, it is equally imperative that the income be high enough to enable women to leave the intimate trades, or to avoid entering them in the first place. This is because the provision of an adequate alternative to intimate labor would prevent the proliferation of market relations. As would the simultaneous provision of needed in-kind goods and services that prevent citizens from having to enter into market relations to satisfy all their basic needs.

This, therefore, concludes the project of the chapter, which has been to show that the criminal law solution to intimate labor should satisfy neither party to the debate, whereas a UBI could. Decriminalization may well preserve autonomy but does not address the liberal's equally pressing concerns about vulnerability and desperation. Criminalization, meanwhile, may on the surface appear to address the communitarian's worry that important social relations should not become relations of capital, but, in fact, ignores the extent to which criminal bans simply turn white markets black. A UBI set at a level adequate to providing an alternative to the intimate trades and provided as part of rather than instead of a broad package of in-kind social supports could allow women to leave the trades or to avoid entering them in the first place without foreclosing the opportunities of any woman to pursue the work of her choice. It could also thereby prevent any number of relations properly defined by altruism or solidarism from becoming relations of capital. A UBI of this sort would demonstrate a commitment to the autonomy central to the liberal project and to the relationality and solidarism essential to the communitarian project. I thus hope to have shown that both liberal and communitarian roads lead away from criminal law and toward basic income.

Notes

1. Canada's Bill C-36, *Protection of Communities and Exploited Persons Act*, SC 2014. www.parl.ca/DocumentViewer/en/41-2/bill/C-36/royal-assent; *Canada's Assisted Human Reproduction Act*, SC 2004, c.2. http://laws-lois. justice.gc.ca/eng/acts/A-13.4/FullText.html.
2. Alex Finkelstein, Sarah Mac Dougall, Angela Kintominas, and Anya Olsen, *Surrogacy Law and Policy in the U.S.: A National Conversation Informed by Global Lawmaking* (Sexuality & Gender Law Clinic, Columbia Law School. Surrogacy Law and Policy in the U.S., 2016), 1–90.
3. Peter de Marneffe, *Liberalism and Prostitution* (New York: Oxford University Press, 2010).
4. Martha Nussbaum, "Whether From Reason or Prejudice: Taking Money for Bodily Services," in her *Sex and Social Justice* (New York: Oxford, 1999); Karen Green, "Prostitution, Exploitation, and Taboo," *Philosophy* 64, no. 250 (1989): 525–534; Alison Jaggar, "Prostitution," in *The Philosophy of Sex: Contemporary Readings*, 1st ed., ed. Alan Soble (Totowa: Rowman & Littlefield, 1980), 348–368; Lars Ericson, "Charges Against Prostitution: An Attempt at a Philosophical Assessment," *Ethics* 90, no. 3 (1980): 335–366.
5. Alan Wertheimer, *Exploitation* (Princeton: Princeton University Press, 1999).
6. Bonnie Steinbock, "Surrogate Motherhood as Prenatal Adoption," in *Surrogate Motherhood, Politics and Privacy*, ed. Larry Gostin (Bloomington: Indiana University Press, 1988); Christine Straehle, "Is There a Right to Surrogacy," *Journal of Applied Philosophy* 33, no. 2 (2016): 146–159.
7. Ronald Weitzer, "Sociology of Sex Work," *Annual Review of Sociology* 35, no. 1 (2009): 213–234.
8. John Stuart Mill, *On Liberty* (Cambridge: Cambridge University Press, 2011), 168–208.

9. Karen Busby and Delaney Vun, "Revisiting *The Handmaid's Tale*: Feminist Theory Meets Empirical Research on Surrogate Mothers," *Canadian Journal of Family Law* 26, no. 1 (2010): 13–93; Angela Campbell, *Sister Wives, Surrogates and Sex Workers: Outlaws by Choice?* (New York: Routledge, 2016); Alexandra Murphy and Sudir Venkatesh, "Vice Careers: The Changing Contours of Sex Work in New York City," *Qualitative Sociology* 29, no. 2 (2006): 129–154.

10. Scott A. Anderson, "Prostitution and Sexual Autonomy," *Ethics* 112, no. 3 (2002): 748–780; Debra Satz, "Markets in Women's Sexual Labor," *Ethics* 106, no. 1 (1995): 63–85; Laurie Shrage, *Moral Dilemmas of Feminism: Prostitution, Adultery, and Abortion* (New York: Routledge, 1994), 99–161.

11. It is important to acknowledge that the philosophical and legal debate has for the most part treated sex work and gestational work separately. Generally, the prostitution debate has pitted liberal feminists against radical feminists, rather than against communitarians. With respect to surrogacy and the sale of reproductive gametes, however, the debate has much more evidently pitted communitarian and relational egalitarian theory against liberalism.

12. Michael J. Sandel, "What Money Can't Buy: The Moral Limits of the Market," *Tanner Lectures on Human Values*, Vol. 21 (Salt Lake City: University of Utah Press, 2000), 87–122.

13. Elizabeth Anderson, "Ethical Limitations of the Market," *Economics and Philosophy* 6, no. 2 (1990): 179–205; Michael Walzer, *Spheres of Justice: A Defense of Pluralism and Equality* (New York: Basic Books, 1984).

14. Charles Taylor, "Atomism," in his *Philosophy and the Human Sciences* (Cambridge: Cambridge University Press, 1985), 187–210.

15. Anderson, "Ethical Limitations of the Market," 189.

16. Elizabeth Anderson, "Is Women's Labor a Commodity?" *Philosophy and Public Affairs* 19, no. 1 (1990): 71–92.

17. Anderson, "Ethical Limitations of the Market," 192–201.

18. Carole Pateman, "What's Wrong With Prostitution?" *Women's Studies Quarterly* 27, nos. 1–2 (1999): 53–64; Mary Warnock, *Report of the Committee of Inquiry Into Human Fertilization and Embryology* (London: HMSO, 1984); Margaret Sommerville, *The Ethical Canary* (Toronto: Penguin Canada, 2000).

19. Margaret Jane Radin, *Contested Commodities* (Cambridge, MA: Harvard University Press, 1996), 123–130.

20. Scott Carney, *The Red Market* (New York: William Morrow, 2011); For these reasons, the World Health Organization (WHO) has recommended the global decriminalization of sex work, see the WHO's *Consolidated Guidelines on HIV Prevention, Diagnosis, Treatment and Care for Key Populations*, 2014. See Sec. 5.1.2, "Critical Enablers." http://apps.who.int/iris/bitstream/10665/128048/1/9789241507431_eng.pdf?ua=1&ua=1

21. Philippe Van Parijs, *Real Freedom for All: What (If Anything) Can Justify Capitalism?* (Oxford: Oxford University Press, 1995).

22. Van Parijs, *Real Freedom for All*, 21–22.

23. Van Parijs, *Real Freedom for All*, 33.

24. Elizabeth Anderson, "Optional Freedoms," *Boston Review*, October 2000.

25. Stuart White, "Liberal Equality, Exploitation, and the Case for an Unconditional Basic Income," *Political Studies* 45, no. 2 (1997): 312–326.

26. Philippe Van Parijs, "Why Surfers Should Be Fed: The Liberal Case for an Unconditional Basic Income," 22, no. 2 (1991): 101–131, at pp. 108–109; Bill Jordan, "Basic Income and the Common Good," in *Arguing for Basic Income: Ethical Foundations for a Radical Reform*, ed. Philippe Van Parijs (London: Verso, 1992), 155–177.

27. Claus Offe, "A Non-Productivist Design for Social Policy," in *Arguing for Basic Income: Ethical Foundations for a Radical Reform*, 61–80.
28. Carole Pateman, "Democratizing Citizenship: Some Advantages of a Basic Income," *Politics & Society* 32, no. 1 (2004): 89–105.
29. Van Parijs, *Real Freedom for All*, 22.
30. Gosta Esping-Andersen, *The Three Worlds of Welfare Capitalism* (Princeton: Princeton University Press, 1990), 21–22.
31. Esping-Anderson, *The Three Worlds of Welfare Capitalism*, 45–46.
32. Xavier Landes and Pierre Yves Neron, "Public Insurance and Equality: From Redistribution to Relation," *Res Publica* 21, no. 2 (2015): 137–154.
33. Gijs van Donselaar, "The Freedom Based Account of Solidarity and Basic Income," *Ethical Theory and Moral Practice* 1, no. 3 (1998): 313–338.
34. To the extent that the presence of self-interest is what is thought to threaten altruism and solidarity, the communitarian argument comes down to a motivational worry. But there is no reason to think that self-interest necessarily silences altruism. Myriad examples would suffice here, but in the present context, consider the sex therapist who works with clients who have a disability: She might reasonably be said to have both beneficent and pecuniary motives, neither eclipsing the other.
35. Jason Brennan and Peter Martin Jaworski, "Markets Without Symbolic Limits," *Ethics* 125, no. 4 (2015): 1053–1077.
36. Debra Satz, *Why Some Things Should Not Be for Sale: The Moral Limits of Markets* (New York: Oxford University Press, 2010), 146–148. This point requires some nuance. With respect to sex work, there are, of course, men in the profession, but who primarily provide their services to other men. In the case of surrogacy and egg sales, the work is done entirely by women, but not always, or not only for men.
37. Catharine A. MacKinnon, *Toward a Feminist Theory of the State* (Cambridge, MA: Harvard University Press, 1989).
38. Julieta Elgarte, "Basic Income and the Gendered Division of Labor," *Basic Income Studies* 3, no. 3 (2008): 1–8.
39. Brian Barry, "UBI and the Work Ethics," *Boston Review*, October 2000.
40. Ronald Weitzer, "Prostitution as a Form of Work," *Sociology Compass* 1, no. 1 (2007): 143–155.
41. Basic Income Earth Network, "Overview of Current Basic Income Related Experiments," October 2017. https://basicincome.org/news/2017/10/over view-of-current-basic-income-related-experiments-october-2017. (Figures used in the body of this paper reflect financial exchange rates from EU to USD and CAD to USD at the time of final editing, November 2018.)
42. Stephanie Talmadge, "College Females Turn to Egg Donation to Fund School," *USA Today*, July 11, 2013; Lois Rogers and Jane Mulkerrins, "Young Women Selling Their Eggs to Pay Off Student Loans," *Sunday Times*, June 5, 2016.
43. Carina Hsieh, "16 Things You Need to Know About Donating Your Eggs," *Cosmopolitan*, September 27, 2017.
44. Leslie Morgan Steiner, "Who Becomes a Surrogate?" *The Atlantic*, November 23, 2013.
45. Cynthia Cole Robinson, "Female Dropouts and Prostitution," *Counterpoints* 302 (2007): 3–19.
46. Evelyn L. Forget, "The Town With No Poverty," University of Manitoba, February 12, 2011. http://nccdh.ca/images/uploads/comments/forget-cea_(2).pdf
47. Joseph Heath and Vida Panitch. "Why Cash Violates Neutrality," *Basic Income Studies* 5, no. 1 (2010): 1–26.

48. L. Chad Horne, "Medical Need, Equality, and Uncertainty," *Bioethics* 30, no. 8 (2016): 588–596.
49. Jordan, "Basic Income and the Common Good," 162.
50. Esping-Anderson, *The Three Worlds of Welfare Capitalism*, 45.
51. Vida Panitch, "Basic Income, Decommodification, and the Welfare State," *Philosophy and Social Criticism* 37, no. 8 (2011): 935–945.

Contributors

Michael Cholbi is Professor of Philosophy and Director of the California Center for Ethics and Policy at California State Polytechnic University, Pomona.

John Danaher is Senior Lecturer at the School of Law, National University of Ireland Galway.

Jessica Flanigan is Associate Professor of Leadership Studies and Philosophy, Politics, Economics and Law at the University of Richmond.

Evelyn L. Forget is Professor in the Department of Community Health Sciences at the University of Manitoba.

Vida Panitch is Associate Professor of Philosophy at Carleton University.

Kory P. Schaff is Lecturer in Philosophy at California State University, Los Angeles.

Frauke Schmode is a PhD student in political philosophy and theory at the Bavarian School for Public Policy.

Justin Tosi is Assistant Professor of Philosophy at Texas Tech University.

Andrea Veltman is Professor of Philosophy at James Madison University.

Matt Zwolinski is Professor of Philosophy and director of the Center for Ethics, Economics, and Public Policy at the University of San Diego.

Index

Printed in the United States
by Baker & Taylor Publisher Services